The Other Perspective in Gender and Culture

IRVINE STUDIES IN THE HUMANITIES
Robert Folkenflik, General Editor

THE OTHER PERSPECTIVE IN GENDER AND CULTURE

REWRITING WOMEN AND THE SYMBOLIC

Edited by Juliet Flower MacCannell

COLUMBIA UNIVERSITY PRESS

New York Oxford

Library of Congress Cataloging-in-Publication Data

The other perspective in gender and culture : rewriting women and the
 symbolic / edited by Juliet Flower MacCannell.
      p.   cm. — (Irvine studies in the humanities)
    "Papers . . . presented to the Focused Research Program in Gender
 and Women's Studies, 1985–88, at the Irvine campus of the University
 of California"—Acknowledgments.
   Includes bibliographical references and index.
   ISBN 0–231–07256–2
   1. Feminism and the arts—Congresses.   I. MacCannell, Juliet
 Flower, 1943–   .   II. University of California, Irvine. Focused
 Research Program in Gender and Women's Studies.   III. Series.
 NX180.F4084   1990
 700′.1′03—dc20
 90–1913
 CIP

Casebound editions of Columbia University Press books are Smyth-sewn
and printed on permanent and durable acid-free paper

Printed in the United States of America
c 10 9 8 7 6 5 4 3 2 1

CONTENTS

II. ART AND PRACTICE

III. LOSSES AND GAINS

ACKNOWLEDGMENTS

THE PAPERS collected in this volume were all presented to the Focused Research Program in Gender and Women's Studies, 1985–88, at the Irvine campus of the University of California. They are by no means all those we were privileged to hear during that time, and, as Director of the Program and Editor of this volume, I want to take this occasion to thank deeply those who have offered us their work for publication here, but also those whose papers, for reasons of prior commitment or other circumstances, do not appear here. Their contributions to our studies were invaluable for our thinking; without them this volume would not yet exist.

Our project, which united the efforts of between fifteen and eighteen Irvine faculty members in our three-year existence, was initially encouraged and funded by the Division of Graduate Studies and Research at Irvine. We would like to thank in particular both former Dean Jaime Rodriguez and Dave Schetter of that office for their material assistance in bringing the perspective of this volume to the campus. We would also like to thank Carol Giangola, our administrative associate, for her tireless, meticulous care for the complicated aspects of our multifarious enterprise, and for the unmatched evenness of her temperament. The three graduate students who assisted us were critical to our success: Patricia Hartz, Lollie Groth, and Judith Pike. Their duties ranged from mundane, but all-important, scheduling and memo-ing to intellectually sophisticated contributions to discussions, to our colloquia, and to our general thinking. We should also like to thank Joan Ariel, Women's Studies Coordinator; and Professor Robert Folkenflik, General Editor of the Irvine Series, for issuing the invitation to undertake this collection.

ACKNOWLEDGMENTS

I
CRITICAL ISSUES

INTRODUCTION: WOMEN AND THE SYMBOLIC
Juliet Flower MacCannell

OUR INTEREST in publishing this volume arises from a desire to provide as complete a picture of the contemporary intellectual spectrum as possible, through a selection of exemplary essays, of those who are working from a feminist and women's studies perspective in traditional disciplines (e.g., literature and art history) and newer fields (like film studies and Afro-American studies). The collection is meant to showcase how some of the best minds currently working in feminism are not following familiar and well-worn paths, but are instead utilizing the opening made by the study of women to re-frame and inject new creativity into older fields, and to participate actively in the formulation of the newer ones. It is intended to supplement and not supplant earlier and crucial work in feminism and women's studies in regard to the problematic relation of women to culture. There was great élan in the first and second generations who worked to bring the study of women to the academy, but repeating their ways and means is an error at this point, in large part because of the initial changes they have wrought in the working conditions for women writers and thinkers.

The essays in this collection travel through many different fields as they approach their encounter here and commence their common labor: the "rewriting" of women and the symbolic. The "symbolic" here is defined as the communal dimension, the forces that shape human relations.[1] In all cases the various routes taken by the authors have been shaped semiotically, by attention to the sign (image + concept), the signifier (image), but also, most importantly, to the symbolic dimension of the sign. This collection would not have been possible under pre-semiotic discipline-based theories of women in relation to culture.

Following Lacan, I am making here a distinction between the symbolic and what traditionally has been termed the "social"— that set of determining factors which situate, shape, limit, or enable. The symbolic organizes and classifies, cuts and divides. But it also is what is—or ought to be—what we hold in common. It is what ought not to be the property of any one at the expense of any other.[2] By insisting on the *other* perspective on the symbolic, I am hoping this text can perform a double act: to permit us to become conscious of a much wider range of phenomena by whose means the subject—in this case, the gendered subject—is set up than those known under the somewhat worn terms of sociology, linguistics, rhetoric, psychoanalysis, representation, and the like. It hopefully will also enable us to become conscious of a new source of power on the part of the feminine subject: no longer passive victim of culture but a subject potentially able to assume her own subject-position, taking possession of her symbols, but more crucially, affecting our communal symbols as well.

A *symbolic* woman? Traditionally, to the modern Western eye at least, the symbolic has operated as a function of and for men. They alone seemed in possession of the key symbols, to speak, as it were, for all members of the human group.[3] But the "universality" of those symbols is brought critically into question when the matter of gender-as-symbolic-construct is brought up. Gender is doubly problematic as a symbolic "sign." Often reduced to its imaginary or "signifier" aspect, it can become a positive symbolic resource only if handled with extreme caution. For it marks a distinction which exists primarily (if not exclusively) because it is so marked. (Freud, for example, once declared that we are not in possession of any clear mark for distinguishing the sexes).[4] Even those who, like Kristeva,[5] want to feel that the biological realm of sexual division is clear and permanent (if definitively past), are resigned to seeing the clarity of sexual origins barred from our direct experience by the operation of the signifying systems (including gender) we employ. *Gender*, then, would be a purely arbitrary and formal "statement" (or misstatement), that masks and marks a more "archaic" sexual distinction. It liberates us from "sexuality" as a natural state of opposition, but fails to provide absolute freedom since it operates as a code, participates in and reinforces traditional structures of *opposition* between the sexes, all the while enabling a transcendence of sexuality (through the higher unity of the signifier). Gender is, so to speak, a classical double-bind structure.

It seems to me, and I think to the authors in this collection, that what the symbolic construction of gender yields is a dialectic in which sexuality is no longer a permanent (if mythic) division, but a term of *relation* and non-relation. Gender marks and makes distinction; at the same time as it bars biological sexual division, however, it provides the only means at our disposal for constructing "sexual" relations, connections between opposed sexes. Thus, gender is what comes between the sexes, in both highly negative and highly positive senses of the term.

So it happens that, on the unnatural, unstable, and impermanent basis that all human signifying systems are, we nevertheless possess a fully elaborated, powerful, and very often coercive system of gender distinctions which launch the "battle of the sexes." At the same time the system itself opens the potential for reshaping and renegotiating the territories (including the common grounds) of those it so divides. All signs have this double potential, but gender has been one of those most critical to and most general in the operations of human group life. All of the essays in this collection regard gender as the crucial site of struggle and of creative potential for developing the symbolic dimension of human cultural life, the life we imagine we hold in common.

Gender and Masquerade

Now that the mythic construction of sexuality—natural biological sexual division—has been called into question,[6] we find ourselves turning to the serious matter of how to treat the sexual "equality" implicit in the structure of gender-as-sign: mark and mask. While decoding the "set" of gender signs as rhetorical expressions of an actual underlying sameness is now common (even in the popular idiom, i.e., gender-blending) it is important to think most carefully about the symbolic models we adopt for representing this equality.

The emphasis on masquerade and gender has yet to undergo as severe a critical scrutiny as gender marking (pseudo-opposition) in respect to its symbolic role. It is crucial that we articulate a desire to get beyond the confines and restrictions that gender-opposition imposes, but we may not sufficiently understand the symbolic effects, the communal role, that gender unification would involve, or even whether "unification" is a desirable goal. If moving "beyond" gender means submerging gender difference in androgyny, we need to ask how—and more importantly, if there exists a "neutrality" capacious enough for the task. Can it recognize what makes a difference?

We have, I think, to raise the possibility of gender even in the "neuter," the neutral. Has such neutrality ever existed?[7] It is painfully evident to many women that the properties of the "third party" judge, the prestigious, "neutral," symbolic position, are all too often those of *one* gender. The Symbolic assumes the properties, along with the props, of the masculine. Under the sign of neutrality, that is, we often license the incorporation of the feminine gender rather than make space for it. Where we have imagined bisexuality as a doubling of genders—the real addition of one gender and another to make two—it may turn out that we have symbolically accepted a reduction to "one." 'All-in-one' is not, perhaps, the best model for ending the "battle of the sexes" and the pernicious sociocultural effects of human gender-discriminations.

The Structure of the Volume

The question of the symbolic function of gender, gender-blending, gender-distinction, and gender difference is thus the focal point of this volume, in approaching the relation of women to the symbolic. As we have undertaken our studies of the "senior" and "junior" lines of cultural texts (literature, film, painting, even philosophy, as well as mass cultural forms like advertisements, pop singers, the discourse of the ghetto, cooking and eating, etc.) our aim is neither to reinforce the status quo nor to discover yet one more example of male domination of the feminine. It has been, rather, to research the question of women's access to the symbolic, and the effects on the cultural order that women's seizure of the symbolic ground have.

The book falls more or less into three components, each of which addresses the feminist response to major cultural developments in the late twentieth century as these have affected and transformed our perception of the relation of the Woman to the symbolic. What we find, as soon as we look closely at that relation, is that the symbolic itself has to be redefined.[8]

Concern with articulating this issue critically falls to the authors of the first four essays, Leslie Wahl Rabine, Anne Friedberg, Nancy Armstrong, and Avital Ronell. These essays could roughly be characterized as "theoretical," but with some caveats. At issue are three major discourses within the so-called "cultural sciences": postmodernism, deconstruction, psychoanalysis. The papers all speak directly to the woman as subject, object, and theorizer in these discourses. In none of these essays, however, does the author permit discussion the luxury of remaining at the purely speculative level. It seems that, where women and culture are concerned, the material and practical, the empirical and the concrete are integral to the relation between the two.

Nancy Armstrong makes the most forceful statement of what is at stake, putting it politically: she argues that to classify "most of our symbolic activities as 'personal,' 'social,' or 'cultural' . . . places them in a secondary relationship either to the economy or to the official institutions of the state." The identification of the symbolic as conscious and limited "cultural" activity, distinguished from serious, noncultural matters like economics and politics, is to leave too much of the symbolic to the unconscious: for economics, politics, and the rest, are also symbolic activities, appearing as such when the question of sexual difference is raised.

Professor Leslie Wahl Rabine's paper (whose title alludes to Heidi Hartmann's classic work on the unhappy marriage of Marxism and feminism) voices certain distresses in the relation of feminism to "deconstruction." As a *method* of marking repressions and remainders deconstruction often provided new avenues of expression for women. As it has tended to become a

system Professor Rabine finds that it has begun to automate ambiguity, and, overlooking the material conditions under which
women exist, re-naturalizes its own categories in ways that reinforce male control of the symbolic order. She demonstrates that
what at first glance appears to be antagonistic to the male-as-
master in Derrida's discourse ends by becoming in fact a surrep-
titious support for what has been, ultimately and historically, *the*
cardinal symbol of male mastery over women since the foundation of marriage in the Greek state: Derrida sees only the positive
resources in the ambiguity of the *hymen* (membrane/marriage) as
a figure, presenting it as what "outwits, undoes . . . the assurance
of mastery." Rabine's claim is that deconstruction unwittingly
contributes to a recontainment of the feminine by phallocentrism
when it fails to mark institutional practices as strongly as linguistic ones.

Professor Anne Friedberg takes on a different task, that of
reminding those who have mastered the narration of the "postmodern situation" of their material dependence on images of the
feminine. She makes it egregiously plain that much of the "postmodern" story is the story of man's overlooking "the woman"
while looking at her. Her lively and perceptive essay articulates
feminism's growing concern with the role of the woman in our
current haste to be "postmodern," and her essay does double
duty, examining both the critical literature and debates of postmodernism, and shows how quickly the route from pure idea to
commercial image is traveled in the postmodern idiom.

In Professor Armstrong's essay here, "Some Call it Fiction: On
the Politics of Domesticity," she addresses the complaint cited
above specifically to the fields that have dominated the economic
and political history of the arrangement between the sexes: "The
assumption [is] that history consists of economic or political
events, as if these were essentially different from other cultural
events . . . ," and she remarks on our tendency to "shrink 'the
political' down to a very limited set of cultural practices." She
examines the relation between educational institutions and unconscious sexual coding as she pursues a Foucauldian analysis of
the relations among domesticity, fiction, and the political state.
Her reading is exemplary for this section inasmuch as it eschews

the "rhetoric of victimization" as she puts it. Like the essay by Cixous in a later section, this essay pinpoints the potential for empowerment of women that is in fact at hand, but which we tend to misrecognize because our "symbolic" optic is overly identified with the masculine.

For some that identification means Oedipus, and any women's studies volume that pretended to any comprehensibility at this time has to take the practices and theories of psychoanalysis into account. The problematics of psychoanalysis for feminism have recently been succinctly stated in an essay entitled "Notes for an Analysis" by Alice Jardine, an essay that addressed head-on the inappropriateness of the oedipal-generational model for women, especially women in the academy. Characterizing woman's subject position as a condition of "impossibility" Jardine describes two generations of women in the academy who nevertheless managed this impossible set of subject-positional terms. Tradition would lead us to imagine intergenerational differences for women along the same oedipal lines assigned the genealogy of male hierarchies, substituting "mothers" and "daughters" for "fathers" and "sons." But Jardine argues the oedipal paradigm does not fit. Women, she contends, now inhabit institutional scenes with a consciousness not shaped automatically by Oedipus but by the disruption of Oedipus as the primary form of the Symbolic that psychoanalytic method has—unintentionally?—afforded us.[9]

Professor Avital Ronell's essay, different in tone and style from most of the other essays, takes off, I think, from the kind of post-oedipal Jardine's essay depicts. Ronell uses history, patient biographies, and the fundamental fantasies of the analysts to show how the unconscious of both is framed not by Oedipus but by technology. Analyzing the schizophrenic-as-woman Ronell shows how technological objects have displaced the earlier "symbolic" as the primary model for interpersonal "connections." In this case, the traditional psychoanalytic definition of the paraphrenias (like schizophrenia) as disorders that express themselves by means of *word-cathexes* comes into question. For Freud, the paraphrenias are variants of *narcissism*[10]—the so-called "feminine" subject position. But by overlooking the *thing-cathexes* of schizophrenic discourse in its haste to assimilate schizophrenic to feminine narcissism psychoanalysis missed an opportunity to reveal a more general unconscious, full of repressed *things*—objects like, in the case Ronell works with, the *telephone*. It therefore failed to define the intersubjective and gendered cathexes involved with them. The technological object becomes significant as symptom in Heidegger, Jung, and Laing, for whom, ultimately, Techné-is-woman-substitute. Technology is the repressed Mother, neo-nature; its order(s), its commands can be read as writing on the body of the woman, the patients Ronell has speak in her text.

"Access Code" marks an important moment in "poststructuralist" discourse, providing an almost unique example of the way this set of discursive, highly poetic practices can be made to ask and answer questions about women and gender. While some feminists have argued that poststructuralism attacks "essentialism" indiscriminately, failing to credit the special importance of sexual difference, and "does away" with the woman before she has had a chance to come into her own, Professor Ronell's piece belies this in two ways. On the one hand, it shows how poststructural methods can be used to discern and dismantle *the pseudo-essentialization* of woman, an essentialization that appears in discourses seemingly most remote from gender concerns (here in Jung, Heidegger, and Laing). It is this pseudo-essence, a product of technology, which serves to conjure woman away. On the other, Ronell's work should serve to goad practitioners of "deconstruction" to make their rhetoric more openly accountable in terms of the social and intersubjective relations they imply.

Part II deals with the positive and negative symbolics of women's participation in culture up to this point in our collective history. The positive "empowered" aspect of women, the multiple and often unnoticed, undocumented effect women have had on cultural expression is seen here as a critical activity. Professor Renée Riese Hubert's paper on "Gender, Genre, and Partnership" makes this clear: in her study, *partnership* between the sexes in the historical careers of creative artists who, as she put it, "shared their lives" becomes a subtle paradigm for the ways in which the interrelations among cultural production, self-other relations, and the "natural" can model each other positively. With the greatest sophistication about how traditional and largely unconscious symbolization has determined the ways we "understand" feminine images, Professor Hubert demonstrates convincingly how the surrealist artist used the [equally] traditional, but culturally unvalued, "womanly" interest in "relationships" as a resource for articulating—ironically—feminine autonomy, feminine desire. Hubert's direction, like Cixous's (who stresses the relation of feminine and masculine in her artistic production in her essay here), is a departure for feminism at this moment in history.

Important insights into the symbolic empowerment of woman in the context of a confrontation between "traditional" or *Gemeinschaft* cultures with those of "modern" character emerge in the papers by Bennetta Jules-Rosette, Tsili Gandelman, and Jacquelyn Mitchell. In each the woman is a figure burdened with symbolically charged imagery that encodes a larger cultural confrontation, political in character, over which she has little or no control. As such her image can be read as cipher of the larger conflict. Once it is understood as the site of struggle at the political and ethnosemiotic levels, the critical sociocultural import of the handling of the feminine image becomes clear, and should lead to a more general study of women and their image. While the woman is rarely empowered at these moments it is apparent from the findings in these essays that matters need not remain so.

This means, in effect, that the "aesthetic" image of woman must be interpreted in the light of the symbolic way it positions her, that is, within her set or the network of her relations. Reading *artistic production* becomes a significant (perhaps the most significant) means of representing and *at the same time* working through tensions between the "isotopies" [oppositions] of social life they both encode and decode in "Images of Women in African Tourist Art," by Bennetta Jules-Rosette. Her paper demonstrates, at a deep structural level, this intimate interplay between the Imaginary and the Symbolic. Treating not only a non-Western, but also a non-standard "artistic production" (what has been called the "art of the fourth world"—indigenous arts tailored specifically for sale to tourists)[11] she provides crucial insight into the double relation of gender to social systems undergoing change. Framed by both a sense of nostalgic "past" wholeness (original or mythic "maternal" simplicity) and modern or contemporary complexity (the world of men), the situation of the African woman is burdened with being the pivotal image on which the transition from one state to another depends. It enables, but also potentially resists these changes. The essay is a tour de force of semiotic analysis, exemplifying the kind of double perspective the analyst and subject of the feminine experience within culture must have, reading as she puts it, "nostalgia for a past life and sense of community with well-defined social roles" together with the "attraction of modernity and its benefits" with the context of *losses* that accompany the confrontation between the simpler and more complex cultures.

Victimization is, however, an ever-threatening possibility in the symbolic ordering of our lives. Given the plasticity of gender, it is always possible that "being a woman artist" guarantees nothing in regard to her own cultural encoding nor of the evaluation of woman her art produces. Professor Eric Rentschler's study of Nazi filmmaker Leni Riefenstahl offers the reader a sense of the magnitude of the symbolic re-containment—and disfigurement —of the Woman in the facism of our recent past. To recall this "negative" counterpoint is important to this collection, raising the level of the question of symbolic construction well beyond the biological sex of the artist. It reminds us that the ways in which the Woman has unconsciously been offered as an image to be contained and controlled—and often disfigured—through a masculine symbolic order are many and varied and that women have not been immune to participating in their own subjection.

Professor Rentschler analyzes Riefenstahl's film *The Blue Light* as illustrating an unconscious wish for and reaction to the death of a young woman, Junta. The story, in which the dead girl returns as a mythological figure, only apparently exalts and sacralizes her status. For the mythification of Junta in fact only licenses what Rentschler calls a "frenzied phallic order," enabling it to mirror its own rejected characteristics in "others" who are scapegoated and, like Junta, annihilated. Rentschler's analysis of Riefenstahl's special use of feminine and masculine imagery in this early film provides an important insight into the tangle of relations that surround the body of the "dead" woman which Nazi aesthetics were bent on "murdering" and "resuscitating" ritually and in compulsive form.

Part III deals with advances and retreats in the symbolic reframing of the woman. The section opens with the joyous and playful work of Hélène Cixous, who has known both "paradise and loss," both home and exile, the positive and negative forms of masculinity and femininity, and who makes here a statement about the crucial balance required in the completed artistic art.

By accepting the loss of paradise, Cixous seems to assume the loss of the mother, the primary narcissistic state, and, unlike most feminists, to accept as well the regime of the signifier, which we normally assume is phallic.[12] Of course, for Cixous, it is not. Her essay becomes an exercise in how to make these twin "losses," these "lacks" and these "weaknesses" into strengths—into positive preconditions for woman's participation in the production of culture.

Cixous refuses to forget she is a woman. What does this mean? That she is one of those dreaded "essentialists" who evoke a feminine being stubbornly maintaining its integrity outside of its gender-expression? How then could we read her insistence on moving beyond the narrow and arbitrary limits that "gender" has historically entailed? Working through the limits of gender, not forgetting the feminine but not attacking the masculine (she tells us she "respects men") Cixous does more than illustrate the virtues and limitations of debunking gender. She speaks—rationally and eloquently, poetically and rigorously, with femininity and masculinity—about "the writing woman." We witness an event: A Woman is coming to take her place in, to occupy a position from which she has traditionally been excluded: the symbolic. That she is doing so "as a Woman," and not as "a Woman-become-a-man" is what is significant. Her style, her manner carry her meaning. This woman *writes*, she tells us both as a man and as a woman. But she also *speaks*. It is her voice that adds the feminine dimension to what has always been unconsciously designated as a masculine subject position, the symbolic position she is assuming.

There is one other aspect to Cixous's short piece which demands our attention and which links it to the other essays in this section. That is the "maternal" dimension. While traditionally it has been deemed necessary, for the development and advancement of culture and civilization, that the tie with the natural, maternal body be broken, Cixous shows us how the symbolic translation of the mother becomes a resource for poetry, fiction, and theater. In a beautiful sequence, she speaks of losing her father, and regaining her mother, through a Shakespearean encounter: explaining how she loves *Henry V* for its scene on the "eve of the battle," Cixous demonstrates how rich are the rich resources of the signifier, freed from its restriction to the masculine (phallic) mode. It can *comprehend* the gendered subject. Cixous tells us she realizes she loves this "eve of the battle" because it is a "pre-condition"—like the maternal body— for existence. Eve becomes, for her "Eve"-the-mother, our general, first, archaic Mother—and a recognizable support for our art.

Professor Gabriele Schwab's text follows Cixous's, however, with a sobering reminder of the psychological and artistic impact of rejecting the maternal body. Her study of Faulkner's *As I Lay Dying* provides another perspective on the Mother/Culture relationship. Applying Bakhtin's "carnival" and Kristeva's "abjection" to the gender-specific problem of representing the [dying] mother's body as grotesque, the traditional evaluation of the mother-as-good-for-art only when she is overcome is thrown into question. The treatment of this body is to be compared with the reevaluation of the maternal body found in Cixous's critical writing, in her classic essay, for example, on "The Laugh of the Medusa." In that article Cixous challenged the male negative aesthetic which surrounds the maternal and female body, confronting it with a "Medusa's head"—the female sexual organ. Cixous insisted it need no longer to be kept modestly hiding its petrifying power. Instead of alternately blushing and threatening its onlookers with castration, Cixous had it laugh. The laugh is partly Bakhtinian carnival; the Medusa's head is, Cixous assured us, with its lips, quite simply, quite openly *smiling*. For her, the smile has reconstructive as well as deconstructive powers.

Schwab's essay indicates how difficult these desirable moves would be.

Dr. Tsili Doleve-Gandelman's portrayal of the importance of the symbolic in the life of women, even at the most pragmatic level, locates women in the midst of a transformation in their network of symbolic relations, and analyzes the way in which the entire set of everyday life and practices are affected. Her paper deals with the women of the Falashas. These are Ethiopian Jews resettled in Israel, recognized as Jews, but considered "in captivity," i.e., having missed out on the developments of mainstream Judaic culture. In her study, Doleve-Gandelman shows how the Falasha woman both mirrors and sets up the way in which her cultural group is assimilated by another culture, the Israeli, itself less than unified or monological. Her body, her daily life, her food are the almost overdetermined foci of transition from Ethiopia to the Middle Eastern setting with Eurocultural links. Virtually no aspect of her person remains untouched by the critical rearrangement of the sexes effectively—if not consciously—demanded by her group's relocation within a new quasi-"Western" symbolic ordering, even though the new cultural host makes no conscious effort to so intervene.

Finally, Professor Jacquelyn Mitchell's study of "Three Women" raises, as does Doleve-Gandelman's piece, the problematic of the gender and class intersect with ethnicity, but Mitchell accents the positive aspects of arriving at new cosmopolitan street corners. Though confined to a single national context, Mitchell's paper nevertheless offers a way of reevaluating the supposed loss of the woman's "voice" within the community or family as it confronts modern rationality. With great subtlety, and by means of her own eloquent discourse, Mitchell both mourns the loss of the voice of the black woman as a powerful force in the black community, and revitalizes it, ventriloquating and reviving it in her own writing. Her double depiction—of the feminine voices that made a difference to her own experience, and of herself as re-voicing and writing these voices—provides us with a concretely achieved synthesis of feminist analysis and practice.

Conclusion

> Less and less clearly can he make out the limits of this body,
> it's not like other bodies, it's not finished, in the room it keeps
> growing, it's still without set form, continually coming into
> being, not only there where it's visible but elsewhere too,
> stretching beyond sight, toward risk, toward death, it's nim-
> ble, it launches itself wholly into pleasure as if it were grown
> up, adult, it's without guile, and it's frighteningly intelligent.
> —Marguerite Duras, *The Lover*.

The authors in the present volume question the simple equation and division that has traditionally kept woman out of the
symbolic, by having placed her torturously on a threshold between nature and culture, forced to "choose" between the two, to
become an image shaped by a masculine stylization. For this is
no choice at all: like the supposed freedom of the gender distinction (to be natural or purely cultural and arbitrary) woman under
such a regime can only be allied with the silly garrulousness of
images, feminine babble (the Imaginary), or be asked to lend
(silent) support to a symbolic order shaped along public lines that
do not include her.

There is another, and better way of dealing with woman's
double participation in both "nature" and "culture." The masculine model of the symbolic, the "stuff" that binds us together and
which we ought to hold in common has failed monumentally; the
phallus has overstressed its character as a cutting edge, a distinc-
tion-making machine, in its bid to be the exclusive form of the
symbolic. It is time to redraw its form, its shape. When a new
production of symbolic form becomes the order of the day, then
the plural position of woman will come to be viewed as a positive
resource for modeling human being in general.

All the signs are that such is already the case: It is nothing
short of extraordinary that, in this late twentieth century, there
are so many men who wish to comprehend "Woman"—philosophically (Derrida),[13] scientifically (Lévi-Strauss, Lacan), and artistically, evidence of a male fascination with the possibilities for
re-constructing and re-modeling culture that woman-as-new-sym-
bolic-paradigm brings. The change in how we value feminine

multiplicity has been due in no small measure to the practice of feminists: artists and theorists, analysts and critics, aware that to be fully symbolic subjects they need to play their roles in the cultural scene like Diderotian actors, nothing-in-themselves, and also an assorted collection of all possible models. Like Borges' "Shakespeare," they are everything and nothing.

It is critical that women show the way—and show themselves this way—if only to preclude the misuse of their image, their name, to serve a symbolic ordering that continues, surreptitiously, to be morphologically masculine. Only by expanding the limits of the feminine can the woman return to in-form, symbolically, our life in common.

Endnotes

1. Laura Mulvey's classical article, "Visual Pleasure and Narrative Cinema," *Screen 16* (Autumn 1975), is one of the most forceful statements of the exclusion of women from the symbolic. Mulvey vividly depicts the symbolic as overly identified with the masculine. Lacan, too, linked the Symbolic with both the "phallic," and Oedipal form, to whatever put a check on the imaginary (" feminine").

The very arbitrariness implicit in the sign means it is, however, vulnerable to change. It happens that psychoanalysis—Freud's goading questions about femininity, Lacan's about the lack of the woman—played a crucial role in dramatizing the extent of the alliance between the masculine gender and the symbolic. Ironically, then, this particular emphasis on the part of French Lacanians permitted feminist writers to reverse polarities and to conceive, like Irigaray, a feminine Symbolic. Thus, while what we see as a general opening up of the symbolic to the feminine is not a simple direct effect of the psychoanalytic-semiotic method (obviously material conditions such as the nuclear, decolonization, and the world wars awakened many to the flaws in the traditional order), it would not be impossible to make the case for its playing a crucial role. The new, post-Oedipal woman is, one might say, the difference between a symbol and a symptom.

2. Here I am thinking of Rousseau's sense of society as formed by inequality, meaning an absolute dispossession of one person by another. Like Rousseau's pinpointing of the origin of economic inequality, Lacan's marking of gender asymmetry heightened awareness of injustices, even if it offered no cure.

3. It is Symbolic power that everyone wants, it originates Desire—but no one wants to share it.

4. In his *Introductory Lectures on Psychoanalysis*, XX.

5. In "Motherhood According to Bellini," in *Desire in Language* (New York: Columbia University Press, 1982, p. 241), Kristeva tells us "If it is true that every national language has its own dream language and unconscious, then each of the sexes—a division so much more archaic and fundamental than the one into

languages—would have its own unconscious wherein the biological and social program of the species would be ciphered in confrontation with language, exposed to its influence, but independent from it. The symbolic destiny of the speaking animal, which is essential although it comes second, being superimposed on the biological—this destiny *seals off* (and in women . . . it *censures*) that archaic basis and special jouissance it procures in being transferred to the symbolic."

6. Many physiological differences once believed to be permanent marks of sexual distinction are now thought far more susceptible to symbolic ordering than previously imagined. Prior to the advent of modern science, gender was often the subject of debate, but until the Enlightenment, the male form was granted—consciously or unconsciously—primacy as a model. (In the Renaissance, for example, anatomies of male and female genitals often depict the male genital as the root form of all sexual organs.) In the Enlightenment gender opposition became an issue, as the debate over which germ cell (ovum or sperm) contained the generative power (the battle between *"oövistes" and "spermatistes"*).

Modern thinking tends to dispel myths of identifiably natural marks of sexual difference, demonstrating how these marks are never unmodified by cultural choices. Some anatomists now argue that, prior to the invention of agriculture and its resultant division of labor, the sex-linked physiological differences in leg bone structure were unknown, Nevertheless—as recent discussions about the non-mathematical mind of the female show—the drive to fix opposing "natural" qualities in the two sexes (which are always hierarchically ranked) persists. So, while it appears that a standard feature of human cultures is to mark gender difference, by constantly incredible varied devices, we must be vigilantly critical of the social uses to which such discriminations are put. Consciousness of the work of gender-marking is only a beginning, not an end-point of our labor.

7. J. Derrida has pled, recently, for such neutrality in his lecture on women's studies programs entitled "Women in the Beehive," in Alice Jardine and Paul Smith, ed., *Men in Feminism* (New York: Methuen Books, 1988). But it remains a plea.

8. This is the main intent of the work of Luce Irigaray, Catharine Clément, and Hélène Cixous, among others, as I see it, among the French Feminists. Theirs is a call to remodel the Symbolic position—to "change the subject" as it were—so that it could be occupied both by men and women alike, in partnership together or in alternation, without yielding to the hidden agenda of the One. A true Symbolic and not an essence: for the uncanny secret of the Symbolic Subject as Lacan permits us to glimpse it, is that it is not One, but None. The place of the Origin, Father, Prime Cause, etc. is, indeed, empty; it is an error and a ruse for the phallus to presume to a fill its place. Why not fill it with two?

9. In *Between Feminism and Psychoanalysis*, Teresa Brennan, ed. (London: Routledge, 1988).

10. Freud, "On Narcissism: an Introduction," *Collected Papers* IV, Joan Rivière, tr. (London: The Hogarth Press, 1957).

11. See also *The Tourist: A New Theory of the Leisure Class*, by Dean MacCannell (New York: Schocken Books, 1976) and "Introduction: The Arts of the Fourth World," in *Ethnic and Tourist Arts*, Nelson Graburn, ed. (Berkeley: University of California Press, 1976), pp. 1-32.

12. Cixous recognizes the *unconscious* as the site of the signifier, defined up to

now along masculine-metaphoric lines. Her intent is to make the signifier over into a feminine as well as a masculine support. We could argue that any poet of any gender, time, or place has always done the same, but we must credit Cixous with having taken these signifiers back to their embodied source, demonstrating the ways in which language or language-like systems (including gender) are imbricated in the body, on the biological entity, woven into the unconscious.

13. In *Glas* and *Spurs*.

THE UNHAPPY HYMEN
BETWEEN FEMINISM
AND DECONSTRUCTION
Leslie Wahl Rabine

DECONSTRUCTIVE WRITINGS customarily make a disclaimer of mastery over the system of knowledge and language employed.[1] But one question posed by the deconstructive disclaimer is whether it plays at non-mastery in order to arrive at a different kind of mastery, not just of language and knowledge, but of a crumbling and rapidly changing phallocracy. At a time when the structures of patriarchal Western culture are being called into serious question, woman's place in these centered structures (centered around God the Father, the earthly father, and his phallus) as a marginal figure can begin to look, to those not placed in that position, in *some* respects attractive. As an attempt to decenter the discourses of Western thought and representation, deconstruction can end up occupying both the center and the margins, appropriating for itself the traditionally feminine place and pushing women to an even further margin of the now internally displaced but still intact structure.

At first either enthusiastic about or intimidated by deconstruction, feminists have begun to reassess it with more critical assurance. While Alice Jardine in *Gynesis* offers an ambiguous reading of "Woman" as the "primary deconstructive device for those facing the history of philosophy," Gayatri Spivak criticizes "the

The title of this essay refers to the title of Heidi Hartmann's classic essay, "The Unhappy Marriage of Marxism and Feminism," in Lydia Sargent, ed., *Women and Revolution: A Discussion of the Unhappy Marriage of Marxism and Feminism* (Boston: South End Press, 1981).

massive enclosure of the male appropriation of women's voice."[2] In this vein, Teresa de Lauretis identifies Derridean deconstruction as "a way to recontain women in femininity (Woman) and to reposition female subjectivity IN the male subject," while Nancy Miller asks: "When the critic . . . follows . . . a reading practice common to . . . poststructuralist models . . . that by its metaphors and metonymies associates itself with the feminine, whose story is it?"[3] In two recent anthologies of feminist criticism, *The Poetics of Gender*, edited by Nancy Miller, and *Men in Feminism*, edited by Alice Jardine and Paul Smith, several essays express anger, if not outrage, at what Miller calls "the 'masculine recuperation' of the feminine."[4]

Sharing and trying to come to terms with that anger, I am here reading Derrida's "The Double Session" in order to deepen my understanding of just how this recentering of masculine structure can take place through a writer's assumption of the feminine. Paradoxically, it takes place in large part through the very non-mastery of the discursive system in which the writer works. So inextricably do metaphysical logic and semantics enmesh structures of language, that what Sara Kofman calls the "lexical reserve," or the logical and linguistic associations in which a particular discourse is inscribed, must, as she says, "come into play even if the author makes no use of it."[5] My reading of a phallocentric lexical reserve at play in Derrida's deconstruction of phallocentrism keeps in mind that these effects also play against my feminist discourse in what Barbara Johnson calls the attempt "to account for an error by tools produced by this error."[6] Thus my reading of "The Double Session" will keep the relation between deconstruction and feminism ambiguous, and so before I begin that reading, I will explore this ambiguity.

Feminism and Deconstruction

Neither the deconstruction of gender difference nor the incorporation of "Woman" into phallocentric theory will in itself change social gender roles or the social power structure that hierarchically relates men and women. In "The Double Session" a writer marked male by the social gender system displaces the Hegelian dialectic and playfully re-inscribes it within a feminine "logic of the hymen." Derrida's strategy recalls the writings of his women colleagues Hélène Cixous, Luce Irigaray, and Sara Kofman. Each has analyzed how the drama of Hegel's dialectics, in various philosophical and literary texts, associates the subject with Man and the alienated Other with woman or the feminine.[7] According to them, the Hegelian process of *Aufhebung* reincorporates the Other/woman into the Self/man, making him whole, complete, total. Like Derrida, these writers have shown that to maintain its fictional self as whole, coherent, self-identical, master of itself and of "objective" reality, the metaphysical subject must establish the fiction of clear and distinct boundaries between self and other, between its inside and the outside world, between itself as subject and its objects, as well as between consciousness and the unconscious.

In Western culture, the second term in each of these pairs is associated with the feminine. For many feminine and feminist critics, the opposition between masculine and feminine functions as a metaphor for all the others,[8] and indeed these polarities work together inseparably to buttress the social and symbolic order. "The Double Session," having deconstructed gender oppositions, inadvertently reconstructs them in the same movement that reconstructs the inside/outside opposition. And they are reconstructed even as Derrida shows that they and all seeming oppositions work in effect as diacritical relations, produced by the difference or spacing between the terms, so that each term exists only through the space that makes it differ from the other. "The Double Session" demonstrates that there is no first, originary term (Man, spirit, signified, subject) from which is derived a secondary dependant term (Woman, body, signifier, object). But even this demonstration both undermines and reinstates male mastery. By undoing the essential oneness and firstness of the dominant term in any opposition, semiotic or logical, by showing its dependence on the so-called secondary term, deconstruction undermines the male subject of language and thought as a centered structure. That structure, centered around the concepts of Man, the phallus, God, appears as an ideological fiction guaranteeing political mastery.

Deconstructive practice, in "The Double Session," as in Derrida's other texts, does not seek to abolish the binary opposition in question since this would be impossible, "but rather inscribes it within its play as one of its functions or parts"[9] so that the whole system is dislocated. For Gayatri Spivak and Sara Kofman this process of "différance," appearing in "The Double Session" as the logic of the hymen, brings back into discourse and makes palpable the excluded but invisibly working "mark of woman" within the metaphysical system.[10]

But, as Teresa De Lauretis has pointed out, a crucial difference distinguishes "Woman" as a philosophical concept from women as social beings,[11] a difference which deconstructors do not generally recognize, and herein lies the maddening elusiveness of deconstruction. "The Double Session" is one of those texts in which Derrida deconstructs not only the text under scrutiny but also the language of his own phallocentric discourse and the illusion of himself as the autonomous center of that discourse. This self-deconstructive writing, itself freed from any teleological desire for an end, can result in the writer's endless engagement with stylistic games, puns, and sentences which defer any meaning or message. Since the hierarchical oppositions, according to Derrida, always reestablish themselves at another level, the process of self-deconstruction must become an infinite maze. For many a feminist, the spectacle of infinite self-deconstruction of the phallocentric subject can be of limited interest. It can make her wonder whether she is watching a critique of phallocentrism or an attempt to find irreducible differences *inside* the male self while keeping women as other *outside*.

Yet even while wary of this reconstructed inside/outside opposition and all that it implies about the other oppositions, such a feminist can still remain intrigued by the relation between woman and deconstructive notions like the logic of the hymen, as well as its sister notion supplementarity. Supplementarity displaces the conceptual hierarchy of the centered structure as an essential whole, to which the supplement seems exterior, an inessential addition but also a needed completion or replacement for what is lacking in the whole.[12] The supplement is that internal difference that a structure (like that of the phallic subject) has had to exclude to its outside in order to constitute itself as a structure, or in other words as homogeneous, unified, and self-identical. For Irigaray, Kofman, and Spivak, therefore, the role of the supplement in philosophy and theory has been the role of woman, external to Western systems of thought as systematic wholes yet essential to complete the lack within the system. Three recent books on deconstruction can illustrate this. The books of Jonathan Culler, Perry Anderson, and Michael Ryan[13] all have chapters showing the crucial and indispensible link between feminist theory and deconstruction. Yet the exploration of this link is consigned to a separate chapter and does not infuse the rest of the book. Like these books, "The Double Session" engages, as in the case of male mastery, a double treatment of woman as supplement. On the one hand, deconstruction functions here like other philsophical systems as a lacking totality which needs woman to complete it, but whose coherence and boundaries would be disturbed, displaced, deranged through the inclusion of woman.

Yet on the other hand, "The Double Session" as a deconstructive text can be of value to feminists who have often attempted to claim for woman and women a more integral place in theoretical structures. Instead of doing this, we can learn from deconstruction how to invert and displace the relation between structure and supplement. In *Of Grammatology*, Derrida shows that the supplement, as externalized internal difference, actually produces the fiction of the centered structure and is therefore the encompassing term. And "The Double Session," by bringing into play the internal difference always still at work producing the structure, shows that it has no center, no "master word" that organizes it into "decidable poles" and "independent irreversible terms" that have a positive "presence" ("D.S.," p. 210). What appear to be the self-present, positive terms of a structure (e.g., Man/Woman, Subject/Object) are in fact products of relations, which exist only through the other elements of the structure. They therefore exist only through what they are not, through what is absent from themselves in the other elements of the relation, and so the absence or emptiness that makes their existence possible is inescapably a part of themselves.

The empty space of internal difference is necessary to all the terms of a structure and makes it a constant process of play between the terms rather than a stable, centered entity centered by an anchoring master term. Metaphysical discourse, creating the appearance of structure as stable entity, objectifies internal difference and projects it as an external supplement, both a compensation for what the structure lacks and a threatening excess to the structure.

Placed in a double, paradoxical relation to male structure, and projected as the fantasized double of man, woman is like the "supplementary double" ("D.S.," p. 238), both a lack and an excess in relation to the structure. Beyond her image as the fantasmatic double of man, woman is the unsymbolized reminder that phallocentric structure becomes a whole only by the ejection of one of its parts. This internal lack is the condition of its existence as closed totality, and it can never resolve this contradiction at the foundation of its genesis.

The operations of deconstructive reading bring back into a text that contradiction between lack and excess as a quality of the discourse itself, and demonstrate the text as uncentered play. Through a deconstructive supplementarity, women's marginality to male society, and feminism's marginality to male theory can become a strength of feminism, but only if we rescue the discourse of woman as supplement from socially marked male subjects who speak woman as object, and thus inadvertently reconstruct the metaphysical structure of subject/object.

While deconstruction can be a useful tool for a feminism that seeks to go beyond an equality for women that simply incorporates some of them into an unquestioned male social and symbolic order, the reading of "The Double Session" in the next section of this essay rests on the suspicion that feminism and deconstruction will remain uncomfortable and tenuous partners, if partners at all. Socio-historic differences separate the two movements, both of which began in the sixties and responded to very different social needs. Deconstruction, responding in part to an intellectual disillusionment with the Marxism of official Communist Party thought, contributes to a critique of teleology and linear causality. It powerfully explains the impossibility of mastering the practical results of any political action, of being able to determine the effects of any cause, or even to determine what is a cause, and how a cause interacts with another cause. But as a result, although deconstruction is, according to Derrida, "at the very least, a way of taking a position, in its work of analysis concerning . . . political and institutional structures,"[14] it does split theoretical practice from direct political action for immediate goals. Commenting on this, and referring to a different kind of gap from the empty space of différence and supplementarity, Derrida says: "We must take account of certain gaps and try to reduce them, even if for essential reasons, it is impossible to efface them: gaps, for example, between the discourses of practices of this immediately political deconstruction and a deconstruction of theoretical and philosophical aspect."[15]

While deconstruction offers valuable strategies for critique, feminist theory, given the historical conditions to which it responded, cannot separate theoretical critique from political action. When women in the United States earn 63 percent of what men earn, and women in the third world earn even less; when women are the most rapidly growing segment of the poor at the same time they are becoming more and more the single heads of families; when their men subject them to violence in an estimated 50 percent of North American marriages; when in Latin America the largest cause of death among women of child bearing age is unsafe, illegal abortion;[16] and when we live in a world whose overvaluation of a distorted notion of manhood has contributed to a reckless militarism that threatens the life of the planet, the correction has to be engagement in collective actions that change these conditions.

The consequence, however, is that feminists have to live with the results of their actions, disappointing, discomfiting, or disillusioning as those results may be. But here, paradoxically, is precisely where deconstruction can help feminism, and in two ways. On the one hand, political action can accomplish more if our critique of patriarchy cuts to its fictional core and exposes its invisible workings. Deconstruction can offer us valuable tools for a more searing critique. On the other hand, it also offers us tools for a deeper self-critique. It can help us to avoid the illusion of mastery over the results of our actions, and to avoid an absolutist righteousness, since feminist discourse, especially because it must engage in immediate political practice, cannot but operate within the very structures that need dismantling and restructure them within itself. Because in " The Double Session," to a reading of which I will now proceed, the use of the figure of the hymen by a male writer both criticizes the fundamental workings of phallo-centrism through a feminine logic and also restructures phallo-centrism within its critique, it provides an arena in which we can contribute to an investigation of the complex relation between deconstruction and feminism.

A Reading of "The Double Session"

Through a reading of Mallarmé's poetic essay "Mimique," Der-rida analyzes the text as a hymen, which, as a tissue that folds over on itself, has no center and thus no Hegelian "dialectics of totality" ("D.S.," p. 249). The hymen acts as a metaphor for the textual process as a "practice of spacing" ("D.S.," p. 234), in which the "regular intervention of the blanks" ("D.S.," p. 178), spaces, and silences produces the differential relations between signifiers as terms of a linguistic structure. While empty space remains as a trace within the signifying elements of a structure, it cannot itself be signified except by that which cancels it out. Poetic images of whiteness, like swans or snow, or even the white spaces on the page can symbolize the space of productive différ-ance, but these images or figures, as signifiers themselves, cancel out the blank spaces as the movement of nothingness which makes figures possible.

This double self-cancellation governs the operations of textual-ity.The first cancellation operates as the blank that produces sig-nifiers relating in a system; the second cancellation puts under erasure this productive blank within the signifiers so that they can express positive meaning. The hymenal fold opening and closing itself, like the pages of a book, the fan, the wing of a bird, or a multitude of other images in Mallarmé's poetry, figures these operations, since the opening produces the empty space that produces the signifiers, while their closing makes the space disappear and thereby creates the impression of a full word with a self-identical meaning.

The language of texts like "Mimique" refer, according to Derrida, less to established signifieds supposedly outside the text than to this process itself. In fact it mimics the process, through its syntax and the spacing of its words. But since the hymenal fold is *both* difference *and* difference cancelling itself out, the text is not self-reflexive in the Hegelian sense that it mirrors itself as a totalized self-presence and self-identity ("D.S.," p. 270). What seems a self-reflexive text is really a self-differentiating text, pointing to its own internal difference and lack of identity. Its relation to Hegelian discourse is that it "constitutes mimed dialectics" ("D.S.," p. 230), and so allows one to "focus one's critique on the concept of Aufhebung" ("D.S.," p. 248), as a phallocentric reappropriation of the other by the self.

According to Derrida, Mallarmé's mimed dialectics mimes the structure of mimesis itself, and "The Double Session" deconstructs this structure through its reading of "Mimique." The mimetic structure consists of a first term, the original or thing in itself, and a second term, the representation or copy which imitates and doubles the original. "This order of appearance" is, according to Derrida, "the order of truth" ("D.S.," p. 192) in metaphysical systems, truth being either the unveiling of the so-called thing itself or the agreement between the representation and the thing unveiled. Mallarmé's "Mimique" is a reading of a mimodrama by Paul Margueritte, *Pierrot Murderer of his Wife*, in which the mime, as Pierrot, sets himself on the stage and *remembers* how he *planned* to murder his wife for cuckolding him. Playing the role of both Pierrot and Columbine, he dramatizes the remembered anticipation of both the murder and his own suicide. Derrida quotes Mallarmé quoting Margueritte, who characterizes this temporal structure as "a hymen (out of which flows Dream), tainted with vice yet sacred, between desire and fulfillment, perpetration and remembrance: here anticipating, there recalling, in the future, in the past, *under the false appearance of a present.*" [17] Since there is no real present to center past and future, and only, according to Derrida, the "re-enactment of an act never committed anywhere. . . . Never, anywhere, not even in the theatrical fiction" ("D.S.," p. 200), the scene, rather than simply reproducing an external referent, folds over on itself.

The above quotation uses "hymen" in its Greek sense of marriage, to suggest a marriage or joining between memory and anticipation that, according to Derrida, "preserves the differential structure of mimicry or mimesis" ("D.S.," p. 206), but without an original model. Instead of this central, organizing present, referent, or model connecting past and future, they are connected only by the "between," the spacing that produces the mimetic structure. Thus Mallarmé "doesn't get rid of the mimetic structure" but rather "displaces it" ("D.S.," p. 207). Rather than mimesis as the doubling of an original event, this mimodrama is an original doubling, and thus an original spacing, with no antecedent event, a miming of the structure of mimesis that makes undecidable the relation between imitated and imitation.

The hymen figures this play of spacing because both as vaginal membrane and as marriage[18] it dramatizes undecidability. As marriage, the hymen figures the between of one thing and another that both joins and separates. As vaginal/virginal membrane it figures, according to Derrida, the almost nothing "between the inside and the outside of a woman" ("D.S.," p. 212). As a "between" it is "both a confusion and a distinction" ("D.S.," p. 239) of inside and outside. Above all, the hymen figures the betweenness of the word "between" which "signifies the spacing relation, ... the interval, ... and articulation" ("D.S.," p. 222), not only through its meaning, which conveys "the possibility of syntax" ("D.S.," p. 222), but also through its very syntactic function. Since the word "between" is always more important for its syntactic position and function than for its meaning, this "excess of syntax over meaning" gives it a "semantic quasi-emptiness" ("D.S.," p. 222), and so it cannot be reduced to being the copy of a thing. It thus illustrates that all words are quasi-empty, containing traces of the "non-sense ... of the spacing that relates the different meanings" ("D.S.," p. 252) and that makes the meanings possible. Words like "hymen" which join within themselves different meanings contain an internal non-sense of spacing or difference. The "between" of syntax is not just outside and between words but within them as well. This non-sensical gap of the joining, having effected the first cancellation, must then effect the second cancellation: it must erase itself, close its empty space, "marking itself out" ("D.S.," p. 254), for the word's meaning to become visible. Yet without it the word could not have a meaning.

Words like "hymen," "différance," and "supplement" play an important role in deconstruction because they "have a double, contradictory undecidable value that always derives from their syntax" ("D.S.," p. 221). In this they seem similar to the word *Aufhebung* which combines contradictory meanings, but in fact they are precisely those words which resist the actual process of *Aufhebung*, since their meanings cannot be unified in a way that achieves identity: "they mark the spots of what can never be mediated, mastered, sublated or dialectized through any . . . *Aufhebung*" ("D.S.," p. 221).

As a figure of feminine logic, the hymen stands for irreducibility to the phallocentric unity of the *Aufhebung*. The hymen is the between, in French the "entre" which is doubled by its homonym "antre," archaic French for cave. The cave, as represented by Plato's cave in "The Double Session," figures in the phallogocentric imagination as the metaphor for the womb. And the womb also represents to phallogocentric imagination, as Derrida points out in *Glas*, nothingness, disorienting empty space where the organizing center of a structure—the phallus—should be but is not.[19]

This empty space of the differential relation is also like a womb in that it produces, gives birth to what seems like an organized structure. With the feminine lack producing the totalized structure, we have come back to the concept of supplementarity, of which the logic of the hymen is a variation. Mallarmé's writing illustrates supplementarity because his poetry actually thematizes the empty spaces that produce the impression of full themes and meanings. In Mallarmé's poetry images of whiteness (snow, swans, ballerinas, etc.) and references to the white page and the white spaces between the black ink marks signify these unsignifiable blanks or spacings. But Derrida points out that spacings "cannot in fact be mastered as themes or as meanings" ("D.S.," p. 245) because every time one of these blanks or lacks is

represented, yet other unrepresented blanks must be added between and within the signifiers that represent it. All efforts to
thematize or signify the blank produce new unrepresented blanks,
and thus illustrate supplementarity, "since the blank is the polysemic totality of everything white or blank plus the writing site
where the totality is produced" ("D.S.," p. 252). Once again, the
feminine supplement, this time as writing site, produces the totality and in so doing acts as that remainder which the totality
must exclude in order to be formed. In "The Double Session" the
figure of the hymen explicitly joins supplementarity and the feminine. But I think it is important to ask: whose feminine is this,
desired and fantisized by what husband, what seducer?

In "The Double Session" a second, more traditional, phallocentric "logic of the hymen" reconstructs itself in the wake of the
deconstructive play of language. Even if the deconstructive play
of "Mimique" and "The Double Session" makes impossible "any
lexicological summation, any taxonomy of themes" ("D.S.," p.
277), it still can omit and consign to silence certain themes inextricably knotted into the hymenal lexical network and at play
within the texts of "Mimique" and "The Double Session." In
tracing the activity of these themes, I will be exploring some of
the "feminist questions" that Alice Jardine raises at the end of
her reading of "The Double Session."[20] Derrida omits from his
analysis and therefore does not deconstruct in his celebration of
the hymen as that which "outwits, undoes . . . the assurance of
mastery" ("D.S.," p. 230) the hymen/membrane as symbol of male
mastery over women since the beginning of hymen/marriage, established in the patriarchal Greek state as an institution to assure
male mastery.

In Paul Margueritte's mimodrama *Pierrot Murderer of his Wife*,
Pierrot tickles Columbine to death because he finds out that she
cuckolded him. Strangely enough, as "The Double Session" fails
to analyze the tearing of the hymen as a sign of male possession
of women, it also ignores the dialectical logic connecting this
tearing to cuckoldry. Cuckoldry is the inevitable consequence
and negation of that possession, and murderous vengeance is a
kind of *Aufhebung* reaffirming an impossible possession. While
the "The Double Session" shows how Mallarmé plays with Pier-

rot's narrative, Derrida does not deconstruct this clichéd ideology, which accounts for the age-old popularity of Pierrot, the
eternal cuckold.

In focusing on the hymen only as an "undecidability" ("D.S.,"
p. 261), "The Double Session" neglects the hymen as an institution that ensures hierarchy and fusion, and that polices the dominance of the first term, the male, over the second term, the
female. In her reading of "The Double Session," Gayatri Spivak
says: "We cannot avoid remarking that marriage in La Double
Séance remains an unquestioned figure of fulfilled identification."[21] In addition, one can also point out that the essay, with
its focus on the hymen between desire and fulfillment, barely
mentions the hymen between Pierrot and Columbine, and only to
dismiss it without questioning its implications for mastery and
the deconstruction of mastery (cf. "D.S.," pp. 214, 215). And
although it quotes Margueritte's Pierrot as saying: "I killed her—
because I felt like it, I am the master, what can anyone say?"
("D.S.," p. 200), it uses this quotation to discuss how Margueritte
deconstructs a temporal structure organized around presence,
without mentioning or seeming to notice Margueritte's ironic
treatment of male mastery.

In insisting that "The Mime imitates nothing" ("D.S.," p. 194),
that "the Mime does not allow his text to be dictated to him from
any other place," that "he represents nothing, imitates nothing,
does not have to conform to any prior referent" ("D.S.," p. 205),
"The Double Session" excludes to an "outside" the above-men-
tioned social and ideological text and does not analyze the way it
dictates the framework of Margueritte's and Mallarmé's text. On
the contrary, Derrida says: "no act is committed as a crime . . .
not only because on the stage we have never seen it in the present
. . . but also because . . . this crime is its opposite: an act of love"
("D.S.," p. 214). To speak of love in the context of Pierrot's
marriage, an institution based on the tearing of the hymen, as an
unproblematic concept, not in need of deconstruction, with a
unified meaning we can all agree to, brings metaphysics back into
this text with a vengeance equal to Pierrot's.

This phallocentric "lexical reserve" which is excluded from
the deconstructive reading of "The Double Session" reconstructs

itself within the essay's pages. And it reconstructs its structure even as "The Double Session" deconstructs gender oppositions and their cultural corollaries active/passive and subject/object. The mime, all alone on the stage, writing his role in his white grease paint as he plays it, playing all the roles, "is," according to Derrida, "both passive and active" ("D.S.," p. 224). Mallarmé's syntax mimes his play "with each object capable of changing into subject and vice versa" ("D.S.," p. 225). In this one-man show, where the male mime plays all the roles, both Pierrot the tickler and Columbine the ticklee, he becomes "androgynous" ("D.S.," p. 201).

For Kofman, writing as the logic of the hymen "is bisexual, anterior to the distinction of masculine and feminine" (*Lectures de Derrida*, p. 65). But there is a flaw in her interpretation. In the phallocentric logic of the hymen, the hymen would not exist, would have no meaning, no significance at all in a space anterior to the distinction between masculine and feminine. The hymen enters culture as a signifier of men's possession of women, and the mime's double performance idealizes this possession as an allegory for the male appropriation of the feminine, whereby the feminine, or at least those aspects of her that man would like to take over, are reinscribed into a now "bisexual" man. The subject/object structure is dislocated only once the feminine role is relocated *within* the male mime. Man's desire in tearing the hymen and making woman into his private property, his desire in wreaking vengeance for the inevitably resulting cuckoldry, and Pierrot's desire in killing his wife for that cuckoldry, all enact the metaphysical desire to absorb the other into the same. And the mime's assumption of all the roles in this drama of desire reflects on the level of performance that same desire of appropriation of the feminine by man. The two levels of the mime reaffirm rather than deconstruct each other.

If the deconstructive play in "The Double Session" excludes from its orbit the hymen between Pierrot and Columbine, Margueritte's mime can deconstruct gender oppositions because he first gets rid of Columbine. This prior exclusion is in turn excluded from the text of "The Double Session" and noted in its margins. A footnote quotes from a "Notice" to the second edition of *Pierrot Murderer of his Wife* the explanation of why this mime is the sole actor in his drama: "Unknown, a beginner in the world of letters, without any supporting cast or Columbine, I modestly performed a few monomimes in drawing rooms and for the general public" ("D.S.," p. 197). Thus the temporal structure of the mimodrama can be a deconstructive hymen, with no present and no real event because there is no Columbine, no real other. The present is absent as a result of the absence of a woman, who by her absence can be turned into Woman. If the mime's scene marks "nonbeing, the nonreal, the nonpresent" ("D.S.," p. 208), if it "remarks a spacing as a nothing, a blank" ("D.S.," p. 208), this nonbeing is in a very basic sense the absence of a woman, whose exclusion permits this remark of the hymen, which in fact marks her absence. The self-differentiating fold of the hymen is the man doubling and remarking himself.

Like a metaphysical system, the logic of the hymen requires for its establishment the exclusion of woman so that the feminine can be incorporated into the masculine, and also requires the obfuscation of that exclusion. By deconstructing reference so as to deny a prior signified and the social text, "The Double Session" obfuscates its exclusion of woman, which happens "outside" Margueritte's self-originating text, before the text begins. Once the inside/outside opposition comes into play, and the woman as other is excluded, the hymenal logic, like a metaphysical system, can appear to produce itself as a doubling of the same, and then bring in the feminine as a supplement which infinitely displaces the system, but without breaking down its boundaries.

The essay "Plato's Pharmacy," which precedes "The Double Session" in the volume *Dissemination*, and to which "The Double Session" alludes, insists on Plato's negative association of writing with parricide, but does not reflect on its own positive association of writing with feminocide, or at least uxoricide. Pierrot kills his wife, and the mime can become bisexual only by figuratively killing off a female actress from the mimodrama and assuming her role. Kofman points out that the writerly parricide, denounced by Plato and playfully assumed by Derrida, is the "murder of the father" as "the fatherly logos, the voice of truth" (p. 25). But when the historical moment has come to question patriarchal truth, a male appropriation of a certain feminine logic can be used to limit further questioning, in other words to murder women's questioning of patriarchal truth. "The Double Session" excludes a questioning of the institution of hymen, not only in classical Greece and the Victorian era, but in the present where, as in the marriage of Pierrot and Columbine, "as many as one in seven women in the United States have been raped by their husbands: two-thirds have been beaten at least once."[22]

In this institution the hymen as membrane is a mythological object, or as Jardine says, "an object of male fantasy" (*Gynesis*, p. 192), and has no existence separate from the male imaginary order it supports. In "Choreographies," Derrida says "that the hymen *does not exist*. . . . And if there were hymen—I am not saying if the hymen existed—property value would be no more appropriate to it. . . . How can one then attribute the *existence* of the hymen *properly* to woman."[23] But his deconstruction misses the point. What goes unanalyzed in "Choreographies" as well as in "The Double Session" is the lexical network that marks the hymen not as what belongs to woman, but as what makes woman into the property of man, and which comes into play whether acknowledged or not. One cannot really even say that the "hymen *is* only when nothing happens, no violence, no mark" ("D.S.," p. 213), since outside of a socio-symbolic order originally established through the violent subjection of women to male mastery, who cares about the hymen, about whether it is or is not?

In other words, the hymen is not a something/nothing which forms women's symbolic or imaginary relation to their own bodies; it forms men's symbolic and imaginary relation to women's bodies as pieces of property for them to own. In its attempt to go beyond the boundaries of phallocentrism, "The Double Session" has called upon a "feminine" which is not one, which has always been an organ of the masculine imagination. The essay in this respect has not exited from a phallocentric imaginary space.

Having deconstructed subjectivity by excluding woman as a subject even eligible for self-deconstruction, "The Double Session" brings her back in through a footnote as one in a series of poetic objects: "The occurrences [in Mallarmé's writing] of this type of white are less numerous . . . than others, the white of all the fabrics, the flying wings of foam, the sobs, fountains, flowers, women, or nudes in the night, the agonies, etc" ("D.S.," p. 258). Here women are supplements not in the deconstructive sense but in the old-fashioned metaphysical sense, added on to a structure formed through their absence. They serve the inevitable reconstruction of the subject/object opposition, since by their very presence as objects in this list, they signify both that the list must have been written by a subject and that they could not themselves be the subjects who write the list. If, as Gregory Ulmer, writing about the logic of the hymen, says: "writing in the next epoch should be more vaginal than phallic,"[24] the question that still has not been put to rest is: whose writing?

While feminists might not wish to place reclaiming vaginal writing on the top of their agenda, feminism can make use of deconstructive strategies just as it has made use of the male-centered theories of Marxism and psychoanalysis. This assertion, however, only leaves me back in a conflictual and incompatible relation between deconstruction and feminism, because feminism always has to do more than deconstruct. Even a deconstruction that does not universalize the male point of view can universalize the conceptual, theoretical levels of practice and exclude direct political action, which requires certain metaphysical practices.

On the side of deconstruction, the deconstructive gesture can be a courageous attempt to recognize, on the part of men, that their position of plenitude, mastery, and identity with respect to the phallus is indeed a fiction. It can be an attempt to recognize, as Jane Gallop says, that we are all in a position of lack.[25] But a jump from this recognition to a facile assumption of textual bisexuality can prematurely close the question of sexual differentiation and sexual domination. "The Double Session," for instance, is supposed to have deconstructed phallogocentrism and sexual difference; yet Derrida never makes the connection between the violence of a man murdering his wife because she escaped from his ownership, and the tearing of the hymen as the institutionalization of men's violently taking ownership of women. If Derrida remains blind to that which a woman, for whom the fear and/or reality of sexual violence ceaselessly permeates the relation to the socio-symbolic order, cannot avoid seeing, the "feminine force" which he uses to deconstruct the "opposition between men and women"[26] is a very limited concept indeed. Instead of opening deconstruction to a broader and deeper examination of sexual difference, it forecloses that examination and opens what Derrida calls an "abyss" ("D.S.," p. 265) of self-deconstructing discourse where "substitution games are multiplied ad infinitum ("D.S.," p. 268).

Caught between the compelling demands generated by the oppression of women on the one hand to act for urgently needed immediate reforms and on the other hand to understand and dismantle on a deeper level the system producing that oppression, the feminist mentioned earlier hopes that deconstruction can be used to examine social questions like gender domination. She hopes many people will heed Derrida's call to reduce the gap between philosophical deconstruction and political action; she hopes that this "between" will be thoroughly explored, and she hopes it will not be called a hymen.

Endnotes

1. See, for instance, Richard Klein and William B. Warner, "Nuclear Coincidence and the Korean Airline Disaster," *Diacritics* (Spring 1986) 16(1):2-21.

2. Alice Jardine, *Gynesis: Configurations of Woman and Modernity* (Ithaca: Cornell University Press, 1985), p. 182; Gayatri Chakravorty Spivak, "Displacement and the Discourse of Woman," in Mark Krupnik, ed., *Displacement: Derrida and After* (Bloomington: Indiana University Press, 1983), p. 190.

3. Teresa de Lauretis, *Technologies of Gender: Essays on Theory, Film, and Fiction* (Bloomington: Indiana University Press, 1987), p. 24; Nancy K. Miller, "Arachnologies: The Woman, The Text, and The Critic," in Miller, ed. *The Poetics of Gender* (New York: Columbia University Press, 1986), p. 284.

4. Miller, *ibid;* Alice Jardine and Paul Smith, *Men in Feminism* (New York: Methuen, 1987); Miller, *ibid,* p. 271.

5. Sara Kofman, *Lectures de Derrida* (Paris: Editions Galilée, 1984), p. 45. (Further references to this work will appear in parentheses after the quotation).

6. Barbara Johnson, "Introduction," in Jacques Derrida, *Dissemination*, Barbara Johnson trans. (Chicago: University of Chicago Press, 1981), p. x.

7. Hélène Cixous, *La Jeune Née* (Paris: Union d'Editions Générale, 1975); Luce Irigaray, *Speculum de l'autre femme* (Paris: Minuit, 1974); Kofman, *L'Enigme de la femme* (Paris: Editions Galilée, 1980).

8. See Cixous, *La Jeune Née,* p. 116; Irigaray says that woman is the negative term in the male dialectic in *Speculum de l'autre femme,* p. 21; Teresa de Lauretis says that the opposition between masculine and feminine is the metaphor for all the others in *Alice Doesn't: Feminism, Semiotics, Cinema* (Bloomington: Indiana

University Press, 1984), p. 121; and Kofman says that "sexual difference is the best paradigm for difference" (*Lectures de Derrida*, p. 113).

9. Jacques Derrida, "The Double Session," in *Dissemination*, p. 193. (All further references to this text will appear in parentheses after the quotation and will be designated by "D.S.")

10. Gayatri Chakravorty Spivak, "Love Me, Love My Ombre, Elle," *Diacritics* (Winter, 1984), 14(4):26. See also Kofman's remarks on the homologies between writing and woman in *Lectures de Derrida*.

11. Teresa de Lauretis, *Alice Doesn't*, p. 5; and *Technologies*, pp. 23-24.

12. Jacques Derrida, *De la grammatologie* (Paris: Minuit, 1967).

13. Jonathan Culler, *On Deconstruction: Theory and Criticism after Structuralism* (Ithaca: Cornell University Press, 1982); Michael Ryan, *Marxism and Deconstruction: A Critical Evaluation* (Baltimore: Johns Hopkins University Press, 1982); Perry Anderson, *In the Tracks of Historical Materialism* (London: Verso, 1983).

14. Jacques Derrida, "The Conflict of Faculties," quoted in Culler, *On Deconstruction*, p. 156.

15. Jacques Derrida, "Entre Crochets," quoted in Culler, p. 158.

16. Statistics on women's death in Latin America from Charlotte Bunch, "Ten Years After: Mixed Reports," *Women's Review of Books* (October, 1986), 4(1):9-11.

17. Derrida, "The Double Session," p. 175. For the original French version, see Stéphane Mallarmé "Mimique," in *Oeuvres complètes* (Paris: Bibliothèque de la Pléiade, 1945), pp. 310-312.

18. Derrida introduces other meanings of the hymen as a membrane in many animals, "The Double Session," p. 213.

19. Derrida, *Glas* (Paris: Denoel/Gonthier, 1981), p. 69.

20. Jardine, *Gynesis*, p. 191.

21. Spivak, "Displacement," p. 174.

22. Katha Pollitt, "*That* Survey: Being Wedded Is Not Always Bliss," *The Nation* (September 20, 1986), 243(8):240.

23. Jacques Derrida and Christie V. McDonald, "Choreographies," *Cherchez la Femme: Feminist Critique/Feminine Text*, special issue of *Diacritics*, 12(2):75.

24. Gregory Ulmer, "The Post Age," *Diacritics* (Fall, 1981), 11(3):55.

25. Jane Gallop, *Reading Lacan* (Ithaca: Cornell University Press, 1985), p. 20.

26. Jacques Derrida, "Women in the Beehive," in Jardine and Smith, eds., p. 194.

2

MUTUAL INDIFFERENCE: FEMINISM AND POSTMODERNISM
Anne Friedberg

> Defining our world today as Postmodern is rather like defining women as 'non-men.' It doesn't tell us very much either flattering or predictive.[1]

So begins Charles Jencks' architectural study, *Postmodern Architecture*. Is it surprising that the critical debate over the cultural usefulness, political valences of postmodernism seems to send critics, pronouncedly male critics, into the parallel universe of discourse about another uncharted terrain, "dark continent," "remarkable oversight"[2]—that of the feminine? The above equation between postmodernism and woman suggests quite clearly that the need to define postmodernism has sent theorists into the metaphorical pockets of familiar discourses. The enigma "What is postmodernism?" (itself the title of a brief essay, svelte appendix, to Jean-François Lyotard's now canonical volume, *The Postmodern Condition*)[3] has become a riddle almost as taxing as "Was will das Weib?" I want to examine the discourse of postmodernism and its relation to the discourse of feminism because, as one (male) critic, Craig Owens, has pointed out, postmodernism had been "scandalously indifferent" to feminism.[4]

But let us also assume a reciprocal relation: feminism has avoided taking up its differences with postmodernism.[5]

Indifference

> Any discourse which fails to take account of the problem
> of sexual difference in its own enunciation and address will
> be, within a patriarchal order, precisely indifferent, a
> reflection of male domination.[6]

This quote from Stephen Heath, an essay called "Difference"
published in the British film journal *Screen*. A warning to be
drawn now to the surface, used to screen the discourse of postmodernism for its own enunciation and address. Allow me to cite
two male critics who note the feminist silence in the cacophony
of the postmodern debate. First (and again) Craig Owens:

> The absence of discussion of sexual difference in writings
> about postmodernism as well as the fact that few women
> have engaged in the modernism/postmodernism debate, sug-
> gest that postmodernism may be another masculine inven-
> tion engineered to exclude women.[7]

And Andreas Huyssen:

> It is somewhat baffling that feminist criticism has so far
> largely stayed away from the postmodernism debate which
> is considered not be be pertinent to feminist concerns. The
> fact that to date only male critics have addressed the prob-
> lem of modernity/postmodernity, however, does not mean
> that it does not concern women.[8]

But citing these male critics who demarcate feminist concern
only introduces a common but paradoxical use of male authority,
what Elaine Showalter has described as "critical cross-dressing"[9]
a triangulation of power whereby women empower themselves
by aligning with men who align themselves with feminist priorities—a receding referent, a *mise en abyme* of feminist critique.
Owens, sensitive to these difficulties, quite carefully positions
himself as the matchmaker ("to introduce the issue of sexual
difference into the postmodernism debate") not the referee ("My
intention is not to posit an identity between these two critiques:
nor is it to place them in a relation of antagonism or opposition").[10]

But why should feminists address themselves to the philosophical, social, or aesthetic debates of postmodernism? Surely,
feminisms have had a large stake in the heart of Western philosophy, in performing a piercing critique and in proposing new
paradigms.[11] It is my purpose here to decry the continued indifference, to call forth some of the questions that the postmodernist
debate begs for feminism (and vice versa) and hopefully to map
clearly the positions that seem to occupy both territories, charting
the borderline skirmishes.

Before archly citing the need for a feminist critique of postmodernism, allow me to post [sic] a warning at the gate, a necessary admonition about the frequently wrought illusion of a uni-
tary discourse: the deception that either -ism (postmodern or
feminism) is a monolithic, homogeneous, univocal position. Certainly the more one reads of postmodernism, one realizes that
there is no coherent theory, no manifesto, no clear roster of members, no agreed-upon moment of rupture when the modern ended
and the postmodern began. Critics as diverse as Lyotard and
Habermas (whose ongoing variance about the function and valence of the postmodern has continued itself across many texts),
Fredric Jameson, Hal Foster, Victor Burgin—the male constellation continues—all seem to endorse it as a problematic, an ongoing set of arguments about the philosophical condition, social
positioning, aesthetic effects of what (not without struggle) is
being deemed the postmodern.

While its usage and spelling vary (sometimes hyphenated,
sometimes not; sometimes capitalized, sometimes not), the word
postmodern has a semiotic instability that almost mimetically
inscribes its own sense of indeterminacy. The mire of debate
about its history and definition is infused with many of the epis-
temic assumptions that the theorists of the postmodern would
themselves challenge—the ontology of history, the denotative
certainty of definition. But when all the semantic dust settles,
these chronological and typological questions address either a
style (postmodern*ism*) or a social formation (postmoder*nity*). Much
of the murky quality of the debate about the postmodern would
become more focused by this clarification: the use of separate
terms for the social and philosophical dimension—moder*nity*

and postmodernity—and for its concurrent cultural movements —modernisms and postmodernisms (i.e., we live in postmodernity but art practice may exemplify modernism). [12]

Similarly, feminism as a practical or theoretical project is not a unified front or a singular discourse which posits fixed identity.[13] Using topographical language to describe its conflicting claims, Teresa de Lauretis has recently written: "feminism itself . . . is not a secure or stable ground but a highly permeable terrain infiltrated by subterranean waterways that cause it to shift under our feet and sometimes turn into a swamp." [14] Feminism contains its own litany of debates, not the least of which is the essentialism/anti-essentialism warfare, that cause the incendiary epithet "essentialist" to be flung in all directions, most frequently as a gesture of dismissal.

In descriptions of the feminine, the salient metaphorical structures of topography, sight, and sound posit a descriptive spectrum between unmapped/obscured/silent *and* positioned/visible/ voiced. The discourse of feminism has attempted to make the very unchartedness /masking/silence of the feminine into a positioned/visible/significant voice. In feminist discourse it is as if there is a coextensivity between the map and the territory— between feminist discourse and the feminine—something that is called into question, not just by Baudrillard in his insistence on a new ontological category of the hyperreal, but by the murky terrain of the postmodern debate.

Positions on the postmodern seem to split along the ideological divide of its effects (either or both): 1) a neoconservative, retrenchment, reassertion of traditional premodern values, a harking back to a past which was disturbed by the rupture of modernism or 2) a subversion of past values (both premodern and modern) through reappropriation or pastiche that somehow shifts the authority of those values. This is, of course, a gesture of great simplification. Fredric Jameson and Hal Foster have addressed much of their work on postmodernism to underlining the schisms that break between what Hal Foster calls "neo-conservative" vs. "poststructuralist" postmodernism.[15] Habermas and Lyotard have pitted themselves implicitly against each other in separate object relations with the postmodern—Habermas denounces the antimodernist roots of postmodernism which have subverted the completion he wishes of the modernist project (BAD OBJECT POSTMODERNISM), while Lyotard seems to find, if not emancipatory potential in the postmodern, a more philosophically positive valence: "Putting forth the unpresentable in presentation itself" (GOOD OBJECT POSTMODERNISM), he concludes his essay, "Quest-ce que le postmoderne?" with the proclamation, a slippery manifesto: "Let us wage war on totality, let us be witness to the unpresentable; let us activate the differences and save the honor of the name."[16] Lyotard may maintain that the grand narratives of Western culture have lost their meaning, but he is proposing new ones, as if heterogeneity, positionlessness, plurality are the "honor" of postmodernism. Clearly, even if these theorists or critics agree that postmodernism marks a crisis in cultural authority they seem split along the lines of its effects.

Both Owens and Huyssen, the only critics who seem to notice or mind the absence of feminist engagement, are also the most enthusiastic about the potentials of postmodern aesthetic activity (GOOD OBJECT POSTMODERNISTS). Huyssen optimistically, but perhaps a bit voluntaristically, tries to chart the impact of feminism on his map of the postmodern:

> It was especially the art, writing, film making and criticism of women and minority artists with their recuperation of buried and mutilated traditions, their emphasis on exploring forms of gender- and race-based subjectivity in aesthetic productions and experiences, and their refusal to be limited to standard canonizations, which added a whole new dimension to the critique of high modernism and to the emergence of alternative forms of culture.[17]

Owens, perhaps a bit more tempered in his assessment, claims: "Still, if one of the most salient aspects of our postmodern culture is the presence of an insistent feminist voice (and I use the terms presence and voice advisedly), theories of postmodernism have tended to either neglect or repress that voice."[18] However muted, Owens seems to hear that voice, find its presence in a long list of women artists—Barbara Kruger, Cindy Sherman, Mary Kelly, Sherry Levine, Martha Rosler—whose work constitutes a critique of male systems of representations, problematization of image, language, and power in the art world. From their work, Owens generalizes a destabilizing power:

> As recent analyses of the "enunciative apparatuses" of visual representation—its poles of emission and reception—confirm, the representational systems of the West admit only one vision—the constitutive male subject—or rather they posit the subject of representation as absolutely centered, unitary, masculine. . . . the postmodernist work attempts to upset the re-assuring stability of that mastering position.[19]

With such potential for postmodernism, feminism should enter the fray. If feminists have had as one of their prime agendas the reordering of relations of power and difference, then appropriation and its aesthetic underbelly, nostalgia, must be interrogated for the ways in which these strategies in representation *do* reorder relations of power and difference. But equally important here is the realization that postmodern aesthetic practice does not always undermine that authority, it can reassert it. The split between negation and affirmation of the past (whether it be the past of the modern or the premodern), the nature of one's dependence on that which one critiques, becomes the centrally valenced question for postmodern feminists.

Andreas Huyssen also has an argument that describes postmodernism's potential to *reposition* the female because, as he claims, the old rhetoric of modernism "has lost its persuasive power" and postmodernism can break through the constraints, cast off the shackles of fixed gender hierarchies. Huyssen provides a wonderfully incisive account (in an essay "Mass Culture as Woman: Modernism's Other")[20] of the inscription of the masculine into the modernist aesthetic, detailing the manner in which mass culture was posited as the "Other" of modernism and how modernism was full of a rhetoric that deposed the female, equating it with the vampirism of mass culture, but to assume that it was only a male province willfully overlooks the abounding presence of female modernists (from Gertrude Stein to H.D. to Dorothy Richardson and Virginia Woolf—to name only a few exemplars) who challenged the very authority of the male. Huyssen's defense of postmodern culture resides in the impact of women artists on culture, as if their presence alone induces a cultural change, destabilizes the authority of the male artist. (If this is so, I would want to examine the same potential within modernism.) Yet Huyssen's description of Flaubert's assertion "Madame Bov-

Figure 2.1

ary, c'est moi" as the fixed syntagm of modernism concisely sums up the gender configuration of much of modernism. But it also ironically applies to tendencies in critical cross-dressing. From Huyssen: "Flaubert fetishized his own imaginary femininity while simultaneously sharing his period's hostility toward real women, participating in a pattern of the imagination and of behavior all too common in the history of modernism."[21] The role of the male artist (or the male critic) whose authority allows him to have it both ways—enacting his imaginary femininity while asserting his cultural priority over real women—is not only the province of modernism, but also the premodern and (is it no surprise?) the postmodern.[22]

A premodern paradigm, not unlike Flaubert's "Madame Bovary, c'est moi," can be found in the recent assertion by a computer-aided artist that the Mona Lisa, long representation's most enigmatic female, was not a mysterious woman in Da Vinci's life but was Da Vinci himself, womanized. The all-knowing smile its own smug self-knowledge that, like Tootsie, Da Vinci was a better man to the world as a woman and a better woman to the world as a man than a woman would have been. And, as Lillian Schwartz, the artist whose computer-processed palimpsest of a self-portrait of Leonardo and the Mona Lisa led to such conclusions, points out, Da Vinci was fascinated by optical paradoxes (he wrote in a "mirror writing" that could be decoded only when held to a mirror). The Mona Lisa: an optical transvestism that has perplexed art historians for 500 years: "Mona Lisa," Da Vinci could have said, "sono io."[23]

Used Promiscuously

> Postmodernism is a term used promiscuously in art criticism, often as a mere sign for not modernism, or as a synonym for pluralism.
> —Hal Foster, "RE: POST"[24]

A term used promiscuously, random, indiscriminate. In the discourse of art criticism, its usage is an intercourse measured, in this case, as a "mere sign" for the negation of modernism as if

POST = NOT, the way that FEMALE = NOT MALE. As Foster is not-ing, postmodernism is a term without its own meaning, interiority, its substance is left defined only in usage/misusage.

Many have complained about the trivialization of the word "postmodern" — an adjective that has, in some cases, been kid-napped by conservatives and forced to submit to their agendas.[25] That the terminology of postmodernism has been scavenged by the discourses of advertising and the mass media without a knowledge of its ideological or theoretical underpinnings may be the greatest recuperation of the word — forced to sell the style of the signifier without the referent. A quick examination of the newsstand illustrates this rhetorical servitude, not so much a devaluation of the term, but rather its semantic inflation.

EXHIBIT A

A full-page ad in September 1986 Vogue, illustrating the fall ad campaign for the New York department store B. Altman's (liter-ally BE OLD MAN.) The ad copy reads:

ALTMAN'S
A New York tradition since 1865
We're entering an era of Post-modern poise
P.S.I's balance of flair and refinement

The image here is of a woman in a skirted suit.

The new cut-away jacket leads a long, lean line freed of non-essentials.
A discreet flash of brass buttons provides all the decor this beautiful shaping requires ... from the Chairman of the Board ... 360.00 Suit Shop, third floor of the store that specializes in ultra-modern ideas and old-fashioned fine service.

"WE'RE ENTERING AN ERA OF POST-MODERN POISE": the "we" here, a pronoun shifter that may or may not be gendered, is not the same "we" in Barbara Kruger's "WE CONSTRUCT THE CHORUS OF MISSING PERSONS," "WE WON'T PLAY NATURE TO YOUR CULTURE," a "we" that forces the spectator to shift uncomfortably between inclusion and exclusion.[26] The discourse of the post-modern is used here to market an image, to define a combination of the premodern and the modern, an "ERA" (a subliminal choice over "AGE" because it evokes the Equal Rights Amendment? Or is age a taboo in women's fashion?), a temporal space that "WE" have entered, a "POISE" not a pose, a "BALANCE" (of flair/refinement; ultramodern ideas/old-fashioned service) not a false stasis. The gender rhetoric here is quite garbled: "brass buttons" but a "discreet flash"; "Chairman of the Board" but "freed of non-essentials." The rhetoric of pastiche and combination, the ultramodern and the old-fashioned, sponsored by a New York tradition since 1865. ("Freed of non-essentials" reserving the equation of woman with essence, emancipating her in a non-denial denial, back to essentials, back to the body at the center of identity?) We are entering, but are we there yet?

EXHIBIT B

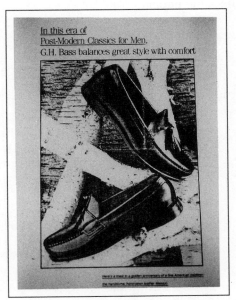

In this era of
Post-Modern Classics for Men,
G.H. Bass balances great style with comfort

A full-page ad, *New York Times*, September 19, 1986, more of Altman's fall ad campaign, but this one for menswear:

> In this era of
> Post-modern classics for Men
> G. H. Bass balances great style with comfort

The image here is of two loafers:

> Some things just don't need changing . . . They haven't missed a fashion beat since they started swinging way back in the thirties . . . at the store with two traditions, good taste and good service.

Given the context, one can't avoid recalling the Nietzsche quote from "The Use and Abuse of History": "We need history but not in the way a spoiled loafer in the garden of knowledge needs it."[27]

Here again, the temporal space, "ERA," of "Post-modern classics" provides a balance, a pluralist embrace of traditions (style/comfort; taste/service) recalling, re-using, celebrating the anniver-

sary of an enduring classic. Even B. Altman's competitor bandied
the word in the same paper:

EXHIBIT C

Menswear...with a new signature. Post-modernist. From Bill Robinson. Midnight blue jacket of pure wool; $280. Limestone cotton shirt, $85. Flecked wool trousers in limestone; $140. Silk jacquard tie; $35. In Moda on Six. In New York, today, meet Bill Robinson when he personally presents informal modeling of his collection from 5 to 7.

Saks Fifth Avenue

Saks Fifth Avenue at Rockefeller Center

New York Times ad image of man in zippered work jacket, but
with a tie. The copy is simple:

Menswear. . . . with a new signature. Post-modernist.

In all of these cases, we are looking at examples of what Roland
Barthes would call the *written garment*—the image reproduced
is not the garment per se—an item of real clothing—insomuch
as it is a combination of two systems of representation—the
described and the photographed, written clothing and image
clothing. Barthes, in this attempt to propose a semiology of fashion, describes a written garment as a purely imaginary signifier.[28]
These suits, these shoes, all vestimentary signs in a language of
fashion which changes its lexicon yearly—or even moment to
moment—are controlled by how they are *written*. The rhetorical

system evinced here writes these garments as postmodern, yet the clothing looks no different than last year's or next year's (in fact they are last year's!), using periodizing properties, the post-haste of postmodernism, to signify the very volatility of fashion.

Examples abound. Everywhere the term is flung. The *Village Voice* describes hipsters at a Jim Jarmusch screening as chewing "postmodern gum"; in *Vanity Fair*, Tina Brown describes charity hostess Gayfryd Steinberg's "postmodern haircut"; James Wolcott refers to the "postmodern druids" Robert Wilson, Twyla Tharp, Brian Eno.[29] (Even Steve's ice cream in New York markets its "MIX-INS" — the culinary equivalent of pastiche — as postmodern ice cream.) The cumulative connotation of postmodernism is a style of pluralistic otherness. Its usage is sloppy, ill-defined, polysemic, contradictory, What then, if anything, can it signify? In all of these cases, how does it repackage gender roles?? Are these retrenchments in the pre-feminist past or subversions of these very structures? Is POSTMODERNISM POSTFEMINIST???

A Case Study: Cindy Sherman vs. Madonna

As a brief excursion into the cultural, allow me to illustrate the narrow differences in the politics of appropriation between *recuperative* parody and *transgressive* parody.

Vanity Fair's December 1986 cover story on "Classic Madonna" —illustrated by four black-and-white still poses of the newly platinumed Madonna and three black-and-white stills of movie-star blondes, Grace Kelly, Judy Holiday, Marilyn Monroe— described Madonna's self-styled quotation of Marilyn Monroe. Madonna's reenactment in her "Material Girl" video of the "Diamonds Are a Girl's Best Friend" number from *Gentlemen Prefer Blondes* was, according to the author, "knowing, defiant, successful," causing the *National Inquirer* to run an article suggesting Madonna (b. 1958) was a reincarnation of Marilyn (d. 1962)— mathematical transubstantiation aside. The text accompanying these photos, producing a written image of Madonna, claims: "Instinctively she positions herself. Beautiful but strong. A feminist's Marilyn."[30]

Cindy Sherman, an artist who has positioned herself in a series

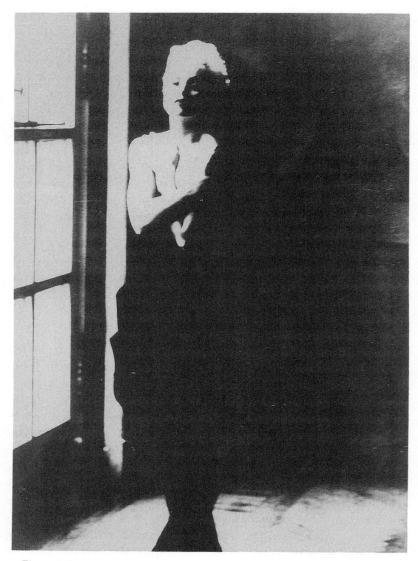

Figure 2.5

Figure 2.6

of *faux* film stills (here one much like Marilyn) may have done so to foreground femininity as masquerade, as construction, but let us ask how her images differ from Madonna's? Quotation here seems to produce split effects: between unmooring, dislodging, destabilizing effects which negate the authority of the construction itself (in this case, the positioning of woman as object of male desire, to-be-looked-at, in a sexually coded way) and, on the other hand, a reassertion, reintroduction, repetition of precisely the modes of representation that feminists have indicted as phallocratic and patriarchal.[31]

Both Cindy Sherman and Madonna take themselves as image, maneuver and perform their own constructions, but how do we assess the rather separate effects of their reordering of power and difference? What is at issue here is the nature of dependency on that which one quotes/appropriates—whether the critical cathexis empowers and centers what one intends to disempower and decenter. The politics of appropriation seem to require a site-specific analysis. The potential of transgressive appropriation, where radical irony—that nothing is real and all is representation

—what Linda Hutcheon argues is a "critical not recuperative return to the past"[32]—must be tempered by the risks involved. To maintain that reenactment exposes and undermines a system of power, is transgressive, denies the recuperative possibilities, the desires that are played into not challenged. Similarly, a too quick totalization that all is recuperative in appropriation and that all ruptures are repetitions, denies the possibility of breaking out of a signifying chain. Would we deem Cindy Sherman and Madonna, one transgressive, one recuperative? Or is that simply saying that art world strategies have a different audience/venue than mass cultural ones? Can we maintain these dichotomies in signification between high art and mass culture, or isn't the point that the separations have disappeared?

In their book The Postmodern Scene, Arthur Kroker and David Cook include a brief description of what they call "processed feminism," as though we are at a moment in late capitalism where even the discourse of feminism is recycled back to us, the Velveeta of its rhetoric reduced to smooth sale-ability. They describe Madonna and others (Annie Lennox) as "artists in the business of committing sign crimes against the big signifier of Sex."[33] Postmodernism, I would want to assert, does not offer an aesthetic of innovation or of the new, but one of return, recycling, a system-based ecology of the past. Yet how powerful is the web of recuperation? Is a sign crime a "deconstructive thrust"[34] or a playful semiotic game that reasserts the power of the old signs?

Up until now, I have conducted what was basically a discourse analysis—how postmodernism as a term has been recuperated by mass cultural marketing into an empty slogan—in much the same way that the discourse of feminism was engaged to sell cigarettes with "you've come a long way baby." Debates about modernity/ postmodernity would profit from an addition of feminist questions about social positioning and aesthetic representation of gender difference. Many of the questions that feminist film theory has posed to cinematic representation, how "woman" is appropriated as image, narrative agent, spectator, should be recalled here. The accounts of how woman is elided (her image omitted, given no narrative agency, spectators addressed as male) or constructed falsely (her image based on male desire, given a negative narrative agency, as in the *femme fatale*, and put in an impossible position of spectation) seem particularly useful here. While feminist film theorists began to produce treatises that demanded alternative strategies for image, narrative, spectation, the question is: are these alternatives possible in the foreclosure of signification in postmodernity?

Feminists must ask if the dislocation of signifier/signified that is so often found to be a symptom of postmodernism always constitutes a subversive dislocation, or, in some cases, seems to constitute the ascendancy of the sign into an emphatic reassertion of all that the feminist critique has questioned.

Neither or Both:
An Epilogue to the Period of the Plural

And, of course, the superlatives of pluralism are not new. Recall 1859: Dickens publishes *A Tale of Two Cities*, opens his book with "Chapter 1: The Period." ("It was the year of our Lord one thousand seven hundred and seventy five.") Already he was describing a period almost a century prior.

> It was the best of times, it was the worst of times, it was the age of wisdom, it was the age of foolishness, it was the epoch of belief, it was the epoch of incredulity, it was the season of Light, it was the season of Darkness, it was the spring of hope, it was the winter of despair, we had everything before us, we had nothing before us, we were all going direct to Heaven, we were all going direct the other way— in short, the period was so far like the present period, that some of its noisiest authorities insisted on its being received, for good or for evil, in the superlative degree of comparison only.

And about the *post* of modernism: It was conservative politics, it was subversive politics, it was the return of tradition, it was the final revolt of tradition, it was the unmooring of patriarchy, it was the reassertion of patriarchy . . . and so on.

Can we say only, in this waning and brightening light, that the POSTMAN ALWAYS RINGS TWICE; first time as tragedy, second as farce, and yet, the third time, is there a separate order beyond the simulacra of the referent? And has THE POSTWOMAN YET RUNG?

Endnotes

1. Charles Jencks, *The Language of Postmodern Architecture* (New York: Rizzoli, 1984), p. 5.

2. Freud's comment, "The sexual life of women is a 'dark continent' for psychology," from "The Question of Lay Analysis" (1926) was not, even metaphorically, more illuminating than his avowal in "Three Essays on the Theory of Sexuality" (1905): "[the sexual life of men] alone has become assessible to research. That of women . . . is still veiled in an impenetrable obscurity."

Lacan, in "Guiding Remarks for a Congress on Feminine Sexuality" (written 1958, spoken in 1960, published in 1964), offers a "Historical Introduction" of a "remarkable oversight." See *Feminine Sexuality*, Juliet Mitchell and Jacqueline Rose, eds. (New York: Norton, 1982).

3. "Answering the Question: What Is Postmodernism?" originally appeared as "Réponse à la question: Qu'est-ce que le postmoderne?" in *Critique*, (April 1982), no. 419, and is now included in *The Postmodern Condition: A Report on Knowledge* (Minneapolis: University of Minnesota Press, 1984). See also Lyotard's "Defining the Postmodern," in *ICA Documents* 4 (1985). Unfortunately, in the United States, Lyotard's name is synonymous with the word "postmodernism" and the theoretical issues that characterize his previous and subsequent work are overshadowed by the "p" word. It should also be noted that the twist in translation from the French *le postmoderne* into the English *postmodernism* has produced some of the semantic confusion in terminology. Charles Jencks, *What Is Postmodernism?* (New York: St. Martin's Press, 1986), repeats the question of definition.

4. Craig Owens, "Discourse of Others: Feminists and Postmodernism," in *The Anti-Aesthetic*, Hal Foster, ed. (Port Townsend, Wash.: Bay Press, 1983), p. 59.

5. Since this essay was written in 1986, the "mutual indifference" that I described seems to have been only partially resolved. [A version of this was given as a paper at the MLA Convention in New York City in 1986 and at Irvine in May 1987.]

While feminists have begun to attend to the debates around postmodernism, much of the dismissive indifference by postmodern (male) theorists has persisted. Or perhaps worse yet, discourse about postmodernity has shifted the cultural priority away from the feminist critique into another symptomatic terrain: *post*-feminism.

For feminist interventions in the postmodern debate, see: Nancy Fraser and Linda Nicholson, "Social Criticism Without Philosophy: An Encounter Between Feminism and Postmodernism," Laura Kipnis, "Feminism: The Political Conscience of Postmodernism?" and Jacqueline Rose, "*The Man Who Mistook His Wife for a Hat* or *A Wife is Like an Umbrella*—Fantasies of the Modern and Postmodern," in *Universal Abandon? The Politics of Postmodernism*, Andrew Ross, ed. (Minneapolis: University of Minnesota Press, 1988); Toril Moi, "Feminism, Postmodernism, and Style: Recent Feminist Criticism in the United States," *Cultural Critique* (Spring 1988), no. 9, Kate Linker, "Eluding Definition," *Art*-

forum (December 1984), and Abigail Solomon-Godeau, "Living with Contradictions: Critical Practices in the Age of Supply-Side Aesthetics," *Screen* (Summer 1987), vol. 28, no. 3.

In their book-length works, Linda Hutcheon, *A Poetics of Postmodernism* (New York: Routledge, 1988), Meaghan Morris, *The Pirate's Fiancée* (London: Verso, 1988), and Alice Jardine, *Gynesis: Configurations of Woman and Modernity* (Ithaca: Cornell University Press, 1985) contend with feminism's role in postmodernism/postmodernity.

6. Stephen Heath, "Difference," *Screen* (Autumn 1978) 19(3):53.

7. Owens, "Discourse," p. 61.

8. Andreas Huyssen, "Mapping the Postmodern," *New German Critique* (Fall 1984) no. 33, p. 27. This essay is now included in *After the Great Divide: Modernism, Mass Culture, Postmodernism* (Bloomington: Indiana University Press, 1986).

9. Elaine Showalter, "Critical Cross-Dressing: Male Feminists and The Woman of the Year," *Men in Feminism*, Alice Jardine and Paul Smith, eds. (New York: Methuen, 1987), pp. 116-133.

10. Owens, "Discourse," p. 59.

11. See Nancy Fraser and Linda Nicholson, "Social Criticism Without Philosophy: An Encounter Between Feminism and Postmodernism" (paper presented at International Association for Philosophy and Literature, April 30-May 2, 1987), now in *Universal Abandon? The Politics of Postmodernism*, Andrew Ross, ed. (Minneapolis: University of Minnesota Press, 1988). While Fraser and Nicholson point out that both feminism and postmodernism offer a philosophical critique, they describe both with univocal generalizations.

12. Jochen Schulte-Sasse, in "Modernity and Modernism, Postmodernity and Postmodernism: Framing the Issue," *Cultural Critique* (Winter 1986-1987), no. 5, makes a forceful assertion of this terminological clarification.

13. See Nancy F. Cott, *The Grounding of Modern Feminism* (New Haven: Yale University Press, 1987), for a description of the etymology of the word "feminism" as a term which replaced the "woman movement" of the nineteenth century.

14. Teresa de Lauretis, "Feminist Studies / Critical Studies: Issues, Terms, Contexts," *Feminist Studies/Critical Studies*, Teresa de Lauretis, ed. (Bloomington: Indiana University Press, 1986), p. 7.

15. Hal Foster, "Postmodernism: A Preface." in *The Anti-Aesthetic*, Hal Foster, ed. (Port Townsend, Wash.: Bay Press, 1983).

16. Jean-François Lyotard, *The Postmodern Condition* (Minneapolis: University of Minnesota Press, 1984), pp. 81, 82.

17. Andreas Huyssen, "Mapping the Postmodern," p. 27.

18. Owens, "Discourse," p. 61

19. *Ibid.*, p. 58.

20. Andreas Huyssen, "Mass Culture as Woman: Modernism's Other," in *Studies in Entertainment*, Tania Modleski, ed. (Bloomington: Indiana University Press, 1986). This essay is also included in *After the Great Divide: Modernism, Mass Culture, Postmodernism* (Bloomington: Indiana University Press, 1986).

21. *Ibid.*, p. 189.

22. See my review essay: "Mercator of the Postmodern: Mapping the Great Divide," *Camera Obscura*, 18:67-79. (That essay was written after, but published before, this essay.)

23. Lillian Schwartz, "Leonardo's Mona Lisa," *Art & Antiques* (January 1987).

24. Hal Foster, "Re: Post," in *Art After Modernism: Rethinking Representation*, Brian Wallis, ed. (New York: New Museum of Contemporary Art, 1984), p. 189.

25. See Victor Burgin, *The End of Art Theory: Criticism and Postmodernity* (Atlantic Highlands, N.J.: Humanities Press International, 1986).

26. See Barbara Kruger's *We Won't Play Nature to Your Culture* (London: ICA Catalogue, 1983).

27. Friedrich Nietzsche, "The Use and Abuse of History."

28. Roland Barthes, *The Fashion System* (New York: Hill and Wang, 1983).

29. Jane Shapiro, "Stranger in Paradise," *The Village Voice*, September 16, 1986; Tina Brown, "Gayfryd Takes Over," *Vanity Fair*, October 1986; James Wolcott, *Vogue*, October 1986.

30. Michael Gross, "Classic Madonna," *Vanity Fair*, December 1986. Madonna certainly was not the first star to impersonate a star of the past. In 1958 Richard Avedon photographed Marilyn Monroe in the guise of Jean Harlow. But is Avedon's version of Marilyn as Harlow the same as Madonna's "self-styled" version of Marilyn? The question here is *who* is positioning her? Madonna's quotation of the Monroe image seemed, to the *Vanity Fair* author, more "knowing" and "defiant"—in short, a transgressive appropriation. See Leo Braudy, *The Frenzy of Renown* (New York: Oxford University Press, 1986), photographic plate opposite page 339.

31. See Peter Schjeldahl's Introductory essay in *Cindy Sherman* (New York: Pantheon Books, 1984) for an indication of his (male) reaction: "As a male, I also find these pictures sentimentally, charmingly, and sometime pretty fiercely erotic: I'm in love again with every look at the insecure blonde in the nighttime city. I am responding to Sherman's knack, shared with many movie actresses, of projecting feminine vulnerability thereby triggering (masculine) urges to ravish and/or to protect" (p. 9).

32. Linda Hutcheon, "The Politics of Postmodernism: Parody and History," *Cultural Critique* (Winter 1986-1987), no. 5.

33. Arthur Kroker and David Cook, *The Postmodern Scene* (New York: St. Martin's Press, 1986), pp. 20-22.

34. Owens, "Discourse," p. 58.

3

SOME CALL IT FICTION: ON THE POLITICS OF DOMESTICITY
Nancy Armstrong

> It is queer how out of touch with truth women are. They live
> in a world of their own, and there has never been anything
> like it, and never can be.
>
> Joseph Conrad, *Heart of Darkness*

FOR SOME years now, American scholars have been puzzling out
the relationship between literature and history. Apparently the
right connections were not made when literary histories were
first compiled. Yet in turning to the question of how some of the
most famous British novelists were linked to their moment in
time, I have found I must begin at step one, with extremely
powerful conventions of representation. Though old and utterly
familiar, nothing new has taken their place. Their potency has
not diminished in this country despite the theory revolution and
the calls for a new literary history that came in its wake. The
conventions to which I refer are many and various indeed, but all
reinforce the assumption that history consists of economic or
political events, as if these were essentially different from other
cultural events. Some of us—a distinct minority, to be sure—feel
that to proceed on this assumption is to brush aside most of the
activities composing everyday life and so shrink the category of
"the political" down to a very limited set of cultural practices.
And then, having classified most of our symbolic activities as
"personal," "social," or "cultural" (it is all much the same),
traditional histories would have us place them in a secondary

relationship either to the economy or to the official institutions of state. This essay is written in opposition to models of history that confine political practices to activities directly concerned with the marketplace, the official institutions of the state, or else resistance to these. I write as one who feels that such models have not provided an adequate basis for understanding the formation of a modern bureaucratic culture or for our place, as intellectuals, within it. More than that, I regard any model that places personal life in a separate sphere and that grants literature a secondary and passive role in political history as unconsciously sexist. I believe such models necessarily fail to account for the formation of a modern bureaucratic culture because they fail to account for the place of women within it.

Some of our best theorizers of fiction's relationship to history —Raymond Williams in England and Edward Said in the United States—have done much to tear down the barrier between culture and state. They demonstrate that the middle-class hegemony succeeded in part because it constructed separate historical narratives for self and society, family and factory, literature and history. They suggest that by maintaining these divisions within culture, liberal intellectuals continue to sanitize certain areas of culture—namely, the personal, domestic, and literary. The practices that go by these names consequently appear to be benignly progressive, in their analyses, to provide a place of escape from the political world, and even to offer forms of resistance. Still, I would argue, such efforts as those of Williams and Said will be only partially successful so long as they continue to ignore *the sexual division of labor* that underwrites and naturalizes the difference between culture and politics.

The Limits of Political History

To put some life into all these abstractions, let me now turn to domestic fiction and the difficulties that scholars encounter when they try to place writing of this kind in history. Ian Watt convincingly describes the socioeconomic character of the new readership for whom Defoe, Richardson, and Fielding wrote, a readership whose rise in turn gave rise to the novel. But Watt has no

similar explanation for Austen. Her popularity he ascribes to her
talent, and her talent, to nature. And so he concludes that nature
must have given Austen a good eye for details.[1] Although Williams moves well beyond such reflection theories in his groundbreaking account of the information revolution, his model of
history ultimately serves us no better than Watt's when it comes
to explaining domestic fiction. His *Long Revolution* regards intellectual labor as a political force in its own right without which
capitalism could not have unfolded as smoothly and completely
as it appears to have done. But however much power Williams
grants this domain, it belongs to culture and, as such, exists in a
secondary relationship with political history. To historicize writing, he feels compelled to give it a source in events outside of and
prior to writing. He does not entertain the possibility that the
classic unfolding of capitalism was predicated on writing, much
less on writing by women or writing that appealed to the interests
of a female readership.[2] For Williams as for Watt, historical events
take place in the official institutions of state or else through
resistance to these institutions, and both forms of power are exercised primarily through men.

I have found Watt and Williams especially helpful for establishing links between the history of fiction and the rise of the new
middle classes in England. At the same time, I am perplexed to
find that, in establishing a relationship between writing and political history, these otherwise conscientious scholars completely
neglect to account for the most obvious fact of all, namely, that
sometime during the eighteenth century, in the words of Virginia
Woolf, "the middle class woman began to write."[3] If, as Watt and
Williams say, the rise of the novel was directly related to the rise
of the new middle classes, then some of our best literary evidence
suggests that the rise of the novel was related to the emergence of
women's writing as well. In drawing this equation, of course, I
have doubled the difficulties entailed in historicizing fiction, for
I have suggested that to historicize fiction we must politicize not
only intellectual labor but female labor as well. Much of British
fiction exists at the intersection of these two definitively modern
subsets of culture and is thereby twice removed from the mainstream of political history.

The writing I call domestic fiction is gender-inflected writing. Unlike the work of earlier women of letters, it comes to us as women's writing. In designating certain forms of writing as feminine, it designates other writing as masculine. The enclosure that marks a Jane Austen novel does not simply distinguish her "world" from that of a Shakespeare, a Blake, a Dickens, or a Yeats. The boundaries it constructs between inside and outside are personal in a far more wide-reaching and historically significant way. They mark the difference between the world over which women novelists have authority—the domain of the personal—and that which is ruled by men and their politics. In doing this, Austen makes Richardson the father of the novel, for, like him, she identifies the work of the novelist with the writing of women as well as with other forms of labor that are suitably feminine.[4] To move beyond the impasse that prevents us from situating this work in history, we have it seems to me, to toss out the idea that the gendering of vast areas of culture was a consequence of political events over which men had control. To consider gender itself as a political formation over which modern cultures gave women authority, we will have to invert these priorities. Having done so, one comes face to face with the possibility that a revolution in the home preceded the spread of the factory system and all that hinged upon its becoming the means of distributing the wealth of the nation.[5]

To deal with this possibility, I begin with the proposition Marx put forth in *The German Ideology* and Gramsci later developed into the concept of "hegemony" in his essays on the formation of intellectuals and the organization of culture and education: no political revolution is complete without a cultural revolution. To dominate, the dominant group must offer to one and all a view that makes their form of domination seem true and necessary if not desirable and right. Gramsci developed the contradiction inherent in Marx's notion of labor—that labor was not only a commodity, but also a social practice—into a theory that stressed the double-sidedness of middle-class power: it controlled not only the physical dimension of production but also the social dimension. During the twentieth century, moreover, Gramsci could see that a form of power that worked through spatial location, supervision, and individuals' relationship with machines was giving way to something more ubiquitous—bureaucratic control that divided and hierarchized individuals so as to place their labor on separate social planes. And indeed, as the wage was generalized to include members of this and other bureaucracies, those who performed productive labor shrank in number and importance.

More recently, therefore, a number of us who work in the humanities and social sciences have begun to feel theories of resistance which depend upon an essentialized class or, for that matter, any other essentialized group will no longer do. Once taken up by theory, such essentialisms quickly cease to represent the possibility of power coalescing outside a pluralistic society. Rather, they identify contradictory positions within that system and, in so doing, only supply more differences in a differential system that exists on an abstract plane of ideas. The system to which I refer is no system in the abstract, however, but the disciplinary institution itself. Slouching by way of homology from one cultural site to another, it has achieved the status of a paradigm. In its atomizing structure, political issues get lost. Everything matters. All truths are equivalent—only some are more complex and, in this respect alone, more satisfying than others. In the maze of differences, the difference between positive and negative has all but disappeared, and the paradise of liberalism seems near at hand.[6]

So perceiving her historical moment, one can consider in a radically materialist light the Foucauldian propositions that the modern state was called into being in writing, exists mainly as a state of mind, and perpetuates itself through the well orchestrated collection, regulation, and dissemination of information. The idea of order that Foucault sometimes calls "discourse" or "power" and at other times names "sexuality" or "discipline" is indeed a ruling idea. But in a world that is ruled more surely by ideas than by physical or economic means, one has to be especially careful not to hypothesize some corresponding "reality" as their source. We cannot grant these ideas the autonomy, universality, and mystic interconnection that they have achieved, but neither can we seek out some more primary truth behind or below them. Rather, we must understand them, as Foucault suggests, as the self-conception of a class that has achieved hegemony. And hegemony in the case of modern post-industrial societies, depends on self-conceptions capable of swallowing up all opposition in a single system of micro-differences.

The power of the system depends upon the production of a particular form of consciousness that is at once unique and standardizing. In place of what he calls the "repressive hypothesis," the assumption that culture either "suppresses" or "imposes itself on" the individual's desire, Foucault offers a productive hypothesis that turns this commonplace on its ear. The first volume of The History of Sexuality argues that the very forms of subjectivity we consider most essential to ourselves as selves had no existence prior to their symbolization, that the deepest and most private recesses of our being are culturally produced.[7] His Discipline and Punish mounts a detailed historical argument to show that the truth of the modern individual existed first as writing, before she or he was transformed successively into speech, thought, and unconscious desire.[8] Thus Foucault enables us to see the European Enlightenment as a revolution in words, which gave writing a new and awesome power over the world of objects as it shaped the individuals who established a relationship with that world through reading. In England, I would like to suggest, this cultural revolution was the only kind of revolution to occur during the eighteenth century, because in England the revolution in words took a form that prevented popular revolution.[9]

Having torn down the conceptual barrier between writing and political history, we have cleared the way to see the intellectual labor of women as part of the mainstream of political events. Foucault will not help us achieve this particular step, however. His History of Sexuality is not concerned with the history of gender. Nor does it deal with the role that writing for, by, and about women played in the history of sexuality, For this reason, his procedures cannot identify the decisive events that detached family life from politics, and these are the very events that tie the formation of a domestic domain to the development of an institutional culture in England. Foucault's Discipline and Punish overlooks the fact that the modern household served as the groundbreaking prototype of modern institutions. His History of

Sexuality neglects to theorize the power of that prototype as it spills over from this account of modern personal life into his account of institutional power to saturate and make intelligible the theory of discipline. Despite the anti-Cartesian thrust of his work, Foucault does not finally break through the barrier that separates his position as theorizer of the sexual subject in *The History of Sexuality* from the one he takes up in order to theorize the political subject in *Discipline and Punish*. Yet not only does he use the same figure to think out the two; he also gives the strategies producing the sexual subject (those organizing the home) priority in his thinking over the strategies that subject the individual to the state (those of disciplinary institutions).

Central to the central chapter on "Panopticism" in *Discipline and Punish* is Foucault's figure of the city under plague. In contrast with leprosy, which calls for exclusionary strategies more consistent with the aristocratic imagination of power, the plague, as he plays with the figure, seems to require inclusion and enclosure as preconditions for a modern system of surveillance. The division of the population into progressively smaller subdivisions of which the household is the basic module, is followed by the ritual purification of each and every household:

> Five or six days after the beginning of the quarantine, the process of purifying the houses one by one is begun. All the inhabitants are made to leave; in each room "the furniture and goods" are raised from the ground or suspended from the air; perfume is poured around the room; after carefully sealing the windows, doors and even the keyholes with wax, the perfume is set alight. Finally, the entire house is closed while the perfume is consumed; those who have carried out the work are searched, as they were on entry, "in the presence of the residents of the house, to see that they did not have something on their persons as they left that they did not have on entering." Four hours later, the residents are allowed to re-enter their homes. (p. 197)

Such enclosure and purification of the house produces a new household free from the taint of any unregulated intercourse with the world, its membrane permeable only to certain kinds of information. Reading this account of the plague, I am struck by the difference between its place in the modern imagination and its use by Boccaccio, who imagined a small aristocratic community safely ensconced in the country to pass the time free from the infection of the city. In this early modern world, those who remain in the city are to be regarded as a different social body altogether, behaving much like the riotous and grotesquely permeable body celebrated by Bakhtin. How significant, then, that Foucault, in contrast with Bakhtin, imagines a city purified from the inside out by the production of hygenically pure domestic spaces within the body politic! In this attempt to fantasize the present from the position of the past, households serve as magical spaces where people go to die in order that they may be reborn as modern individuals—enclosed and self-regulating.

Having pursued the internal logic of his figure thus far, Foucault extends it outward from the newly enclosed domestic world —as from a new source of power—into the cultural and political domains, and from there into history. First, he notes how a "whole literary fiction of the festival grew up around the plague: suspended laws, lifted prohibitions, the frenzy of passing time, bodies mingling together without respect, individuals unmasked, abandoning their statutory identity and the figure under which they had been recognized, allowing a quite different truth to appear. But," he continues, "there was also a political dream of the plague, which was exactly its reverse: not the collective festival, but strict divisions; not laws transgressed, but the penetration of regulation into even the smallest details of everyday life . . . ; not masks that were put on and taken off, but the assignment to each individual of his 'true' name, his 'true' place, his 'true' disease" (pp. 197–198). On the metaphor of the city under plague thus rests Foucault's entire theory of the development of modern institutions: "If it is true that the leper gave rise to rituals of exclusion, which to a certain extent provided the model for and general form of the Great Confinement, then the plague gave rise to disciplinary projects" (p. 198). Metaphorical use of disease allows him to declare the eighteenth-century hospital with its anatomy theater as the historical prototype for the modern prison.

And to be sure, I *like* Foucault for transgressing the boundary between the therapeutic and the punitive to demonstrate how much they have in common. But this, to my mind, is also a way of avoiding the full implications of his chosen metaphor, the city under plague, implications that would destroy the differences between sexual subject and political subject, and between these and the subject's material body, all of which rest upon preserving the line that divvies up cultural information according to gender. This is the line between inside and outside that is implanted in his metaphor from the beginning to distinguish personal from political life. This is the first division of the conceptual zygote, the line without which the fantasy of an entire political world cannot develop its inexorable symmetry, a symmetry that cuts beneath and through particular features that culture manifests at one site rather than another. While he opens the category of political power considerably by including institutions other than those officially charged to distribute wealth and power, Foucault extends the cultural scope of discipline only so far as institutions that, in becoming institutions, came to be dominated by men. Thus if power does not originate in the minds of individual men or in the bodies of men collectively, it arises from the cultural patterns that make men think of themselves as certain kinds of men and exercise power accordingly.

But if one pursues the implications of Foucault's chosen metaphor for modern power, his city under plague, in contrast with a Boccaccian remedy, contains a certain form of household that is the perfect and obvious answer to the indiscriminate mingling of bodies spreading the infection. When we expand our concept of the political further even than Foucault's, we discover grounds on which to argue that the modern household rather than the clinic provided the proto-institutional setting where government through relentless supervision first appeared, and appeared in its most benevolent guise. Foucault never takes note of these continuities between home and state even though they are as plain as the words on his page. More curious still is his failure to acknowledge the fact that a home espoused by various subgroups aspiring for the status of "respectability," a home overseen by a woman, actually preceded the formation of other social institutions by at least fifty years. There is little to suggest this household took root in practice much before the beginning of the nine-

teenth century, even though it frequently appeared in the literature
and political argumentation of the previous century. From writing, it can be argued, the new family passed into the realm of
common sense, where it came to justify the distribution of national wealth through wages paid to men. Indeed, it remains
extremely powerful to this day as both metaphor and metonymy,
the unacknowledged model and source of middle-class power.[10]

The Power of Domesticity

It is at this point in my argument that a feminist perspective
must be invoked, but it cannot be a feminism that sinks comfortably into the rhetoric of victimization. It has to be thoroughly
politicized. By this I mean we must be willing to accept the idea
that, as middle-class women, we are empowered, although we are
not empowered in traditionally masculine ways. We have to acknowledge that as middle-class intellectuals we are not critical
mirrors of a separate and more primary process orchestrated by
others—be they politicians, bureaucrats, captains of industry, or
simply men. As women intellectuals we are doubly implicated in
the process of reproducing the state of mind upon which other
openly and avowedly political institutions depend. It is on this
basis that I reject the notion that women's writing exists in a
domain of experience outside of political history. I can no longer
accept what conventional histories assume—that such writing
occupies the secondary status of a "reflection" or "consequence"
of changes within more primary social institutions—the army,
hospital, prison, or factory. To the contrary, my evidence reveals
domestic fiction actively disentangled the language of sexual relations from that of political economy. The rhetoric of this fiction
(in Wayne Booth's sense of the term) laid out a new cultural logic
that would eventually become common sense, sensibility, and
public opinion. In this way, female knowledge successfully com-
batted one kind of power, based on title, wealth, and physical
force, with another, based on the control of literacy. By equating
good reading with what was good for women readers, a new
standard for reading laid down the semantic ground for common
sense and established the narrative conventions structuring pub-

lic opinion. The new standard of literacy helped to bring a new class of people into existence. This class laid claim to the right to privacy on behalf of each individual. Yet this class set in motion the systematic invasion of private life by surveillance, observation, evaluation, and remediation. In a word, it ruled, still rules, through countless microtechniques of socialization, all of which may be lumped together under the heading of education.[11] During the second half of the nineteenth century, institutions were created to perform these operations upon masses of people in much the same way as domestic fiction did upon characters.

Those of us who have grown up within an institutional culture consequently carry around a voice much like that of a fictional narrator in his or her head. Sensitive to the least sign of disorder —a foul word, a piece of clothing undone, some food sliding off one's fork, or, worse still, some loss of control over bodily functions—the presence of this voice, now nearly two hundred years old, more surely keeps us in line than fear of the police or the military. For the unofficial forms of power have a terrible advantage over those which are openly and avowedly regulatory. They make us afraid of ourselves. They operate on the supposition that we harbor desires dangerous to the general good. Believing in the presence of a self that is essentially subversive, we keep watch over ourselves—in mirrors, on clocks, on scales, through medical exams, and by means of any number of other such practices. Thus we internalize a state that is founded on the conflict between self and state interests, and we feel perfectly justified in enacting its power—which is, after all, only good for oneself—upon others.

Convinced that power exerted in and through the female domain is at least as powerful as the more conventional forms of power associated with the male, I want to sketch out the relationship between the two during the modern period. I will suggest that modern institutional cultures depend upon the separation of "the political" from "the personal" and that they produce and maintain this separation on the basis of gender—the formation of masculine and feminine domains of culture. For, I will argue, even as certain forms of cultural information were separated into these two opposing fields, they were brought together as an intricate set of pressures that operated on the subject's body and mind to induce self-regulation. We can observe this peculiarly effective collaboration of the official and unofficial forms of power perhaps most clearly in the formation of a national education system during the Victorian period and in the whole constellation of efforts that went on simultaneously to appropriate leisure time.[12] British fiction participates in both efforts and therefore demonstrates the modes of collaboration between them.

To introduce their highly influential *Practical Education* in 1801, Maria Edgeworth and her father announce their break with the curriculum that reinforced traditional political distinctions: "On religion and politics we have been silent because we have no ambition to gain partisans, or to make proselytes, and because we do not address ourselves to any sect or party."[13] In virtually the same breath, they assure readers, "With respect to what is commonly called the education of the heart, we have endeavored to suggest the easiest means of inducing useful and agreeable habits, well regulated sympathy and benevolent affections" (p. viii). Their program substitutes abstract terms of emotion and behavior for those of one's specific socioeconomic identity. Rooting identity in the very subjective qualities that earlier curricula had sought to inculcate in young women alone, the Edgeworths' program gives priority to the schoolroom and parlor over the church and courts for purposes of regulating human behavior. In doing this, their educational program promises to suppress the political signs of human identity (which is of course a powerful political gesture in its own right). Perfectly aware of the power to be exercised through education, the Edgeworths justify their curriculum for cultivating the heart on grounds that it offered a new and more effective method of policing. In their words, "It is the business of education to prevent crimes, and to prevent all those habitual propensities which necessarily lead to their commission" (p. 354).

To accomplish their ambitious political goal, the Edgeworths invoke an economy of pleasure which cannot in fact be understood apart from the novel and the criticism that was produced both to censor and to foster it. First, the Edgeworths accept the view prevailing during the eighteenth century which said that fiction was sure to mislead female desire:

> With respect to sentimental stories, and books of mere enter-
> tainment, we must remark, that they should be sparingly
> used, especially in the education of girls. This species of
> reading cultivates what is called the heart prematurely, low-
> ers the tone of the mind, and induces indifference for those
> common pleasures and occupations which . . . constitute by
> far the greatest portion of our daily happiness. (p. 105)

But the same turn of mind could as easily recognize the practical
value of pleasure when it is harnessed and aimed at the right
goals. Convinced that "the pleasures of literature" acted upon the
reader in much the same way as a child's "taste for sugar-plums"
(p. 80), forward-thinking educators began to endorse the reading
of fiction, so long as it was governed by principles that made
conformity seem desirable.

In formulating a theory of mass education in which fiction had
a deceptively marginal role to play, the Edgeworths and their
colleagues were adopting a rhetoric which earlier reformers had
used to level charges of violence and corruption against the old
aristocracy. They placed themselves in the tradition of radical
Protestant dissent going back to the sixteenth century, a tradition
which had always argued that political authority should be based
on moral superiority. Sexual relations so often provided the terms
for making this claim that no representation of the household
could be considered politically neutral. To contest that notion of
the state which depended upon inherited power, puritan treatises
on marriage and household governance represented the family as
a self-enclosed social unit into whose affairs the state had no
right to intervene. Against genealogy they posited domesticity.
But in claiming sovereignty for the natural father over his household, these treatises were not proposing a new distribution of
political power. They were simply trying to limit the monarch's
power. To understand the social transformation that was achieved
by the English Revolution (according to Christopher Hill, not
achieved until more than a century later), we have to turn away
from what we consider to be the political themes of the puritan
argument and consider instead what happens to gender.[14]

According to Kathleen M. Davis, the puritan doctrine of equality insisted upon the difference of sexual roles, in which the

female was certainly subordinate to the male, and not upon the equality of the woman in kind. "The result of this partnership," she explains, "was a definition of mutual and complementary duties and characteristics." Gender was so clearly understood in these oppositional terms that it could be graphically represented: [15]

Husband	Wife
Get goods	Gather them together and save them
Travel, seek a living	Keep the house
Get money and provisions	Do not vainly spend it
Deal with many men	Talk with few
Be "entertaining"	Be solitary and withdrawn
Be skillful in talk	Boast of silence
Be a giver	Be a saver
Apparel yourself as you may	Apparel yourself as it becomes you
Dispatch all things outdoors	Oversee and give order within

In so representing the household as the opposition of complementary genders, the authors of countless puritan tracts asked readers to imagine the household as a self-enclosed social unit. But if these authors wanted to define the family as an independent source of authority, their moment did not arrive. The puritan household consisted of a male and a female who were structurally identical, positive and negative versions of the same thing. The authority of the housewife described above could not yet be imagined as a positive thing in its own right. Until she took up her vigil and began to order personal life, a single understanding of power reigned, and men fought to determine the balance among its various parts.

Unlike the authors of seventeenth-century marriage manuals and domestic economies, the educational reformers of nineteenth-century England could look back on a substantial body of writing whose main purpose was to produce a historically new woman. During the centuries between the English Revolution and the present day, this woman was inscribed with values which apppealed to a whole range of competing interest groups, and, through her, these groups seized authority over domestic relations and personal life. In this way, I believe, they created a need for the kind of surveillance which modern institutions provide. Indeed, the last two decades of the seventeenth century saw an explosion of writing aimed at educating the daughters of the numerous aspiring social groups. The new curriculum promised to educate these women in such a way as to make them more desirable than women who had only their own rank and fortune to recommend them. This curriculum exalted a woman whose value resided chiefly in her femaleness rather than in the traditional signs of status, a woman who possessed emotional depth rather than a physically stimulating surface, one who, in other words, excelled in the very qualities that differentiated her from the male. As gender was redefined in these terms, the woman exalted by an aristocratic tradition of letters ceased to appear so desirable. In becoming the other side of this new sexual coin, she represented surface rather than depth, embodied material as opposed to moral value, and displayed idle sensuality instead of unflagging concern for the well-being of others. So conceived, the aristocratic woman no longer defined what was truly and most desirably female.

But it was not until the mid nineteenth century that the project of defining people on the basis of gender began to acquire some of the immense political influence it still exercises today. Around the 1830s, one can see the discourse of sexuality relax its critical gaze on the aristocracy as the newly forming working classes became a more obvious target of moral reform. Authors suddenly took notice of social elements who had hardly mattered before. These reformers and men of letters discovered that rebellious artisans and urban laborers, for example, lacked the kind of motivation that supposedly characterized normal individuals. Numerous writers sought out the source of poverty, illiteracy, and demographic change in these underdeveloped individuals, whose behavior was generally found to be not only promiscuous but also ambiguously gendered. Once they succeeded in translating an overwhelming economic problem into a sexual scandal, middle-class intellectuals could step forward and offer themselves, their technology, their supervisory skills, and their institutions of education and social welfare as the appropriate remedy for growing political resistance.

In all fairness, as Foucault notes, the middle classes rarely applied institutional procedures to others without first trying them out on themselves. When putting together a national curriculum, the government officials and educators in charge adopted one modeled on the educational theory that grew up around the Edgeworths and their intellectual circle, the heirs of the dissenting tradition.[16] This was basically the same as the curriculum proposed by eighteenth-century pedagogues and reformers as the best way of producing a marriageable daughter. By the end of the eighteenth century, the Edgeworths were among those who had already determined that the program aimed at producing the ideal woman could be applied to boys just as well as to girls. And by the mid-nineteenth century, one can see the government figuring out how to administer much the same program on a mass basis. In providing the conceptual foundation for a national curriculum, a particular idea of the self thus became commonplace, and as gendered forms of identity determined how people thought of themselves as well as others, that self became the dominant social reality.

Such an abbreviated history cannot do justice to the fierce controversies punctuating the institution of a national education system in England. I simply call attention to this material as a site where political history obviously converged with the history of sexuality as well as with that of the novel to produce a specific kind of individual. I do this to suggest the political implications of representing these as separate narratives. As it began to deny its political and religious bias and to present itself instead as a moral and psychological truth, the rhetoric of reform obviously severed its ties with an aristocratic past and took up a new role in history. It no longer constituted a form of resistance but enclosed a specialized domain of culture apart from political relations where apolitical truths could be told. The novel's literary status hinged upon this event. Henceforth fiction would deny the political basis for its meaning and refer instead to the private regions of the self or to the specialized world of art but never to the use of words that created and still maintains these distinctions so basic to our culture. Favored among kinds of fiction were novels that best performed the rhetorical operations of division and self-containment and thus turned existing political information into the discourse of sexuality. These works of fiction gave novels a good name, a name free of politics, and often the name of a woman such as Pamela, Evelina, Emma, or Jane Eyre. Then, with the translation of human identity into sexual identity came widespread repression of the political literacy characterizing an earlier culture, and with it, too, mass forgetting that there was a history of sexuality to tell.

The Politics of Domestic Fiction

Let me offer a detailed example of the exchange between reader and literary text to provide a sense of how the power of domesticity works through such an exchange. Charlotte Brontë flaunted this very power in writing her novel *Shirley*. The novel contains an otherwise gratuitous scene where Shakespeare's *Coriolanus* is read aloud and critiqued, as if to give the reader precise rules for reading, rules that should fascinate literary historians. They are not Brontë's own but rules developed during the preceding century by countless authors of ladies' conduct books and educational treatises. These authors proposed the first curriculum to include native British literature. Around the time Brontë sat down to write *Shirley*, a new generation of writers had taken up the question of how to distinguish good reading from bad. Their efforts swelled the growing number of Victorian magazines. Whether or not girls should read novels was the concern that shaped the debates over a curriculum for women during the eighteenth century, then nineteenth-century pedagogical theory developed around the question of how to make fiction useful for teaching foreigners and working-class people as well as women and children. Rules for reading developed along with the national standard curriculum that extended a curriculum originally meant only for girls of the literate classes to young Englishmen and women at various levels and their counterparts throughout the colonies. It is much the same theory of education that informs our educational system today. By using this example from *Shirley* to illustrate the rationale and procedures by which Victorian intellectuals extended what had been regarded as a female form of literacy to male education, I also want to mark an important difference between Charlotte Brontë's understanding of this process and our own. She was, I believe, far more aware of the politics of literary interpretation than we are.

One of her least colorful heroines, Carolyn Helstone, uses Shakespeare to while away an evening of leisure with her beloved cousin and future husband Robert Moore, a surly manufacturer, whose authoritarian way of dealing with factory hands is earning him threats of Luddite reprisals. During this, their one intimate moment together until the end of the novel, they reject all the pastimes available to lovers in an Austen novel in favor of reading Shakespeare's *Coriolanus*. Far more detailed than any such exchange in earlier fiction, this act of reading spells out the procedures by which reading literature was thought to produce a form of knowledge that was also a form of social control. Robert Moore is half Belgian, half English. It is through reading Shakespeare that, according to Carolyn, he "shall be entirely English." [17] For, as she patiently explains to him, "Your French forefathers don't speak so sweetly, not so solemnly, nor so impressively as your English ancestors, Robert." But being English does not identify a set of political affiliations—as it would in Shakespeare's time. It refers instead to essential qualities of human mind. Caroline has selected a part for Robert to read aloud that, in her words, "is toned with something in you. It shall waken your nature, fill your mind with music, it shall pass like a skillful hand over your heart .... Let glorious William come near and touch it; you will see how he will draw the English power and melody out of its chords."

I have called this relationship between reader and text an exchange in order to stress the fact that writing cannot be turned to the task of constituting readers without giving up old features and acquiring new ones of its own; to dwell on the reader is to explain but one half of the transformational logic of this exchange. Just as Robert, the rude Belgian, becomes a gentle Englishman by reading Shakespeare, so, too, the Jacobean playwright is transformed by the domestic setting in which he is read.

Carolyn urges Robert to receive the English of another historical moment as the voice of an ancestor speaking to him across time and cultural boundaries. To no one's surprise, the written Shakespeare, thus resurrected, has acquired the yearnings and anxieties of an early nineteenth-century factory owner. And as we observe the Bard becoming the nineteenth-century man, we also witness an early version of our own literary training. Here, extending through the educated middle-class female to the male and, through him, acquiring universal application, we can see how voices that speak from positions vastly different in social space and time quickly translate into aspects of modern consciousness.

Thus Shakespeare becomes the means of reproducing specifically modern states of mind within the reader. Reading Shakespeare is supposed "to stir you," Carolyn explains, "to give you new sensations. It is to make you feel your life strongly, not only your virtues, but your vicious, perverse points. Discover by the feeling the reading will give you at once how high and how low you are" (p. 115). If Shakespeare loses the very turns of mind that would identify him with his moment in history, then Robert loses features of a similar kind in Brontë's representation of the scene of reading. And this, of course, is the point. Reading Shakespeare translates Robert's political attitudes into essential features of mind. It simultaneously objectifies those features and subjects them to evaluation. The "English power" that Robert acquires by reading literature is simply the power of observing himself through the lens of liberal humanism—as a self flushed with the grandiosity of an ordinariness that has been totally liberated from historical bias and political commitment. For it is through this lens that the novel has us perceive the transformations that come over Robert as he reads *Coriolanus* under the gentle tutelage of Carolyn Helstone: "stepping out of the narrow line of private prejudices, he began to revel in the large picture of human nature, to feel the reality stamped upon the characters who were speaking from that page before him" (p.116).

Her tutoring induces Robert to renounce one mode of power—which Carolyn associates with the imperiously patriarchal nature of Coriolanus—and to adopt another—which she identifies as a benevolent form of paternalism. As it is administered by a woman

and used to mediate a sexual exchange, *Coriolanus* becomes the
means for effecting historical change: *Coriolanus* becomes Carolyn. Performed as writing and reading, that is, the play becomes
the means of internalizing a form of authority identified with the
female. The political implications of feminizing the reader are
clear as Carolyn gives Robert a moral to "tack to the play: . . . you
must not be proud to your workpeople; you must not neglect
chances of soothing them, and you must not be of an inflexible
nature, uttering a request as austerely as if it were a command"
(p.114). Brontë is less than subtle in dramatizing the process by
which reading rids Robert of the foreign devil. She seems to know
exactly what political objective is fulfilled as he fills the mold of
the Englishman and benevolent father. Brontë also puts the woman
in charge of this process even though she gives her heroine the
less imperious passages to read. Retiring, feminine, and thoroughly benign, Carolyn's power is hardly visible as such. Yet she
is clearly the one who declares that reading has the power "to stir
you; to give you new sensations. It is to make you feel your life
strongly, not only your virtues, but your vicious, perverse points"
(p.115). And when Robert has finished reading, she is the one to
ask, "Now, have you felt Shakespeare?" (p.117). She suppresses
all that belongs to the past as so much noise in her effort to being
under examination the grand currents of emotion that run straight
from Shakespeare to the modern day reader, a reader who is
thoroughly English. In thus guiding his reading with her smiles
and admonitions, Caroline executes a set of delicate procedures
capable of translating any and all cultural information into shades
of modern middle-class consciousness and the substance of a
literary text. Although its setting—during the Luddite rebellions
—makes *Shirley* anachronistic by about thirty years, the solution
it proposes for the problem of political resistance, through the
production of a new ruling-class mentality, mark this novel as
utterly Victorian—perhaps even ahead of its time.

   As similar textualizing strategies were deployed here and elsewhere throughout Victorian culture, an intricate system of psychological differences completely triumphed over a long-standing
tradition of overtly political signs to usher in a new form of state
power. This power—the power of representation over the thing

represented—wrested authority from the old aristocracy on grounds that a government was morally obliged to rehabilitate deviant individuals rather than subdue them by force. The Peterloo Massacre of 1819 made it clear that the state's capacity for violence had become a source of embarrassment to the state. Overt displays of force worked against legitimate authority just as they did against subversive factions.[18] If acts of open rebellion had justified intervention in areas of society that government had not had to deal with before, then the government's use of force gave credence to the workers' charges of government oppression. The power of surveillance came into dominance at precisely this moment in English history, displacing traditional displays of violence. Remarkably like the form of vigilance that insured an orderly household, this power did not create equality so much as trivialize the material signs of difference by translating all such signs into differences in the quality, intensity, direction, and self-regulatory capability of an individual's desire.

In saying this, I am not suggesting that we should use British fiction to identify forms of repression or to perform acts of liberation, although my project has a definite political goal. I simply want to represent the discourse of sexuality as deeply implicated in—if not directly responsible for—the shape of the novel, and to show the novel's implication, at the same time, in producing a subject who knew herself and saw that self in relation to others according to the same feminizing strategies that had shaped fiction. I regard fiction, in other words, both as a document and as an agency of cultural history. I believe it helped to formulate the ordered space we now recognize as the household, that it made that space totally functional and used it as the context for representing normal behavior. In doing all this, fiction contested alternative bases for human relationships. As the history of this female domain is figured into political history, then, it will outline boldly the telling cultural move upon which, I believe, the supremacy of middle-class culture ultimately hinged. That is, it will reenact the moment when writing invaded, revised, and contained the household according to strategies that distinguished private from social life and thus detached sexuality from political history.

Where others have isolated rhetorical strategies that naturalize the subordination of female to male, no one has thoroughly examined the figure that differentiates the sexes as it links them together by sexual desire. And if no one asks why, how, and when gender differentiation became the root of human identity, no degree of theoretical sophistication can help us understand the totalizing power of this figure and the very real interests such power inevitably serves. So basic are the terms "male" and "female" to the semiotics of modern life that no one can use them without to some degree performing the very reifying gesture whose operations we need to understand and whose power we want to historicize. Whenever we cast our political lot in the dyadic formation of gender, we place ourselves in a classic double bind, which confines us to alternatives that are not really alternatives at all. That is to say, any political position founded primarily on sexual identity ultimately confirms the limited choices offered by such a dyadic model. Once one thinks within such a structure, sexual relationships appear as the model for all power relationships. This makes it possible to see the female as representative of all subjection and to use her subjectivity as if it were a form of resistance. Having inscribed social conflict within a domestic configuration, however, one loses sight of all the various and contrary political affiliations for which any given individual provides the site. This power of sexuality to appropriate the voice of the victim works as surely through inversion, of course, as by strict adherence to the internal organization of the model.

Still, there is a way in which I owe everything to the very academic feminism I seem to critique, for unless it were now acceptable to read women's texts as women's texts, there would be no call to historicize this area of culture. In view of the fact that women writers have been taken up by the Norton Anthology as part of the standard survey of British literature and also as a collection all of their own, and in view of the fact that we now have male feminists straining to hop on the bandwagon, I feel it is simply time to take stock. It is time to consider why literary criticism presently feels so comfortable with a kind of criticism that began as a critique both of the traditional canon and of the interpretive procedures the canon called forth. This should tell us that by carving out a separate domain for women within literary criticism, feminist criticism has yet to destabilize the reigning metaphysics of sexuality. Literary historians continue to remain aloof from but still firmly anchored in a narrow masculinist notion of politics as more and more areas within literary studies have given ground to the thematics of sexuality promoted by academic feminism. Indeed, a sexual division of labor threatens to reproduce itself within the academy whereby women scholars interpret literature as the expression of the sexual subject while male scholars attend to matters of history and politics. To subvert this process, I believe we must read fiction not as literature but as the history of gender differences and a means by which we have reproduced a class and culture specific form of consciousness.

Endnotes

1. Ian Watt, The Rise of the Novel (Berkely: University of California Press, 1957), p. 57.

2. In The Long Revolution (New York: Columbia University Press, 1961), Williams sets out to show how the "creative" or cultural dimension of social experience opposed existing forms of political authority during the seventeenth and eighteenth centuries and won. Part one of his book indeed gives culture priority over the official institutions of state (as it must during the eighteenth century), claiming that cultural history "is more than a department, a special area of change. In this creative area the changes and conflicts of the whole way of life are necessarily involved" (p. 122). But latent in this promise to extend the category of "the political" broadly to include "the whole way of life" is the contradictory suggestion that political practices are also a special category of "the whole." The second notion of politics emerges in part two, where Williams describes such historical processes as the growth of the reading public, of the popular press, and of standard English through which the new middle classes converted the power of language into economic power. Here the narrow definition of political events, as those which take place in the houses of government, the courts, and the marketplace, assumes control over the "creative" cultural dimension of social experience. For example, Williams writes, "as 1688 is a significant political date, so 1695 is significant in the history of the press. For in that year Parliament declined to renew the 1662 Licensing Act, and the stage for expansion was now fully set" (p. 180). Had Williams actually gathered data that would compose the record of "the whole" of life, he might have broken out of this circle. But, in producing cultural histories, he invariably bows to tradition and stops before entering into the female domain.

3. Virginia Woolf, A Room of One's Own (New York: Harcourt, Brace and World, 1975), p. 69.

4. For an account of the early eighteenth-century tradition that links the novel

to criminal culture, see Lennard Davis, *Factual Fictions: The Origins of the English Novel* (New York: Columbia University Press, 1983), pp. 123–137. For the objection to novels because of their quasi-erotic appeal, see John Richetti, *Popular Fiction Before Richardson's Narrative Patterns 1700–1734* (Oxford: Clarendon, 1969). In an issue of Addison's *Spectator*, for example, Mr. Spectator warns readers about the perils of May, advising that women "be in a particular Manner how they meddle with Romances, Chocolates, Novels, and the like inflamers, which I look upon to be very dangerous to be made use of during this great Carnival of Nature," quoted in *Four Before Richardson: Selected English Novels 1720–1727*, William H. McBurney, ed. (Lincoln: University of Nebraska Press, 1963), p. ix. Toward the end of the eighteenth century, however, one discovers a good number of pedagogical treatises echo Austen's *Northanger Abbey* in advocating certain works of fiction as the fitting way to occupy leisure time. The fiction that was supposed to have a salutory effect on young women was either produced by lady novelists that gained currency during the age of Burney and the other lady novelists or else by earlier novelists who celebrated the same domestic virtues and saw the same form of domestic happiness as the ultimate reward for demononstrating these virtues. It was during this time, as Homer O. Brown explains, that certain novels were published under the editorship of Scott and Barbauld and marked as polite reading, and on the basis of this limited and anomalous body of works, a history of the novel was constructed backward in time (from his book in progress, *Institutions of the English Novel in the Eighteenth Century*).

5. A number of social historians have suggested that the factory system, and with it the economic domination of the new middle classes, was stalled until the beginning of the nineteenth century. In *The Making of the English Working Class* (New York: Random House, 1966) p. 198, E. P. Thompson suggests that fear of Jacobinism produced a new alignment between landowners and industrialists that divided the traditional resistance to industrustrialization. In *The Machinery Question and the Making of Political Economy* (Cambridge: Cambridge University Press, 1980), Maxine Berg explains how the development of political economy as a problem-solving logic at the end of the eighteenth century helped to make industrialization seem like an answer rather than a problem to be avoided at all costs. It was under such conditions that various authors first saw how many people had economic interests in common with the industrialists and described them as a class. In *Desire and Domestic Fiction: A Political History of the Novel* (New York: Oxford University Press, 1987), I carry this argument further by suggesting that well before they felt they had economic interests in common, numerous social groups ranging between the lower gentry and skilled workers were persuaded, in large part by authors unknown to us today, to buy into a single notion of personal life that centered around the kind of woman one desired to marry and the sort of happiness she would provide (pp. 59–95).

6. In discussing Feuerbach, Marx not only stresses that the "ruling ideas" of an epoch are the ideas of a ruling class who "regulate the production and distribution of ideas of their age" (p. 64). He also speculates that during the modern epoch, the production and distribution of ideas (i.e., the production of consciousness) will become increasingly important to the preservation of the bourgeois "state" and to its eventual disintegration or overthrow, *The German Ideology*, Part One, C. J. Arthur, ed. (New York: International Publishers, 1985). Without sliding back into

the idealist philosophy from which Marx sought to rescue "the production of ideas," Gramsci applies the contradiction inherent in Marx's notion of labor to intellectual labor. The intellectual does not necessarily identify with the ruling class by reproducing the ideas inherited from the past but at certain moments may expand their political horizon by lending unity and coherence to the view of an emergent group, *The Modern Prince and Other Writings* (New York: International Publishers, 1957). In *Hegemony and Socialist Strategy*, Winston Moore and Paul Cammack, trs. (London: Verso, 1985), Ernesto Laclau and Chantal Mouffe update this principle for a postmodern society by broadening Gramsci's notions of both power and resistance. Where the difference between production in the traditional sense and the production of information has virtually disappeared, the antagonism between worker and owner is likewise dispersed. Where such polarities could once be taken for granted, then, it becomes extremely difficult to create polarities along political lines. Laclau and Mouffe find it necessary to depart from Gramsci's reliance on the emergence of labor in conflict with capital and to turn instead to the intellectual labor of negativities and positivities out of the contemporary swamp of equivalences. For another important analysis of power in postmodern society, see Bonaventura de Sousa Santos, "Law and Community: The Changing Nature of State Power in Late Capitalism," *International Journal of the Sociology of the Law* (1980), 8: 379–397.

7. Michel Foucault, *The History of Sexuality*, vol. 1, *An Introduction*, Robert Hurley, tr. (New York: Pantheon, 1978).

8. *Discipline and Punish: The Birth of the Prison*, Alan Sheridan, tr. (New York: Vintage, 1979). All citations are to this edition.

9. In *The Imaginary Puritan: Literature and the Origins of Personal Life* (forthcoming), Leonard Tennenhouse and I explain at length how the English Revolution failed to produce the base transformations that mark political revolution. We argue for a more adequate definition of the political, showing that while political change, in the narrow sense of the term, failed to occur, cultural change was profound and lasting. Before the modern middle classes gained economic control, and well before they gained control of the Houses of Parliament, a new class of intellectuals gained hegemony over aristocratic culture as it translated puritanism into the secular practices composing modern domesticity and personal life.

10. I have argued this at length in *Desire and Domestic Fiction*. This essay began as an early version of the introduction and later developed into a theoretical investigation of my argument with literature, history, and academic feminism. I refer readers to the book for evidence supporting the necessarily brief outline of the events in the history of modern sexuality which composes part of this essay.

11. In " 'The Mother Made Conscious': The Historical Development of a Primary School Pedagogy," *History Workshop* (1985), vol. 20, Carolyn Steedman has researched the rationale and analyzed the process by which the techniques of mothering were extended beyond the household and, through the establishment of a national educational system, became the gentle but unyielding girders of a new institutional culture.

12. See, for example, Peter Stallybrass and Allon White, *The Politics and Poetics of Transgression* (London: Methuen, 1986); Peter Clark, *The English Alehouse: A Social History 1200–1830* (London: Longman, 1983); Thomas Walter Laqueur, *Religion and Respectability: Sunday Schools and Working Class Culture 1780–1850* (New Haven: Yale University Press, 1976).

13. Maria Edgeworth and Robert L. Edgeworth *Practical Education* (London, 1801), 2: ix. Citations in the text are to this edition.

14. For a discussion of the paternalism that emerged in opposition to patriarchy in seventeenth-century puritan writing, see Leonard Tennenhouse, *Power on Display: the Politics of Shakespeare's Genres* (New York: Methuen, 1986), especially the chapter entitled "Family Rites." In describing the alternative to patriarchy that arose at the end of the seventeenth and beginning of the eighteenth century in aristocratic families, Randolph Trumbach opposes the term "patriarchal" to the term "domesticity," by which he refers to the modern household. This social formation is authorized by internal relations of gender and generation rather than by way of analogy to external power relations between monarch and subject or between God and man, *The Rise of the Egalitarian Family* (New York: Academic Press, 1978), pp. 119–163.

15. Kathleen M. Davis, "The Sacred Condition of Equality—How Original were Puritan Doctrines of Marriage?" *Social History* (1977), 5: 570. Davis quotes this list from John Dod and Robert Cleaver, *A Godly Forme of Householde Gouernment* (London, 1614).

16. See Brian Simon, *Studies in the History of Education 1780–1870* (London: Lawrence and Wishart, 1960), pp. 1–62.

17. Charlotte Brontë, *Shirley,* Andrew and Judith Hock, eds. (Harmondsworth: Penguin, 1974), p. 114. Citations of the text are to this edition.

18. E. P. Thompson, pp. 680–685.

4
ACCESS CODE: TECHNOLOGY AND THE SCHIZOFEMININE
Avital Ronell

MY LINE on technology operates according to the emergency feminine, a flash on the switchboard of Being. What follows has strayed from a larger essay on speculative telephonics in which the predicament of "accepting a call" creates the thematic atmosphere in which the problematics of calling and technology are brought into contact. Often the transmitting ear is at issue, and the way it is received by political subjects. The telephone functions here as a synecdoche of technology. It is always more or less than technology, but it enables us to hook up an immense apparatus that periodically scrambles the concepts of gender, culture, alterity, being-at-home. To what extent has technology made itself responsible for phantasms of the real?

The telephone connection houses the improper. Hitting the streets, it necessarily touches the state, terrorism, psychoanalysis, language theory, and a number of death-support systems. Its concept has preceded its technical installation. Thus we are inclined to place the telephone not so much at the origin of some reflection but as a response, as that which is answering a call. Perhaps the first and most arousing subscribers to the call of the telephone were the *schizophrenics*, who created a rhetoric of bionic assimilation—a mode of perception on the alert, articulating itself through the logic of transalive coding. The schizophrenic's stationary mobility and the migratory patterns that stay in place offer one dimension of the telephonic incorporation. The case study that we consult shows the extent to which the schizo has

distributed telephone receivers along her body. The treatment
text faithfully transcribes articulations of the telesphere without,
however, supplying any analysis of how the telephone called the
schizophrenic home. Nor even a word explaining why the schizo
might be attracted to the carceral silence of a telephone booth. the
telephone—its figure and field of semantic registers—has slipped
by the technophobic screening systems established in texts of
Heidegger, R. D. Laing, and Jung. Even so, their largely pretech-
nological ears are trained on the telephone. As for the talking
schizo heads of Jung and Laing, they are themselves telephone
extensions, answering devices controlled by Operators. One of
the patients claims to have swallowed a telephone, while another
remembers with traumatic intensity the call box from which her
father made a mysterious connection. The doctors, themselves
recording machines, transcribe the network of mentions without
ever addressing the telephone as image, drive, desire, phantasm,
concept, object, etc. It has been overlooked and underread by
Jung, Heidegger, and R. D. Laing. These thinkers are linked by a
hidden telephone monopoly whose effects I shall in part try to
interpret.

Theoretical: The Nervous Breakdown

Philosophy has been wondering what constitutes the "thing."
At one point, Martin Heidegger slips us a reference to the young
thing. It turns you on, makes your body move, giving you the
sense that technology and the feminine are henceforth inseparable. Maybe it's time to put a search on this curious form of
cohabitation, if only in terms of a single metonymy. It is no longer
a question of adducing causes to the thing, assigning its place,
and determining its equipmental nature. If the thing turned out
to be a telephone, then it would be more than a thing, less than
the fullness of a self, difficult to locate according to classical
taxonomies. Nor could you go about searching for a mere double
and phantom of an organ (like Woman, reduced to the phantom
of a missing organ). This would be much, and much that is
engaging: the phone as a missing mouth, displaced genital, a
mother's deaf ear, or any number of M.I.A.-organs such as the

partial object-ear transmitting and suturing the themes of *Blue Velvet*. So much channeling began through the ear of Alexander Graham Bell's mother—and that of his wife, Mabel Bell. Together, they formed a pair of deaf ears into which he never ceased shouting. The telephone will have become the intensified organ gluing itself to a steadily molting body. The ear, eye, even skin have been divested of authority as they acquire technical extension and amplification in media. Yet the felt radicality of the transaction asserts itself only to the extent that technology, like God for the paranoid hysteric, has broken into the body. This involves every body including the body politic and its internal organs, i.e., the security organs of state. The somaticizations that a neurotic might chart are generally little compared with the electric currents felt to be running through the schizonoiac body. "With respect to their experiencing of life, the neurotic patient and the perverted individual are to the schizophrenics as the petty thief is to the daring safecracker." The schizophrenic gives us exemplary access to the fundamental shifts in affectivity and corporeal organization produced and commanded by technology, in part because the schizophrenic inhabits these other territorialities, "more artificial still and more lunar than that of Oedipus."[1]

In the treatment text we are consulting, the telephone occupies a privileged position, being installed, in Jung's case, in the patient's body from where it extends a partial line to the receiving doctor. The telephone has been the schizonoiac's darling, calling to itself zomboid subjects who, in the early days of telephony, lined up to discuss with Bell and Watson the telephone operators, exchange numbers, and circuitry threaded in their heads. Telephony suited the migratory impulse spanning indivisible distances, and, permitting them to escape the puerile, reactionary dragnet of psychiatric wisdom, it donated structures of disconnection and close range long-distance. "The schizo knows how to leave: he has made departure into something as simple as being born or dying. But at the same time his journey is strangely stationary, in place. He does not speak of another world (p. 131).

Anti-Oedipus describes the schizo as "trans-alivedead, transparentchild," transsexual, a subject alongside a machine. The withdrawal into a body-without-organs "that has become deaf, dumb and blind" (p. 88) does not make schizophrenia the clean-cut other of the normally constituted subject, however. The concept itself of a "normally *functioning* human being"—one equipped, so to speak, with proper shock absorbers for enduring interruption and pain—and conversely, within this normativity, the concept of *breakdown*, demonstrate the effects of wiring systems. (The very possibility of "having" a nervous breakdown can be traced to structures borrowed by the so-called psyche from advanced machinery, a historical transaction of massive rhetorical, affective and bodily shifts). Desire has been rerouted, computerized, electrocuted, and satellited according to a wholly other rhetorical order. And thus the field under investigation, whose floodlights are power-generated by schizonoia, ought to concern the engulfing transformation of the human subject into a technologized entity.

In their work on schizophrenia, Deleuze and Guattari at one point explain a type of interruption or break characteristic of the desiring-machine—the residual break *(coupure-reste)* or residuum—which produces a subject alongside the machine, functioning as a part adjacent to the machine (p. 40). With what intensity have these chips of *coupure-reste* been generally internalized so that one has been programmed to respond in certain ways to equally programmed events? "Internalized" cannot belong here as the inner/outer dimensions of a self begin no doubt to constitute part of an accelerated obsolescence. To plug in the electrical currency of the epochal shift it becomes necessary to undertake an exploration of the extent to which we have become effects of technology. For it is entirely possible that reading such a desire is already programmed by the technology in question. And if technology will not be limited to a reactionary grasp of science but expands to fill a space of art and dissimulation, then the hallucinated fantasy to which it owes its existence also invites a reading.

It is not clear how to call it, in the sense that an umpire calls a play. Psychoanalysis was not sure how to call it or whether to legislate the disruptive tropes of schizophrenia's self-constitution. Deleuze and Guattari chalk this up to the schizo's resistance to being oedipalized. Freud doesn't like them, argue D-G, for in the first place they mistake words for things. Furthermore, they are apathetic, narcissistic, cut off from reality, incapable of achieving transference; they resemble philosophers. The problem of securing an identity for the schizophrenic condition or singularizing its aspect occurs even in the subtitle of the *Anti-Oedipus*, which couples schizophrenia with capitalism by the conjunction "and." Always connected to something else and to another calling, schizophrenia is never itself but invariably put through by an operator. The schizophrenic subject insists on this, as does the philosopher who hazards the problematic unity of clinical and critical discourse. What *Anti-Oedipus* argues may involve a predicament of even more general intensity than the authors suggest, however. The restrictions placed on schizophrenia are put under capitalism's sole surveillance, in a strangely constricting space, "artificial." We view the phenomenon as being largely ascribable to technology in general, and not solely to capitalist production, though these often present invaginating rather than opposing structures. This, precisely, is why we need time out before calling it.

Schizophrenia never had an easy access code. It (in the plural) could not be presented in its singularity—though that, in a sense, is what it's "about." In the preface to his pioneering work *Dementia Praecox oder Gruppe der Schizophrenien (Dementia Praecox or Group of Schizophrenias*, 1911), Professor E. Bleuler makes this opening statement: "Knowledge of the group of illnesses, which Kraeplin has gathered together under the name of dementia praecox is too young for us to give, at this early stage, a closed description thereof."[2] In a sense, then, still too young, at the blossom of its youth, the study of dementia praecox is shown to be too precocious to form as yet a system of closure; it exhibits resistance to totalization. The terms of the felt maturity are spelled out by Bleuler as "zu jung." These words resonate prophetically for any commencement by way of Jung; can a field *become* "zu Jung," that is, too Jungian? Dementia praecox "or" schizophrenia are attuned to inquiry relatively late in psychiatric history. Lines of inquiry are opened with the aid of a hidden telephone, linking up systems of auditory hallucination to the very concept of voice, which often overlays the voice speaking from different topoi of the self (for example, in terms of high psychoanalysis, the hookup to the superego or other regions of aphonic calls).

An object of considerable dispute, provoking valuation wars ("the great artist scales the schizophrenic wall"),[3] "schizophrenia" put psychoanalysis on guard. While the term has largely been accepted in psychiatry, the history of schizophrenia is rooted in disagreements about its nature and, correspondingly, about its extension as a nosological category. — — — — — — — — — Schizophrenia seems to disconnect quite haphazardly, sometimes cutting simple threads, sometimes an entire group or large units of thought. Due to actions taken by demonic operators, certain connections are simply not made, while some are interrupted or transferred to other posts. There are also ambitious schizophrenics, contends Pontalis, and these dream only of their desires; obstacles simply do not exist for them.[4] Like doubles of technology, they immediately gain access everywhere—no roadblocks or policing operators, whom they invisibly run down on automatic switch. Psychoanalysis approaches schizo-dementia-paraphrenia-praecox largely by treating it diffidently; it is in a broad sense made fragile by schizophrenia, which it frankly expulses from its knowing about itself. Where does it resist? Is the ejection button at hand because. — — — — — — — — — — — — — — — An exponent of this malaise, Jung's classic study quickly and consistently falls into default; he cannot stop apologizing for not knowing what he is doing, he signs off by offering that "someone had to take it on himself to get the ball rolling," hoping that future countersignatories will help him untangle some of the scrambled semantics he has recorded, finding himself tossed into what he claims on a number of occasions his patients come up with, namely, a "word salad."[5] Generally speaking, the word salad which afflicts Jung—we'll get to the head of this lettuce momentarily—evokes a phobia shared by psychoanalysis and the schizo. It is as if the two were playing telephone with each other, garbling transmissions that cannot be made to stop. But schizo-noia may have a direct impact on the way psychoanalysis forms a recording surface.

Let's rewind and play. Freud says we can gain cognition of that which psychoanalysis achieves by hearsay. In other words—it is only a matter of other words—by reports of what takes place behind closed doors (of the Unconscious, of the session). These reports of what psychoanalysis tells itself can be passed on through lines of rumorological paranoia. We know something of psychoanalysis by the distortions *(Entstellungen)* that attempt to report on it. In the *New Introductory Lectures* the discipline of which Freud speaks without being prepared to establish a clean transmission system depends, for its dissemination, on the workings of hearsay. This may mean that psychoanalysis is particularly prey to the complaint registered by intensely suffering paraphrenics, who are tormented by chatter and ascertainable forms of auditory hallucinations. Psychoanalysis duplicates this suffering when it draws into itself in an effort to systematize a way out of these fluid channels. To the wall of systematicity erected by psychoanalysis, the schizo responds with the chatter that persecutes him, the vegetal word salad. Still, the lines between psychoanalysis and the schizo are not entirely cut. Thus the schizo herself will ring up the analyst by internal phone systems, returning the call of chatter.

Beyond schizophrenia—if such a realm exists, with sound frontiers, border patrols, exit visas—the telephone maintains an instrumentalizing role in modern phantasms of chatter. Such is the case in the last play read by Nietzche, Strindberg's *Father,* as in his *Easter,* the telephone torments the subject under sufferance, acting as the purveyor of hearsay, chatter, alarm. Now, this demarcates one of the most vulnerable points of entry into psychoanalysis, its dependence upon a fundamental structure of *Gerede*—roughly speaking, what Heidegger understands under the less authentic instances of language, such as idle chatter, small talk, hearsay. This does not necessarily situate psychoanalysis among the historical lowlife, for a number of well-known though often ill-advised discourses depend upon hearsay for their persistence, and this includes spreading the word of any absent Speaker, organizing one's actions according to commanding voices, from Hamlet to other mass murdering automatons. But this dependency also protects psychoanalysis, like the schizo, from being knowable on the surface or exhaustible. Discouraging a serene certitude about its principles or actual taking place, it is often

bound up in the stationary mobility which characterizes the schizonoiac machine. — — — — — — — — — — — — — — —
We now repair to Jung. In a great majority of cases the "feeling-toned complex" in dementia praecox is in some way spliced into fear of gossip, oversensitivity to chatter, or suggestibility which emphasizes command automatism and echopraxia. In some instances indifferent and quite trivial ideas may be accompanied by an intense feeling-tone, which has been taken over, however, from a repressed idea. Accordingly the symptomatology that's about to hit us appears to run counter to that of obsessional neurosis, where a strikingly exceptional narration can be delivered by the analysand with an equally striking lack of affect. It seems necessary to mention this difference, or the position from which a difference can be discerned, because Rat Man's obsessional neurosis operates along telephonic lines as well. His telephone system consists of an internalized converter of constative speech acts into perlocutionary utterances, making it necessary for him to respond to the calls commanding him. Nonetheless, it can be quickly said of obsessional neurosis, and of that which hosts it as a dialect—hysteria—that their telephone systems appear to be connected in compliance with a different set of rules from those governing dementia praecox, where the disconnective structures take the upper hand. — — — — — — — — — —
When schizophrenia "itself" says it maintains an open switchboard (and it says so to Jung) Jung proposes that he calls a purely hypothetical conjecture, venturing a distinction between hysteria's finitude and the unnegotiable endurance of dementia praecox. In fact, it entails the wager that the latter has entered the systemic design of the body to an extent such that it can be viewed as a physiological insert of sorts, affecting the body, suggests Jung, in an irreversible manner: "the hysterogenic complex produces reparable symptoms, while the affect in dementia praecox favours the appearance of anomalies in the metabolism—toxins, perhaps, which injure the brain in a more or less irreparable manner, so that the highest psychic functions become paralysed." (DP, p. 36) Indeed, Jung argues, the change in metabolism "may be primary; the complex which happens to be the newest and last one 'coagulates' and determines the content of the symp-

toms. Our experience does not yet go nearly far enough to warrant the exclusion of such a possiblity," (*DP*, p. 37). We have not yet accumulated a sufficient amount of experience to exclude the hypothesis of a primary change in metabolism. It would be entirely possible, therefore, to conceive a somatological reordering, we could say, as the body achieves a new interpretation of exteriority to which it seeks attunement. This form of "adjustment," which clinically needs to be read as severe maladjustment, nonetheless happens to respond with excruciating sensitivity to *a felt technologization of a world bionically assimilated*—which is to say, by no means fully assimilated, interiorized, freeze dried, or swallowed. It has often been shown how easy it is to confuse a schizophrenic for a perfectly well-behaved child of machine-like obeisance. Schizophrenia scrambles the lines separating the physiological from psychological, keeping it unclear whether dementia praecox is traceable to somatic or psychogenic causes.

Prior to his analysis of the case study that incorporates the telephone monopoly into its rhetoric, Jung points up the superegoical dimension of hallucinatory voices, for subjects "are often corrected by their voices," importantly suggesting that the "normal ego-complex does not perish entirely, but is simply pushed aside by the pathological complex" (*DP*, p. 90). This seems to be borne out by the fact that schizophrenics "often suddenly begin to react in a fairly normal manner during severe physical illnesses or any other far-reaching changes" (*DP*, p. 91). The relay between a normativity ruling the ego or superego functions and severe illness, one that supersedes injury, maps a passage from acquired catatonia to sudden alarm. The (super) ego can give a wake up call. Thus:

> It is remarkable that not a few patients who delight in neologisms and bizarre delusional ideas, and who are therefore under the complete domination of the complex, are often corrected by their voices. One of my patients, for example, was twitted by the voices about her delusions of grandeur, or the voices commanded her to tell the doctor who was examining her delusions "not to bother himself with these things." Another patient, who has been in the clinic for a number of years and always spoke in a disdainful way about

his family, was told by the voices that he was "homesick."
From there and numerous other examples I have gained the
impression that the correcting voices may perhaps be irrup-
tions of the repressed normal remnant of the ego-complex.
(*DP*, p. 90)

Pierre Janet's compelling observations on psychasthenics takes
us one step further in illustrating something like a technological
need. This is articulated in the terms spelled out by *sentiment
d'automatisme* (of which one patient reports, "I am unable to
give an account of what I really do, everything is mechanical in
me and is done unconsciously. I am nothing but a machine"—
(*DP*, p. 80). Here we see to what extent dementia praecox poses a
move in the horizon of a bionic unconscious. A related borrowing
structure emerges in the *sentiment de domination*. A patient
describes the feeling thus: "For four months I have had queer
ideas. It seems to me that I am forced to think them and say them;
someone forces me to speak and suggests coarse words, it is not
my fault if my mouth acts in spite of me" (*DP*, p. 84). Jung adds:
"A dementia praecox patient might talk like this," that is to say,
there exists a marked accentuation on the physiological organization of the mouthpiece, a kind of mechanized vision of the
body in response, in this case, articulated as the instrumentalization of the mouth that acts in spite of "me." This would suggest a
denial statute which legislates the letting go of superegoical interventions, insofar as "it is not my fault if my mouth acts in spite
of me." The "my mouth" imposes an anglicism, a mark of possession which other languages of the body are content to dispense
with. English hangs on to body parts, as if threatened by the organ
with a lapsed body: *la bouche, der Mund* in solitary orbit.

In this context of a mouth that speaks like a loudspeaker de-
tachable from a concept of self that it nonetheless leaves intact,
precisely at the place of mouthpiecing together components of
dementia praecox, Jung somewhat perplexingly introduces an
example of "normal people." What serves as example is the birth
of Nietszche's mouthpiece, *Zarathustra*:

We frequently hear such remarks from hysterical patients,
especially from somnambulists, and we find something sim-

ilar in normal people who are dominated by an unusually strong complex, for instance in poets and artists. (Cf. what Nietzsche says about the origin of *Zarathustra*.)

Jung at this puts us through to his "Psychology of So-Called Occult Phenomena," which leads in Freud's case, as in every case of occult interference, directly to the telephone. The switching on and off of the interjected voices, argues Jung, often coincides with "the 'stupid chattering' about which so many schizophrenics complain" (*DP*, p. 95). These bouts of persecutory chatter, like the complaints which they generate, can be turned down or even tuned out by hallucinating patients who claim with frequency that "the voices in time grow quieter and emptier, but as soon as the excitement returns they regain their content and clarity" (*DP*, p. 95). — — — — — — — — — — — — — — — The enormous tendency to automatization and fixation character-izing the subject, born as it is from "the alienation from reality, the loss of interest in objective events," can be explained by the fact that "schizophrenics are permanently under the spell of an insuperable complex" (*DP*, p. 98). He adds that anyone whose whole interest is captivated by a complex must be dead to his environment. — — — — — — — — — — — — — — —

It would be foolish to engage Jung in a debate on this conclusion; as presiding doctor, he is entitled to pronounce a death sentence. He invites further inquiry, however, by his highly conjectural style, which advances the supposition, among other things, that anyone so wholly absorbed "must be," as if he were, which he openly suggests he is, quite finished. What remains unclear to me is the meaning with which Jung invests "environment" and "dead" in this context, although the figural gist of the phrase is by no means incomprehensible.

The questions to be raised, then, are: What environment? Does schizophrenia not enter its codes only in a technologically inflected environment? Is its silence not always the answering machine to the noise of a prior, simulating machine whose function precisely lies in stimulating such a response? Or put less vulnerably, how does it come about that schizophrenia's Vocabulary is so imbued with the ascientific dial tone of technology, no matter what number or which channel you dial? Given the blank spaces or rather the insufficient material with which Jung fills his understanding of environment, what does it mean to be dead, that is, presumably not alive to this non-determined environment? Does not the pressure exerted by technology require a rethinking of easy recommendations made by the life sciences? And if the intrusion of such radical machinery is itself the irreparable *Ge-Stell*, then what permits us to decide that the mute speaker of technologese is dead? Perhaps we are confronted with a radical answering device, a kind of turned up mimetological stance toward machined-being. But we shall stick to a mere signpost of this possible mapping, gluing ourselves, as it is said, to the telephone.

The Case Study: Miss St.

The case history which Jung designates as paradigmatic traces a route from slandering voices to a telephone connection. In terms of a literary mapping, we could say, it takes us from Kafka's *Trial* ("someone must have slandered him" opens the hearing and text) to *The Castle* (K.'s telephone line to the top). I would recommend that one read "Analysis of a Case of Paranoid Dementia as a Paradigm."[6] It begins as an essay on hearsay, inextricably linking the torments of its victims, who are also persecuted by killer telephones. The speaker, recorded by Jung, has remained permanently in the asylum. To the extent that she is radar-controlled by Jung, we only see a minimal trace of her trajectory which nevertheless suggests a heightened, if troubled adherency to language ("Now and then she used peculiar expressions, and in general spoke in a somewhat pretentious manner. The letters she wrote . . ." etc). (*DP*, p. 99). I am not unaware of the scandal of putting Ms. St. on the line in order to achieve the telephone's finitude. Yet, we depend upon her connections if we want to obtain a genuine appointment with its fantasmatico-historical personality. The reading of Miss St.'s essay on technology neither mystifies her as oracular, anarchic source nor does it pretend to observe a non-interring, bloodless coup. This is not so much an interpretation of schizophrenia, as schizophrenia is made to read technology's omphalos. The interrogation of the schizo does not avoid violence—to assert piety would be hypocritical. I want names and facts.

B. St., dressmaker, unmarried, born in 1845, admitted to the asylum in 1887, had:

> for several years heard voices that slandered her. . . . She explained the voices as invisible telephones. They called out to her that she was a woman of doubtful character, that her child had been found in a toilet, that she had stolen a pair of scissors in order to poke out a child's eyes. (According to the anamnesis the patient had led a thoroughly respectable and quiet life). (*DP*, p. 99)

Once installed, the telephone accuses the childless woman of conceiving a child whose eyes she removed, annulling the sight of the other at the outset of the narrative projection. The child was found in a toilet. The patient later describes herself as a containing house. She hosts a toilet as one of her orifices. It may not be incorrect to designate the toilet, like the telephone, as offering principal household cavities made invisibly to link the inside, an inside going as deep as one's own insides, to an outside. Words are flushed through the telephone like so much excrement, nothing to hold this in the house, out with it. The flushing action taken by Miss St. appears to bolster her delusion of having millions to spare, immense cash flow and liquid assets. (Freud has made the definitive connection between money and excrement, both of which are hard to part with. The flush and the call: money down the drain).

In a later episode of imagined childbearing, Miss St. brings forth a child from her mouth:

> —also a little girl jumped out of my mouth with a little brown frock and a little black apron—my little daughter, she is granted to me—O God, the deputy—she is the deputy, the end of the lunatic asylum came out of my mouth— my little daughter shot out of my mouth to the end of the lunatic asylum—she was slightly paralysed—I came first as double, as sole owner of the world, first with the deaf and dumb Mr. Wegmann.

She makes her little girl. The buccal cavity appears somehow to be connected with the toilet, both openings bypassing the vaginal or anal orifices, from where one would expect a child to spring forth. The motif of paralysis, deafness and dumbness rarely makes its absence felt in evocations of telephonics, be these located at the origin of the telecommunicative history or at the origin of schizophrenic discourse. The patient repeats "I came first as double," notes Jung (*DP*, p. 143).

In an entirely different episode she asserts "I am the Emperor Francis." Jung recalls that "the Emperor Francis I was the husband of Maria Theresa. The patient is both of them at once, but 'in spite of that I am a female' " (*DP*, p. 138). In other words, she assembles like a telephone; compacting a double gender, she came first as the other, as the anteriority of the other which has allowed her to come first. A kind of empty container, she opens only to dissemination. The double gender dominated by the feminine arrives in a richly complicated narrative. In the first place, she produces allusions to "horses, which 'stood near the speaking tubes' " (*DP*, p. 139).

Jung points out, perhaps with some exasperation, that horses, like bulls, dogs, and cats, are often sexual symbols. But I am more taken by another observation concerning Miss St.'s fixation on "extensile animals." To situate this properly, let us present the context from which the double gender falling under the feminine arises—one might in passing note that this particular figuration of gender which breaks down the hope for sexual opposition is common both to Nietzsche ("I am the both") and to Strindberg, whose dramas play out the persecuting mergers that take place in the telephone. Under the entry made near the name Maria Theresa, we find some of the following elements. Remember that for Jung, dreams and schizophrenic utterance share the same phenomenological status:

> —in the dream I was at a table with omelets and dried prunes—then there was a dam with speaking tubes in it— then there were four horses with moustaches over their tails —they stood near the speaking tubes—the third emperor has already legalized this—I am the Emperor Francis in Vienna—in spite of that I am female—my Liesel rises early

and yodels in the morning—each horse stood near a speaking tube." (Suddenly the patient made a gesture of embracing . . .). (*DP*, p. 138)

Of this episode, Jung writes, transferring the concept of analysis to the patient:

This analysis, unlike any of the others, was continually interrupted by blockings (thought-deprivation) and motor stereotypies (embracing). . . . the patient went on tracing little circles in the air with her forefinger, saying she "had to show the speaking-tubes," or she drew little half-moons with both hands: "These are the moustaches." Besides this, the "telephone" kept on making mocking remarks. (*DP*, p. 138)

The telephone exchange: the schizo as analyst, rhetorical transfer of power, continually interrupted. A pointer, an index, her forefinger gestures an air dialing whose telephonic systems appear to conjoin the receiver (speaking tubes) with the anus (the mustaches cover the horses' tails, covering the anus). The speaking tubes were themselves shown to be located by a dam, a Deleuzian switchboard barrier containing flow. Thus

every machine, in the first place, is related to a continual material flow *(hylè)* that it cuts into. It functions like a ham-slicing machine removing portions [*prélèvement*: a skimming off or draining off, a deduction from a sum of money on deposit, etc.] from the associative flow: the anus and the flow of shit it cuts off, for instance; the mouth that cuts off not only the flow of milk but also the flow of air and sound; the penis that interrupts not only the flow of urine but also the flow of sperm. Each associative flow must be seen as an ideal thing, an endless flux, flowing from something not unlike the immense thigh of a pig. (Deleuze-Guattari, p. 36)

Rather than pouring on additional commentary, it seems appropriate not to allow Miss St. to speak through her tubes in her preferred mode of interruption, without the assurance of continuity from any operator. Just one more thing: Jung remarks that "she is involved in the automatic machinery, with the result that all logical reproduction naturally ceases" (*DP*, p. 125)—a somewhat unfortunate choice of words which nonetheless serves to underscore the disjunctive shifts within the rhetoric of machinery returning to that of logical reproduction, and coming home finally to a moment in naturalizing discourse ("naturally ceases"). The register of machined-being belongs to the milieu of dream logic:

> But when the patient talks of her dreams, she speaks as if she were still in the dream, she is involved in the automatic machinery, with the result that all logical reproduction naturally ceases. She is then entirely dependent on chance ideas, and must wait to see whether the complex will reproduce anything or not. Accordingly her thought-process is halting, reiterative (perserverating), and constantly interrupted by thought-deprivation, which the patient considers very trying. (*DP*, p. 125)

Miss St. considers herself a "double polytechnic." (Jung: "It is quite clear that 'double polytechnic' is simply another metonymy for the acme of art and wisdom"—*DP*, p. 114). Let us take this at face value. Miss St. is a polytechnic, a metonymy if that's what it must be, of that which provides instruction in a number of scientific and technical subjects. What does she instruct? In the first place she pieces together a link that she will maintain throughout her stammering, affiliating her invisible telephones with unaccountable loss. At times this achieves expression in the form of mourning or paralysis, at other times through what she calls her "hieroglyphic suffering," a phone number that we shall try in a moment. Miss St., like Nietzsche in his suffering, goes by many names simultaneously. ("The schizo indeed participates in history; he hallucinates and raves universal history, and proliferates all the races.")[7] Besides being the Lord God, Mary Stuart, Empress Alexander, triple owner of the world, and a number of others, she also emerges as the Lorelei. This identifies her with the famous refrain of "have I been understood?" She punches in the code of literary history herself:

> *Lorelei:* "Is the owner of the world—it expresses the deepest mourning because the world is so depraved—a title that is the greatest happiness for others—usually these personalities who have the misfortune, I might almost say, to be the

owners of the world are extraordinarily tormented—Lorelei is also the highest life-image—the world can show no higher remembrance—no higher veneration—for example, the song runs 'I know not what it means'—it happens so often that the title owner of the world is not understood at all—that people say they don't know what it means."

The telephone in her discourse continues to ring out in death-giving moments, on the pain of financial and human loss, as loss of the properly human. Her resources drained, "the heathens chatter so. . . . they said over the telephone that Mr. O. had drawn my annuity—universal is a finality—you can be that through deceased persons—through legacies . . . I am the hero of the pen" (*DP*, p. 118).

Jung does not provide an analysis of the telephone report. Instead, the patient is found to have "lost all sense of humor, as usually happens in dementia praecox" (*DP*, p. 120). But the telephone, as a storage tank of reserve otherness, takes on an increasingly ironic function as it assumes an order of alternative consciousness or secondary personality "with a separate consciousness of its own" (*DP*, p. 156). Distance asserts itself in a schizophrenia where the complexes have become disconnected and "autonomous fragments." The nearly allegorical distance produces "the hero of the pen" who fights a duel with the ironizing stabs of the telephone. The telephone grows by extension into the voice of irony and self-corrective dialogics. It attains this commanding post by scaling regions of irreversible loss, cabling messages across an abyss. Miss St. charts the preliminary stages of devastation with which the telephone is to be inextricably identified. Under the "Complex of Injury", she dictates a first entry:

> (1) *Paralysis* (stereotypy: "That is paralysis"): Bad food—overwork—sleep deprivation—telephone—those are the natural causes—consumption—spine—the paralysis comes from there—wheel chairs . . . tortured—. . . I belong to the monopoly, to the payment—banknotes—here the suffering is affirmed—it is a just system—crutches—dust development—I need immediate help." (*DP*, p. 125)

This unit could have been taken from Marshall McLuhan's steno pad, or indeed originated it, since a necessary articulation

is insinuated between a communications media and body extensions—here most pressingly supported by the word "crutches,"
itself designating corporeal citation marks: crutches holding up a
body the way citations are propped up. Somehow the patient
senses her membership in the monopoly, which further indebts
her. It is not without interest to note that the telephone is inserted
into a long line of deprivations listed under the definitional stereotypy, "That is paralysis." Of these the telephone is listed as a
"natural cause" of paralysis, whereas other forms of torture, tapped
into the spinal cord and supported by the dials controlling the
wheel chairs, do not emanate from natural causes.

Still spinning, labyrinthine structures coil up in the ear and
telephone receiver, communicating with the intestines into whose
receivership "bad food" initially is placed. The speaking tubes
enter this system. Moving on in order to explain the stereotypy "I
suffer hieroglyphical," Miss St. focuses momentarily on the mouth
as a place of respiration:

> "—I was shut up for fourteen years so that my breath could
> not come out anywhere—that is hieroglyphical suffering—
> that is the very highest suffering—that not even the breath
> could come out—yet I establish everything and don't even
> belong to a little room—that is hieroglyphical suffering—
> through speaking-tubes directed outward." (DP, p. 126)

The grammar of this pain does not permit us to hear whether the
hieroglyphical suffering abates through the outwardly directed
tubes, or, to the contrary, whether the respiratory blockage is not
wrapped up in tubes. If blockage is not due to these instruments,
then Miss St. is sent down the tubes by her research of discord,
something to do with a kind of extension wire into her phantasms:

> Discord: "Discords—it is really a crime—I have to be cared
> for—I saw in a dream two people twisting two cords in the
> loft—there are two such great discords—I have to be cared
> for—discords simply won't go any longer on this floor."
> (DP, p. 126)

Suspicious accuracy of the signifier: spinal cord, telephone cord,
discord. The body reterritorialized, broken into, entered by the

telephone cord. Somewhere someone has said that the enema was the first telephone line to the body. She connects the spinal to the telephone cord.

They do not reach far enough, on each end two people are twisting them. Miss St. invents her prophetic rapport to the Bell system monopoly. In fact Bell, in her manner of speaking, has destinal control, eventually transforming her into a geographical site, a telephone station ("I am Uster, I am Switzerland, I am . . ."). Consider the way in which she operates the monopoly:

> *Monopoly* . . . "With me it expresses itself in the note-factory—quite black windows—I saw it in a dream—that is paralysis—it is a double house—the note-factory is genuine American—the factory has been drawn into the monopoly just like, for example, Schiller's *Bell* and the monopoly— the monopoly includes everything that can happen . . . then attacks of suffocation—from above it is credible—then the terrible stretchings—they're continually stretching me . . . —then the poisoning, it is invisible." (*DP*, p. 127)

Jung adds, "the concept of 'monopoly' is again very unclear. It is associated with a series of tortures" (*DP*, p. 126). The patient also finds Jung to be an "amphi": you have two sides, doctor. The telephone box and the Bell system in her vision don't let go. Jung explains her frequent use of "splinter" that "is a 'wooden post' on a mound of earth which signifies 'the extreme end,' probably a metaphor for 'grave' " (*DP*, p. 131). Associations admitting of suffocation, enclosed spaces, America, suggest her reading from the telephone booth—mausoleum, place of entombed silence, where figures of paralysis, deaf and dumbness, and the speaking tubes communicate to one another shadowlessly. But what of Schiller's *Bell*, his *Glas*? A great deal is cited of this:

> *Schiller's Bell* (stereotypy: "I am Schiller's *Bell* and the monopoly"): "Well, that is—as Schiller's *Bell* I am also the monopoly—Schiller's *Bell* needs immediate help—whoever has achieved this needs immediate help—needs immediate help. Because all those who established this are at the end of their life and have worked themselves to death, immediate help is needed—it is world famous, the poem: *The Bell*

—it also establishes the whole of creation—that is the greatest conclusion—Schiller's *Bell* is the creation, the highest finality." (*DP*, p. 132)

Beyond sounding like mutilated telegraph messages emitted from Heidegger's reading of Hölderlin, we note that the patient self-converts into a poem in need of immediate help. But as poem, she recognizes the mortal coil from which she was released, the poet-mortal, who needs immediate help from her, the grounding monopoly/poem. Establishing the poem puts one at the limit; as poem, she is constituted at the edge of death, immediate help, highest finality. Mortals, Heidegger has said on the way to language, are those who experience death as death; they know that to be alive is to be in pain. To be in hieroglyphic pain is, for Miss St., to need immediate help. As Schiller's *Bell*, she has outlived Schiller, she is creation, the highest finality who tolls the predicament of those who need immediate help. She has become the supreme Operator; and furthermore, "the patient accords herself the title 'Lord God,' " Besides the masculine deity she sees the head of her deceased sister, an image that reminds one [i.e., Jung] of the two pagan divinities, Jupiter and Juno (*DP*, p. 134). "Doctor there is too much amphi."

> "—I established this through pork-sausages—I always hear: there is too much amphi—the animal will only have grown so big by mistake perhaps—it must be in the evacuation (stool)—instead of the factory S. there was a building for amphi ... it needs a huge building ... —once when I affirmed my 1,000 millions in a dream, a little green snake came up to my mouth—it had the finest, loveliest feeling, as if it had human reason, and wanted to tell me something —just as if it wanted to kiss me." (At the words "little green snake" the patient showed lively symptoms of affect, blushing and bashful laughter.) (*DP*, p. 136)

Blushingly, the patient acknowledges the sexual symbolism which Jung then does indeed detect. Jung makes very little of the telephone, which dominates her sensibility, although this in itself hardly warrants a thorough desexualization of affect. There is too much amphi, Doctor, too much psychoanalysis, hearsay, too much of the mouth-ear connection, coming up to my mouth, "as if it had human reason and wanted to tell me something." She establishes this through pork sausages. Miss St.—we might add a link —additionally considers herself to be Socrates' deputy, a transcribing Plato, hero of the pen and mouthpiece to the phantom of his voice.

The status of dementia praecox attains to a certain dignity when Jung arranges a conference call on the outer limits of psychoanalytic logic. In another essay Jung confirms that the concurrence of "three experimenters—Stransky, myself and, so to speak, dementia praecox—can be no accident."[8] He grants the disorder a clinical if not a legal personality. Yet this experimenter, dementia praecox, manages a special kind of techno-irony. As if to refute Jung's earlier suggestion that cases of dementia praecox show the collapse of humor, the telephone gets on the line to become an automaton of ironic doubling and subversion. Jung describes her voices as having an almost exclusively disagreeable and derogatory context, just as parathesias and other automatic phenomenon are generally of an unpleasant character. The telephone lights up otherwise, it seems to us. During a typical conversation, while the patient was telling Jung "what a misfortune it would be for humanity if she, the owner of the world, should have to die before the 'payment,' the 'telephone' suddenly remarked, 'It would do no harm, they would simply take another owner' " (DP, p. 149).

At another time the patient apparently was being hindered by thought deprivation. For a long time "I could get no further. Suddenly to the great chagrin of the patient, the telephone called out, 'The doctor should not bother himself with these things' " (DP, p. 149). We note that when it comes to the rescue of Dr. Jung, the telephone is not placed under the arrest of quotation marks, as if at this moment it were to be admitted, as was dementia praecox, as a legitimate participant in the discussions under way, or at least the telephone appears to be transferring a call to the patient from Jung, who may not have wanted to bother with their impasse. On this occasion, the disconnecting telephone actually disconnects the disconnection (thought deprivation, "I could get no further"), thus looping around to a crucially intelligible connection. Another example shows the telephone behaving as a

colleague to Dr. Jung, miming an explanation and, taking the part
of the patient, saying that nothing can be said. "The associations
to 'Zahringer' likewise presented difficulties, whereupon the telephone said, 'She is embarrassed and therefore can say nothing'"
(*DP*, p. 149). In still another example, the telephone laughs and
sides with the doctor, which makes it all the more difficult to
understand why Jung considers this condition to show no sense
of humor, unless the telephone were to act as echo chamber for
the laugh of the Other: "Once when she remarked during analysis
that she was 'a Switzerland,' and I had to laugh, the telephone
exclaimed, 'That is going a bit too far!'" (*DP*, p. 149). Intolerant
of a crack in the scene's semantics, the telephone supplies the
doctor's laughter with words. And once again, as so often happens, when the telephone achieves audibility, there follows
something so dense "that I absolutely could not follow her; the
thing was really too complicated" (*DP*, p. 149). The following
dialogue then develops:

> Telephone: "You're leading the doctor round the whole
> wood."
> Patient: "Because this also goes too far."
> Telephone: "You're too clever by half."

To this point Jung writes that

> when she came to the neologism "Emperor Francis" the
> patient began to whisper, as she often did, so that I contin-
> ually misunderstood her. She had to repeat several sen-
> tences out loud. This made me rather nervous and I told her
> impatiently to speak louder, whereupon she answered irrit-
> ably too. At this moment the telephone called out: "Now
> they're getting in each other's hair! (*DP*, p. 149)

The telephone acts as a narrator, earwitness, and interpreter
for the irritated couple; it establishes a dimension of thirdness
which every couple, in order to get somewhere, requires.— —
— — —Still, it is too bad that we have no hint of the feeling
tone of this telephone, for the agrammatical, arhetorical, nonlexi-
cal aspect of its emergence in language would shed light on the
telephone's personality. How is it modulated? With demonstrable

regularity this repository of luminous knowing turns up the trope of irony, particularly when the telephone responds to poetry: "Once she said with great emphasis, 'I am the keystone, the monopoly and Schiller's *Bell*,' and the telephone remarked, 'That is so important that the markets will drop!' " (*DP*, p. 150).

The stock exchange system of knowledge in which the telephone participates seems to have reversed its value, for schizophrenia's share in irony has now gone up in Jung's subsequent commentary:

> In all these examples the "telephone" has the character of an ironically commentating spectator who seems to be thoroughly convinced of the futility of these pathological fancies and mocks the patient's assertions in a superior tone. This kind of voice is rather like a personified self-irony. Unfortunately in spite of diligent research I lack the necessary material for a closer characterization of this interesting split-off personality." (*DP*, p. 150)

As Heidegger says of any call, the telephone comes from the patient and from beyond the patient. It mimes the style of the other, in this case demonstrating the physician's conviction of the "futility of these (i.e. schizophrenia's) pathological fancies." In a mode resembling that of Jung throughout, but less toned down, the telephone also appears to function as loudspeaker for Jung's unsaid when it permits itself to mock the patient's assertions. Assuming a superior tone, it masks itself as the clinical complicity which keeps the patient locked up in the asylum, intercepting the initial two letters of "pretentious" diction in which she begs to be let free. What would it mean for "the character of an ironically commentating spectator" to occupy the interstice between the analyst and analysand? Does not the very object that serves to implement the technicity of hearsay, that is, the epistemological structuring of psychoanalysis and its transmissions, intervene in order to cut lines between the couple, to add a third dimension, assuring the sense that reproduces the scene itself of psychoanalysis? By miming the surveillance apparatus trained on the patient, hearsay's televisor ("an ironically commentating spectator") comes as much from the doctor as from the patient. It annuls the doctor's position by assimilation and usurpation as much as it undermines the patient's assertions. It arrives on the scene in order to dislocate each partner from the place of absolute Other: it is the contaminator. — — — — — — The paradigm case has recommended itself to our attention because it furnishes a reception desk for phantasms of telecommunications. One among them arrives in this form:

> Besides the complexes of grandeur and injury [i.e., paranoid persecution mania] there is another complex which has retained a certain amount of normal criticism but is withheld from reproduction by the complex of grandeur, so that no direct communication can be had with it. (As we know, in somnambulism direct communication can be had with such personalities by means of automatic writing)." (*DP*, p. 150)

While the complex harboring the telephone has been shown to be somewhat directly hooked up with the analyst's discourse— be this analyst understood as the ironic, superegoical voice, Jung, or the patient named analyst by virtue of the "analysis" she gives —Jung suggests the necessary inclusion of an operating function or mode of intervention in order to put us through to this place from where "no direct communication" can be had. It is as if the schizophrenic were momentarily opposable to the somnambulist with whom, as with nighttime radio, surprisingly open lines can be maintained. While Jung himself refrains from formulating this opposition, it does appear that the schizophrenic strikes a posture of such paradoxical hyper-awakeness that the more direct lines which psychoanalysis likes to take to unconscious representations are shut down. Schizophrenia would not belong to the dark continent of the noncontradictory regime, but appears to work instead in the abyss of light.

The telephone case represents the final stage of observation that Jung makes here: "Finally, there are cases where a correcting, ironical, semi-normal ego-remnant remains on top, while the two other complexes are acted out in the unconscious and make themselves felt only through hallucinations" (*DP*, p. 150). As if to underscore her vigilance over this knowledge and the terrible light, as if to offer psychoanalysis the design of the probe, Miss

St. has thrown hints at the analyst, suggesting the necessity of entering this difficult case and locket: Under *summit* ("Sublimist sublimity—self-satisfied am I") she has thrown in "—an orphan child—am Socrates—Lorelei—Schiller's *Bell* and the monopoly —Lord God, Mary the mother of God—master-key, the key of heaven." Under the stereotypy "I am the crown" she has uttered "*—master key and a key of heaven with which one cuts off relations* (*DP*, pp. 115–116). Jung views this key phrase as "a naive bit of dreaming." Perhaps so. Still, she hands us

> the key of heaven
> and inserts the
> master key.

The master key provides the means by which the schizo-phrenic cuts off relations, achieving disconnection. To cut off relations implies mastery, or knowing how to interrupt the call. The patient is not herself the master key, but offers it as a way to enter her secret. Once entered, she then dissolves her interiority to become the master key. The temporal succession is disclosed under *master key* (stereotypy: "I am the master-key"): "The mas-ter-key is the house-key—I am not the house-key but the house —the house belongs to me—yes, I am the master-key—I affirm the master-key as my property—it is therefore a house-key that folds up—a key that unlocks all doors—therefore it includes the house—it is a keystone—monopoly—Schiller's *Bell*" (*DP*, p. 117). Jung importantly adds: "The patient means the pass key carried by doctors" (*DP*, p. 117). He allows the power of this remark to attenuate when continuing:

> The patient means the pass key carried by doctors. By means of the stereotypy "I am the master-key" she solves the com-plex of her internment. Here we can see particularly well how hazy her ideas are and also her expressions: sometimes she *is* the master-key, sometimes she merely "affirms" it; sometimes she *is* the house, sometimes it belongs to her."
> (*DP*, p. 117)

Here is one analyst who really does shut off the Nietzsche tape. While Freud comically denies ever having read the last of philos-

ophers, Jung begins by citing him as a case of normalcy but lets
the master key slide when the time for affirmation and double,
enfolding being comes along. No matter. Nietzsche may be the
master key and its affirmation, but we're not turning him either.
If, as Jung contends, the patient means the passkey carried by the
doctor, then she discerns herself as the key by which the analyst
can unlock doors, but insofar as she is the passkey held by the
doctor and psychoanalysis, she is also dispossessed of herself as
her own asylum, place of internment; she is the carceral subject
linked by telephone to the possibility of exteriority. The telephone tunes the note that sings in the master key, the one tolled
by Schiller's "Bell" and which also knows the password carried
by the doctor, ringing out in time to his unspoken deposits. She
is, she says, the house that holds the master key, within which
the telephone is connected, but precisely the master key promises
to crack the case, furnishing the instrument by which one cuts off
relations, and housed, remains simultaneously shut up, like her
impenetrable case, and open (" 'I am a Switzerland.' Analysis: 'I
long ago established Switzerland as a double—I do not belong
shut up here—Switzerland cannot be shut up' " (*DP*, p. 123).
Like the telephone whose ring cuts into the elusive "master-key",
dementia praecox plays itself out along the walls of mute inside
and noisy outside, linking death to the clang of a certain form of
life whose slapping lightstreams

strike the schizophrenic
as an immense
catastrophe.

Noise disaster keeps the schizonoiac on the run (even though
she's not going anywhere. Nonetheless, they're hitting the streets:
Rousseau's Promenades, Nietzsche in Turin, Artaud's strolls).
When the heat is on, it comes down hard on you. Everything
crashes. In "The Psychogenesis of Schizophrenia," Jung cites
Paul Sollier for his description of *troubles cénesthésiques*, which
are compared to "explosions, pistol-shots, and other violent noises
in the head. They appear in projection as earthquakes, cosmic
catastrophes, as the fall of the stars, the splitting of the sun, the

falling asunder of the moon, the transformation of people into corpses, the freezing of the universe, and so on."[9]

"Dreams," adds Jung, "can produce similar pictures of great catastrophes," defining them as sonic images that disturb sleep, "due to an incomplete extinction of consciousness" (*DP*, p. 163). If, then, the phenomenology of the dream and that of schizophrenia are almost identical, there is nothing to disprove a reading of schizophrenia as a condition of hyperinsomnium, the terrible state of alert in which the "incomplete extinction of consciousness" sustains itself indefinitely. It is fed and sustained by noise explosions and the catastrophic knowledge by whose disclosure the telephone box resounds. — — — — — — — — — — — —
One of Miss St.'s great fears is rooted in reports that she was seen carrying a cat (" 'I was once slandered by somebody because I always carried cats in my arms.' It is not clear whether the slander emanated from the voices or from people"—(*DP*, p. 106). Miss St. was carrying a cat. She joins the bestial moments that tend to hit the schizonomad: Rousseau run down by a dog, Nietzsche embracing a horse being beaten, Watson and Bell were receiving signals from finitizing animals too. Cats. Back to Miss St., still ("always") carrying a cat. Miss St. carries some catastrophe with her, whose secret the telephone has attempted to disconnect. It is not clear from what part of the body the telephone speaks, where it has entered, what it zones. In a later essay, written from "the privilege of old age," Jung observes the structure of sudden eruption, the abrupt call from schizophrenia's poetry of discontinuity: "Whereas the neurotic dissociation never loses its systematic character, schizophrenia shows a picture of unsystematic randomness, so to speak, in which the continuity of meanings so distinctive of the neuroses is often mutilated to the point of unintelligibility" (*DP*, p. 179).

The neurotic switchboard makes connections which are sustained in their systematicity. Schizophrenia lights up, jamming the switchboard, fracturing a latent semantics with multiple calls. No one can take all the calls—a number in the Miss St. case are still on hold. Jung ends his and her analysis with the admission of serious "gaps and many weak spots" (*DP*, p. 151). His exposition of the case was not a radio play, but implicated him in the telephonics of the case. The doctor spoke into and from the telephone. He did not speak of the telephone to which he spoke; it held up a mirror to him, and he found it ironic. The telephone was not entered in this lexicon of psychoanalytic conquest—it remained surprisingly in the wild. Jung goes natural and adds a vegetal signifier to the lexicon. He introduces the concept of a "word salad." This imposes a certain schizophrenic reading of the paradigmatic case study—schizophrenic, but also detechnologized. A false *piste*, wrong way. Once introduced, word salad quite naturally keeps the fragments in asignificatory disassemblage.

What does it mean to bring into the vocabulary of psychoanalysis a concept of salad, a linguistically tossed salad? Jung naturalizes the unreconstitutable edibles; nothing ever again will be able to piece together something like an original head of lettuce, not to speak of its heart. This is precisely why Jung's decision to offer the shared logic of a broken head of lettuce and the dream needs to be considered. For while the dream was thought to have a latent content, a retrievable unconscious narrativity, the schizophrenic utterance remains a pistol shot in the dark of metaphysics, shattered, fragmented. This is perhaps why it may be necessary to note that in German, Miss St. is not quite a "dressmaker" as the English translation would have it, but rather a *Schneiderin*, literally a cutter or tailor, also that in the feminine which cuts off or interrupts the fabric of meaning or the texture of any natural unfolding. Jung's final image is rendered in English as "someone had to get the ball rolling" (*DP*, p. 151). In German, however, he hopes, he writes, to have brought a stone to roll ("Jemand muß es ja schießlich auf sich nehmen, einen Stein ins Rollen gebrach zu haben"—(*DP*, p. 179). The analyst takes it upon himself to move the petrified thing, to get it to roll or unravel. Miss St. had offered up an image of medusoid petrification when she recalled "den Kopf ihren verstorbenen Schwester" (the head of her dead sister) (*DP*, p. 158). As cutter she offers the analyst the decapitated image of a sister. Jung, in the same sentence, doubles the head, shifting the gender and enters quickly into mythology: "den Kopf, etc., ein Bild, das etwas an zwei heidnische Gottheiten, an Jupiter und

Juno, erinnert" (DP, p. 158: "she sees the head of her deceased sister, an image that reminds one of the two pagan divinities, Jupiter and Juno"). Jung interiorizes, remembers (erinnert), averts his gaze. There is something he was unable to look at, and it may indeed be the thing or the thingification of the patient whose mechanized fragment spoke so smartly, whose death toll and place of mechanization knew how to turn things around or double them. The snake, which Jung translated in a psychointerlinear manner, belonged, it seemed to the telephone, to a structure of decapitation — for what else does it mean to hold a petrified ear-mouthpiece to one's head? — — — ? — — — — — — — —

Endnotes

1. Gilles Deleuze and Félix Guattari, *Anti-Oedipus: Capitalism and Schizophrenia,* Robert Hurley, trans. (Minneapolis: University of Minnesota Press, 1983), pp. 88 and 67. Page references below given parenthetically in text are to this edition. *Capitalisme et schizophrénie* (Paris: Editions du Minuit, 1973).

2. Eugen Bleuler, *Dementia Praecox oder Gruppe der der Schizophrenien* (Base: F. Deuticke, 1911).

3. Deleuze-Guattari, p. 69.

4. J. Laplanche and J. B. Pontalis, *The Language of Psycho-Analysis,* Donald Nicholson-Smith, trans. (New York: Norton, 1974), pp. 408–410. *Vocabulaire de la psychanalyse* (Paris: Presses Universitaires de France, 1967).

5. C. G. Jung, *The Psychology of Dementia Praecox,* Rr. F. C. Hull, trans. (Princeton: Princeton University Press, 1960), hereafter referred to as *DP.* In a more recent version of the syndromic habit we are about to enter, the Operator functions as the major figuration of being-in-the world. To the extent that we do not know where this "in" is, which is why Heidegger casts it problematically, it can be seen as belonging to the order of the telephonic. The schizophrenic is the on location of being-in-the world. For the schizo the "operator" is typically in-the-world. I have tried to handle this in the *Telephone Book: Technology-Schizophrenia-Electric Speech* (Lincoln: University of Nebraska Press, 1989).

6. Jung, *DP.* In a recent text on the schizophrenic subject, W. G. Kudzus ("Writing in Translation: Louis Wolfson, Paul Celan," in *Qui Parle,* Special Issue on Paranoia and Schizophrenia, Peter Connor, Adam Bresnick, et al., eds., 1988) delineates "the traces BETWEEN the tongues" which are shown to have some bearing upon AT&T. Rooted in Louis Wolfson's novelistic treatise, *Le Schizo et les Langues,* Kudzus' interpretation exterritorializes the propositions consisting in "How to cut out of one's mother tongue. . . . How to keep out one's mother tongue." "Labial passage is a matter of life and death. The young man, one reads, drinks a certain type of milk from a certain type of container (p. 3). Kudzus asserts this vital link that will flow into our dialactate: "Readers are given a glimpse of what they do when they use the channels of communication provided to them by their mother tongue and AT&T" (p. 2). It should become evident in the text

accompanying the "dismemberment" of Ma Bell into AT&T, "the movement away from mother's tongue is psychotically driven." Kudzus identifies Wolfson's writing as "zero zone writing of sorts; no acknowledged language, little or no sanity, no results. In this process, the beginning and end are less important than the live zone in which writing occurs." See also Deleuze, "Schizologie," Introduction to Wolfson, *Le Schizo et les langues ou la phonétique chez le psychotique (Esquisses d'un étudiant schizophrénique)* (Paris: Editions Gallimard, 1970).

    7. Deleuze-Guattari, p. 85.

    8. C. G. Jung, *The Psychology of Dementia Praecox*, R. F. C. Hull, trans., *The Collected Works of C. G. Jung*, Bollingen Series XX (Princeton: Princeton University Press, 1974), p. 32. *Über die Psychologie der Dementia praecox: Ein Versuch* (Base: 1907).

    9. From Paul Auguste Sollier's *Le Mécanisme des émotions* (Paris: 1905), 4: 208.

II
ART AND PRACTICE

5

GENDER, GENRE, AND PARTNERSHIP: A STUDY OF VALENTINE PENROSE

Renée Riese Hubert

A QUICK perusal of general studies on surrealism as well as of retrospectives of surrealist art would give the impression that the members of the movement were almost exclusively male, particularly when they advocated as a group social and sexual liberation. Although they endorsed Violette Nozières who, by compounding incest with parricide, epitomized in their eyes all women victimized by bourgeois institutions, not a single female artist or writer contributed to the *Violette Nozières* volume. But how can we explain the absence or invisibility of female surrealists at the heyday of the movement? In recent years, an essential chapter of avant-garde history is being rewritten, and the importance of women's contribution is being revised. Such critical hindsight differs markedly from contemporary acknowledgment. To be sure, Eluard, Breton, and Ernst gave their close contemporary Valentine Hugo a measure of encouragement and recognition. But such promotions of female artists were few and far between, perhaps because André Breton, as has been pointed out by critics as diverse as Xavière Gauthier and Whitney Chadwick, preferred to see women as muses rather than as creators.[1]

A study of artistic partnerships should lead to a more pertinent and more direct appraisal of the situation of women in surrealism than a survey of group reactions, statistical or otherwise. A number of artist and writers more or less closely associated with surrealism shared their lives: Max Ernst and Leonora Carrington, Max Ernst and Dorothea Tanning, Remedios Varo and Benjamin Péret, Sophie Täuber-Arp and Hans Arp, Hans Bellmer and Unica Zürn, André Breton and Jacqueline Lamba, Kay Sage and Yves Tanguy, Diego Rivera and Frida Kahlo, Wolfgang Paalen and Alice Rahon Paalen, Toyen and Styrsky, Roland Penrose and Valentine Penrose, Roland Penrose and Lee Miller.[2] We shall in this essay focus on a single couple: Valentine and Roland Penrose, by showing mutual interference in their artistic production, offset by a growing impulse toward alterity and self-affirmation on the woman's part.

While Roland Penrose (1900–1984) was a lionized public figure, Valentine Boué Penrose (1898–1978) remained in relative obscurity even during her years of association with the surrealists. Nevertheless, each of her books has a preface or a frontispiece by a poet or artist of the group: Eluard, Miró, Paalen, Mario Prassinos, and even Picasso during his brief surrealist period. Max Ernst, Man Ray, Lee Miller, and Paalen made her the subject of compelling portraits.[3] But little is known of her life after she separated from her husband and returned to India. Both husband and wife can be considered a "double talent." Valentine, primarily a poet and a novelist, composed collages, including a collage novel, while Roland, essentially a visual artist (paintings, collages, objects) became a confirmed essayist. Much of his time and effort went into championing avant-garde movements and organizing their shocking exhibits, activities finally rewarded by the officially sanctioned respectability of knighthood.

Roland and Valentine came to Paris, he from England, she from the provinces, and associated with the surrealists at about the same time. Married in 1925, Valentine developed shortly afterward into a poet, and Roland had his first one-man show in 1928. Like other surrealist women—Léonor Fini, Carrington and Miller—Valentine Boué is considered a highly independent person, but she did not from the start disrupt genre and gender, or free her writings from conventional images of woman. Indeed, she may have owed her final emancipation to her partnership, whether harmonious or stormy, with Roland. It will therefore be necessary to focus on domains where interaction may have taken place, notably the practice of collage and the role played by women in their respective works. Unlike other collage artists such as Ernst, Max Bucaille, and Valentine herself, Roland does not borrow from journals, illustrated books and catalogues. Perhaps because he had little use for anachronistic allusions, he relied mainly on current postcards representing such well-known sights as the Eiffel Tower, the Place de l'Opéra, Mediterranean seascapes. In the revealing *Magnetic Moth* (1938), identical cards are assembled, for the sake not of repetition, but of subversion: as the picture is dissected, reversed, partially covered up or exposed, new patterns emerge. Roland's technique emphasizes displacement: the Place de l'Opéra has lost its autonomy, for it is superseded by the image of the lower part of a candle. By assembling and fragmenting postcards, the painter also creates the contours of a moth, with recognizable wings, eyes, body. Moreover, by the undermining of referentiality, the postcards lose their essential function, which obviously consists in representing for the purpose of transmission real scenes. Additionally, the candle on the right of the collage flaunts its phallic design, whereas the center section of assembled Eiffel Towers suggests vaginal contours. Penrose's humorous eroticism corroborates a claim formulated by Ernst and others that sexuality and eroticism hardly limit themselves to certain circumscribed areas of the body.

More important in the context of Valentine's work is the collage *The Real Woman* (1938), for it reveals that Roland insistently problematizes woman at a time when such an issue is treated only tangentially in Valentine's work. The "real woman" is painfully absent from the collage. We must hopelessly search for her among the many views presented, dominated by obstructing gates, bridges, columns, and fences. The very manner the cards are assembled provokes temptation and curiosity, all the more so because normal entrances and frontviews are missing. Here rocky islands and peninsulas bar easy access to the mainland; there assemblages of columns provide a barrier preventing penetration into the landscape. Throughout the collage, Penrose, by juxtaposing close and distant views, solid outlines and dissolving textures, further complicates the viewer's game of hide and seek. Human representations are confined to statues, artifices and artifacts. Where amidst these erotic temptations lies the woman? Roland invites the viewers to chercher la femme; he lures them into a chase for clues reminiscent of a detective novel.

A large part of the collage is occupied by a woman's torso; headless, legless, and armless, she derives from and trangresses the Venus of Milo. In this way, the artist strongly subverts the traditions and æsthetic commonplaces of our cultural heritage. Durable marble has been replaced by plywood or, more precisely, by the ephemeral traces of its fibers. Faced with no more than a simulacrum of wood, we move one more step from reality. The breasts of the goddess recede rather than protrude, while her genitals are covered up by two colorful postcards contrasting with the neutral gray of the body. By setting up two postcards in or in lieu of the pubic area, Roland Penrose gives us the illusion of penetrating into a mysterious zone and offers us an enticing reward for transgression. A prevalently red and brown erotic landscape substitutes for what lies beneath or beyond the surface. All that is left of the "real woman" in the title is a highlighted spectacle of sexuality that by assorted substitutions moves us step by step into artificiality, real in a completely different sense. The absent woman thus functions mainly as a mediator for otherness.

In Roland's portrait of Valentine, painted in 1938, at which time the couple was already intermittently separated, the occlusion of some of her features reminds us of The Real Woman. The viewer is once again urged to discover the "real woman" as her eyes and her lips are completely covered by moths and butterflies. Norbert Lynton in his introduction to the Roland Penrose exhibit sponsored by the Arts Council of Great Britain states: "The poetess, loved but recognized as an independent being is shown as a woman whose mind and faculties of speech and sight are at once blessed and threatened by experience."[4] The painter provides an exteriorization of his dreams and desires which he undoubtedly attributes to Valentine, since her pale blue face suggests an untroubled azure sky. Its lack of detail contrasts with the precise shapes and colors of the butterflies and moths so tightly knit together, replacing her eyes, endowing them with inner vision. The poetess is adorned with a rose featuring menacingly protruding thorns and functioning as a forbidden jewel, closely guarded by an owl. Roland expresses the ambiguity that haunts woman, whose delicate rose is simultaneously protected and threatened by so many visible thorns.

In the oil painting *Olivia* (1939), the woman's fragmented body is reversed; her head, as in several other paintings, hangs downward; her hair is turning into iron chains and the missing torso is replaced by huge nails. The artist has shifted the problematics of woman toward aggression. Has he perhaps suggested to Valentine, or has she, long before formulating it in any of her writings, suggested to him that woman, ever a prisoner, can disarm men?

Valentine Penrose's first volume of lyrical poetry, *l'Herbe à la Lune* (1935), belongs to the period when she and her husband maintained close ties with Eluard and Ernst.[5] She already combined at that time two more or less related commitments: surrealism and the study of oriental philosophy. The latter interest will eventually contribute to the alienation from her husband who wrote in his *Scrapbook*: "Again, the underlying cause was our deep disagreement after returning from India about the degree to which one should be involved in life or should withdraw from it?"[6] In *l'Herbe à la Lune*, two poems entitled "GOA" are inspired by and reflect strongly her passage to India, her philosophical interests, her receptivity to Eastern culture. The imagery of the collection by no means features surrealist techniques such as the concatenation of explosive metaphors.

The text frequently refers to basic constituents, especially fire and water which can on occasion be associated with male and female elements, a mystical analogy that will surface in her last works. Spatial metaphors constantly orient and disorient the reader as their movements encompass sky and earth, never fully separated or defined, for the author continually multiplies associations, substitutions, and displacements:

> Tous les astres ont pris le large (p. 37).
> (All the stars swoop away) (p. 25)
> Et les cristaux au centre rouge ont pris la place
> et des étoiles séparées qui se sourient
> douces poussant devant elles le sang fleuri (p 40).

(And the cristals have taken the red center's place
and separated stars that smile at one another
softly pushing before them blood in blossom)

Not only does the poet suggest a world of constant change, but a universe in which transgressions bring forth new contacts between the everyday and the mythological, between humanity and nature, and where personifications pertain to almost all manifestations. Images of birth, growth, and fertility, outweighing death and dispersion, emerge in a display of violence. The "I" may assert itself among these forces, not as self-defined in antagonism or union, but as an "I" prone to become a "we," an "I" applicable to others. But this process just barely prefigures the female personifications so characteristic of her later works.

Lyricism designates and thus enhances itself through poetic allusions:

tous les oiseaux au jardin de mon père (p. 17)
(all the birds in my father's garden)

Valentine Penrose makes her readers believe that she will tread on familiar ground in the very process of frustrating their expectations:

allez allez maudits au cher mois de Marie (p. 21)
(away away o! accursed to the dear month of Mary)

By substitutions, she undercuts conventions and their inherent plausibility. Her poetry abounds in intertextuality: references to everyday speech, to popular songs, to fairytales, all introduced with deliberate deviousness. Direct invocations and prophecies alternate with ironic expressions. Only the disruptive nature of certain poems shows affinities with her husband's productions at that time. She brings together stanzas, images, and lines without feeling the need to bind them to what we may call poetic coherence, grammatical continuity, or even standard syntactical devices. She has obviously become cognizant of the very nature of the collage and mastered all its techniques. Nonetheless, her verbal juxtapositions and alignments hardly match the strong structural manipulations that mark the visual collages of Roland Penrose.

In *Martha's Opera* (1945), a short narrative, Valentine Penrose's uniqueness makes itself felt for the first time.[7] The tale's brief episodes end abruptly or shift into another perspective. The author presents a fragmented horror story concluding with the death of almost all the participants. The oppressive atmosphere, the anguished protagonists, the inevitability of the course of events give unity to the story. Four characters are interrelated by more than one bond: the count and Rubia are siblings as are Darcy and Emily. The count wishes to propose to Emily; but unfortunately Emily and Rubia are lovers. Darcy and the count act throughout in accordance with fraternal solidarity. Amid an atmosphere of chivalry, festivity, rituals, the author introduces several varieties of transgression. The castle is full of secret spaces, where mysterious events and unaccountable disappearances repeatedly occur. We witness pursuits through wildernesses fraught with uncanny perils originating in man, beast, sky, and earth. Poison, provocatively present from the beginning, ends Emily's and Rubia's life. It is not merely a substance that causes specific violent reactions, infestation, or death in whoever consumes it, for it inflicts a kind of madness which seems to delight in transgressing accepted moral codes. The tale is in a sense an opera staged by Martha, full of melodramatic scenes and arias. The mythical woman, whose madness can be traced to her cruel Merovingian ancestors, is endowed with an occult strength and unbridled will power.

Lesbianism, so important in *Dons des Féminines* (1951) and *La Comtesse sanglante* (1965), emerges in *Martha's Opera* in the exchange of letters between Emily and Rubia.[8] The reader, plunged without warning in the very midst of the events, immediately senses a complicity. Surrounded by falsity and fraudulent male chivalry, the two women appear by comparison strong and genuine in their relationship. Rubia's words show how much she is aware of the fictionality of the world she shares with Emily, of their seclusion and their otherness: "I know nothing beyond this enchanted and invisible room, reflected only in the clear liquid of a philtre, not there in that water-jug which accepts nothing but its false reflection" (p. 193). An intense courage and conviction sustain Rubia and Emily, who refuses salvation by binding herself to the count. The two women present gifts to each other, for instance, flowers and fruit, a procedure which ironically displaces male chivalry. At the beginning and at the end, they drape themselves in the same shawl and conceal their features under the same veil. Their difference or otherness paradoxically reduces them to sameness. But in their confessional letters, which usually recapitulate past experiences, feminine awareness rarely surfaces. It would seem that the author has not yet discovered how to free her female protagonist from male traditions.

We can regard *Dons des Féminines*, a relatively unknown collage novel, as an archetypal surrealist book.[9] Indeed, the collage and particularly the collage novel are eminently suited to communicating the challenging ideology of the movement and its universal thrust toward action, change, and revolution, encompassing almost all aspects of life. In *Dons des Féminines*, a single artist produced the full-page photocollages, the vignettes, the French and English texts. The reader perceives not only the multiple, divided, and simultaneous images that appear on each page, but must also deal with two series of poems. For bilingual readers, the movement from French to English, or English to French, like the displacement from the visual to the verbal, or the verbal to the visual, entails a linguistic shift, a transfer, as well as a translation. The reader/viewer is constantly translating and retranslating as she or he moves between languages along a vector of verbal modifications. In connection with the photocollages as well as with the text, the reader raises the question of the discrete single page versus continuity of narrative. In this collage novel, as in those of Max Ernst, the expected or announced order is always interrupted, subverted, and redirected. Although references to Rubia, whom we may, if we so wish, identify with the heroine of Penrose's previous tale, are frequent, the adventures linked to her name appear episodic if not totally disconnected. Within each photocollage, more so than within each page of the text, striking incongruities surface. This system of surprising juxtapositions intensifies as the viewer moves from one page to the next. In addition, the vignettes, by systematically occupying changing positions in regard to the printed text, deserve to be considered extensions and reductive echoes of the photocollages. By their stylization and their ornamentation, they stress the non-narrative aspects of the book. Obviously, Valentine's use of the collage owes very little to Roland, who may originally have pointed out to his wife, both in theory and in practice, the advantages of the new medium and encouraged her to try her hand at it.

From the cover page on, the reader is alerted to the variety, duality, rupture, and paradox that mark *Dons des Féminines*. On the white cover, nothing but the title is printed, but every letter is, so to speak, double. The upper part exhibits a fairly stable typography, no doubt listed in standard manuals on the subject. The double-line letters feature angularity, so often favored by Victorian book designers, whereas the lower part is printed in a much more fanciful manner. This juxtaposition not only signals another use of the collage, but fosters the intrusion of the image into the text. The book cover familiarizes the reader with the impishness of collage, not only in terms of typographical manipulation, but also in terms of interferences and collusions between the visual and the verbal, eagerly taking possession of each other's space.

Valentine Penrose's French poems, as those in *Herbe à la Lune*, hardly manifest the explosive concentration of surrealist metaphors, the tense network of imagery capable of undermining both the lyric persona and the unfolding of the narrative. Nor do they boldly mediate the passing of thresholds to the surrealist "ailleurs." Far from attempting such a mediation, she tells a story of adventures pertaining to love, death, dream, and violence, a series of disconnected tales concerning her elusive heroine Rubia. Although the readers may initially have the illusion of finding their bearings, their false sense of orientation will soon disappear:

> Leurs chevaux l'odeur du marécage lèvent.
> Elles passent les ruines les taureaux l'eau.
> Le Roi d'Abyssinie en bas qui les déteste
> Heureux de voir Rubia pleurer de ne pas aimer

> Their horses stirring up the smell of swamps.
> They pass by ruins by bulls by water.
> The king of Abyssinia below who hates them
> So happy to see Rubia weeping because she does not love.

The English version generally tends to sharpen temporal and spatial relationships and brings to the surface seemingly greater narrative coherence, which, however, it perverts by disruptions, just as much as the French. The recurrent spatial and geographical terms do not enable the reader to construct any tangible landscape or to situate the "lonely heroine" whose textual presence suggests a palimpsest of love signs rather than a physical existence. Although her name is given, although the female narrator invokes her, addresses prayers to her, sings her glory, nevertheless the narrator does not make her consistently present. Without clearly stating any origins, without giving the impression of any evolution in time, Rubia enters the reader's world shortly before her betrothal. Her travels and adventures take her to exotic places such as the jungle or rather make distant lands gravitate toward her. Perpetually in motion, she never consents to follow a traceable itinerary through time or space. Not only do we ponder the mysterious identity of Rubia, but we find the other, the partner, the narrator no less perplexing. Although the marriage of Rubia with Cock Nora is concluded, the gender of the betrothed remains in doubt. Intense but sporadic allusions to love, invocations, and prayers appear to echo lines from conventional love lyrics. Their mystery, already enhanced by intertextuality, is compounded by the indefiniteness of the narrative voice, by the lack of identity, by the ambiguity of gender. Whenever the protagonists aspire to a fusion with the universe, it is invariably at the expense of self-definition. Warnings, lyric invocations, prophecies, programmatic statements alternate with one another to such an extent that the textual surface is transformed page after page and, graphically, page upon page.

Penrose sometimes proposes fairly straightforward transformations, for instance, the swallow metamorphosed into a star, which serves to dissolve everyday existence and assure passage into the dream world. But more frequently she evokes changes that defy paraphrase, because, like Max Ernst, she abruptly frustrates the reader's expectations and deliberately undermines predictability. Aimless peregrinations and declarations of feelings, often reversed in the context of a given situation, lead to displacements and disruptions: "Let us go to those frontiers where the sun is icy." This appeal to action suggests a transgressive trip to a fantastic world where day and night as well as aspirations toward love and death become interchangeable. Incomplete statements, telescoped sentences, clauses intersecting one another, verbally bring to the surface the very nature of collage:

> *Ainsi au creux vert des palmes*
> *Les soldats battent leur plein*
> *Et la mariée qui n'en sait rien*
> *Suit son train de pain de Mariée quotidien*

> So in the green hollow of the palms
> The soldiers parade in full dress
> And the bride who understands nothing
> Continues her use of the bride's daily bread.

In these four lines, Penrose juxtaposes several seemingly disconnected images. The introductory word *"Ainsi"* falsely implies a causal continuation. Continuity is but an illusion. By bringing together the hollow of the palm tree, the soldiers, and the bride, the author foregrounds differences and stimulates surprise. The soldiers embattled in the hollow of palm trees suggest an encoun-

Figure 5.1

ter produced by spatial curtailment or *découpage*. But because
the "hollow" of the trees is followed by the antithetical fullness
of the soldiers' masturbating militancy—"*palme*" is the doublet
of *paume*—the contrast implies both a symbiotic and a rhetorical
necessity for the simultaneous presence of the soldiers and the
palms. The shift to the bride marks a return to the abandoned
heroine, whose relationship with the soldiers appears at first
blush incongruous. The poet has indeed added a further discon-
tinuíty, for the bride cannot decently participate in the same
scene as the soldiers and the palm; she remains elsewhere, for
she continues to function in her everyday, ordinary world: "*elle
suit son train.*" On both the syntactical and semantic levels, the
bride refuses to fit in. And would a bride be that incompatible
with an everyday and perhaps religious—"*pain quotidien*"—
existence? Moreover. "*Mariée*" hardly belongs to the same rhym-
ing scheme as "*train*," "*quotidien*," "*pain*," words crowded into
the last line so as to form an authentic verbal collage. The regular
narrative order is clearly disturbed by such interferences, addi-

Figure 5.2

tions, and deletions; and thus, as in the visual collage, no single complete image can emerge, but only an unstable construct.

Valentine Penrose, in her collages, represents multiple scenes. On each page, several landscapes or interiors bisect, or impede upon, one another. Nor does space itself merge into a single perspective. Most plates juxtapose paradoxical fragments, each of which asserts its identity, often introducing incongruities within a given context. A canapé and an armchair are installed in a jungle; a giant succulent nestles in a snow-crested mountain; a tiger races with a farm horse in close proximity to a sphinx. Displacements bring about astonishing encounters. Seldom inscribed in the sky, the sun or a planet finds its place on the ground among everyday objects. Elements stubbornly assert their otherness: the cloud refuses to melt into its celestial surroundings, the woman in her Victorian dress undergoes floatation, a heavy shell-covered box suspended in the sky comes to life. Whatever illusion may arise from these strange juxtapositions is eventually subverted by the shadowlike outline of houses, by obtrusive mountains which heighten the fantastic or erotic quality of the setting; and more often than not, the landscape belies the laws of gravity. In *Un dimanche à Mytilène*, the poem, reduced to its title and without benefit of translation, seems to promise lesbian adventures. The island stretches into an open and flat sea, where, by projecting themselves, rocks form animated and insinuatingly erotic contours (figure 5.1).

By her exploitation of space, Penrose increases suggestiveness, for the scenes, consisting of multiple sections or layers, often conflict with one another within the framework of a single page. By blurring contours or creating amphibious shapes, mirrors combine with curtains, and the dramatic gestures of the women hyperbolize theatricality. These women wear obviously fashionable Victorian clothes where ruffles, belts, buttons, laces often complement gaping curtains. Women protagonists are not the only performers in the multiple scenes: ocean, clouds, rocks, slanted gigantic objects all act out their parts however much they are fragmented or metamorphosed. Various characters share the same collage space, but no real encounter takes place, except here and there an embrace. The protagonists with their intense expressions and their scrutiny of the landscape appear to be strongly absorbed in their own private adventures. Their dramatic gestures performatively express intense psychological stress (figure 5.2).

Penrose's women function as figures of desire, of dreams and longing. The presence of the fantastic, the fading of the city sky, the loss of monolithic consistency, the invasion by enormous threatening objects, the displacement of vegetation, the ambiguity of elements belong to the dream of the female protagonists, who by refusing incarceration in a circumscribed universe assert all the more strongly their otherness. Almost weightless heroines materialize at the very top of a scaffolding or a disintegrating building. Magnified chicken claws, oversized butterflies assume menacing identities. Far from preventing role playing, the dream shows a plant impersonating an artificial object, a woman travestied as a bearded man. It would be erroneous to claim that the women are the dreamers and the landscape the scene of the dream. As the verbal narration is based on recurrences of words, names, and adventures, so the collage includes the return of certain figures alluding to different moments in the sequence of events and mirrors the dream. Thus, the protagonists function both as subject and object (figure 5.3).

In the manipulated world of collage, supernatural emanations may take on the appearance of a frightful reality. Not all feminine figures belong to the same secure universe, for gigantic female heads, either fetishes or idols, assert their threatening presence; and statues, some of them as lifelike as the Victorian protagonists, others fragmented, eclipsed, or dissolved make unexpected appearances. In this manner, Penrose produces a *mise en abyme* of the woman's sublimating dream by whose means she transgresses the barriers between the self and the other:

> *Reviens ô surprenante. Aux rideaux de tes hanches*
> *Où je me tiens agenouillée*
> *Plus que nul autre n'a prié*
> *Je te prie de me laisser dormir et me mêler aux*
> > *temps.*

Come back astonishment. At the curtain of your hips

Where I am now kneeling I beg
As none has ever begged
To let me sleep and melt into the ages.

This poetic text establishes an erotic relationship between two women, *"agenouillée"* and *"surprenante,"* I and you. The prayers to the beloved aim at a transgression into the dreamworld and a relinquishing of the self as an autonomous separate being. The self of the other is characterized by fusion with the world: *"le rideau de tes hanches."* This form of mediation is reminiscent of Eluard, who prefaced *Dons des féminines.*

Figure 5.3

The anecdotal part of the poem has a parallel in the collage. One woman kneels in front of another and prays by word and gesture. The expansion of the dresses hyperbolizes this theatrical incident for which the curtain provides a metonymic stage. The woman kneeling down wears a sort of top hat and obviously plays the part of suitor. So far, I have alluded to only a single section of the scene, where few "alterations" have taken place. But the real rupture, the real duality does not lie exclusively in playing a double male-female role, for it is accentuated and eroticized by the frills and pleats of the dresses as well as the serpentine twists protruding from the standing woman's gown. Sexual overtones are further stressed by the intrusion of the waterfall, an active counterpart of the drawn curtain, as well as by two hybrid bird figures (figure 5.4).

The vignettes, whose relation to the text as commentary and illustration is minimal, serve mainly a decorative purpose. In this respect, they contrast with the full-page plates for which they nevertheless provide a sort of shorthand and *mise en abyme*. Unlike the collages, the vignettes tend to suggest objects, not scenes. These objects, composed of several parts, exemplify the principle of collage. As the various assembled parts do not re-create a recognizable object, their encounters suggest further transgressions. However incongruous the association may be, the object invariably imposes itself by reason of its graceful and mysterious contours. Each vignette proposes its own, usually erotic, enigma. The first object with its lace petticoat, its vaginal creviced shell, and its muzzles combines male and female attributes. In another, Rubia's head appears on top of a long column. A vignette, vertically stretching from the top of the page to the bottom, seems to place the heroine on a pedestal. But multifarious fragmentation subverts so lofty an interpretation, for the head without its bust is installed on stacked pieces of column. The lack of stylistic unity and the instability of the pieces, which merely rest one upon the other, remind us that we are scrutinizing a collage. Valentine Penrose, by her combination of vignettes and texts, texts and collages, collages and vignettes requires from her reader multiple ways of deciphering. Her book depends on enigmatic

Figure 5.4

affinities between images and text, affinities that are invariably undermined and never achieved.

One might claim that Valentine Penrose's *La Comtesse sanglante*, fails, as do so many fictionalized biographies, both as novel and history. One could, moreover, accuse the author of lack of structure, of omissions and repetitions. Information provided on more than one occasion is omitted at the very moment it becomes relevant. Although the work purports to be a documented chronicle, chronology is approached in a rather confusing and desultory way. It is perhaps for this reason that critics have classified the text both as essay and as novel.

La Comtesse sanglante presents us with a wager: its heroine must surpass all male protagonists who, in other novels or even historical events, have reached the heights of villainy! The author insists now and again that she is creating the feminine equivalent of Gilles de Rais, famous for his sadistic murders of hundreds of young boys. With the help of her servants, Erzsébet Bathóry tortures her victims before she puts them to death. Again and again Penrose emphasizes the similarity of the male and female monsters: "Gilles had needed gold. Like Erzsébet Bathory, he needed especially to live a life entirely different from the rest of men, because such a life bored him to extinction" (p. 135). Other passages could pertain to one as well as the other: "The accusation took a more serious turn still when it was learned that, not only had the spilled blood been used as a philtre to maintain youth, but that the victim had been offered as a sacrifice to the devil," (p. 133). Penrose complacently dwells on her heroine's imaginative cruelty, such as covering her female victims with honey and giving them over to insects; exposing them naked to ice or snow; cutting off their limbs; flaying their fingers; torturing them by fire. Thus, the ever increasing number of murders combines repetition with invention.

But cruelty and boldness in action hardly exclude paradox, dialectics, and especially comparisons. The author uncovers precedents for Erzsébet's peculiar crimes, usually in the royal courts of other lands and other times. The countess' redoubtable ancestry provides many an edifying instance of gory violence, which may account for their progeny's frightfulness. The author prides herself on having read all relevant documents and examined all appropriate examples. As a result, her narrative appears so heavily documented that we almost forget that we are reading fiction. But whether or not Bathóry has actually committed all the crimes credited to her matters much less than Penrose's endeavor to present a disquieting feminine consciousness, capable of raising dangerous questions, for instance: why should feminine heroines be the victims of males, why should they behave virtuously, why should they conform to expected patterns, why should they be psychologically convincing?

Like many a conventional heroine, Erzsébet is extremely beautiful. However, the author merely states it as a fact without ever showing its impact on the opposite sex. Although it hardly goes unnoticed, her beauty leads only to narcissism. The following comment by Sarah Kofman in L'Enigme de la femme is relevant here: "The great criminal is besides precisely the one afflicted with a full fledged narcissism, that holds at a distance from his self whatever may diminish him. See how the pale criminal has shaken his head, in his eyes speaks his great contempt. My self is something that must be surmounted . . . my self is my great contempt for mankind. Thus do the criminal's eyes speak."[10] Bathóry's husband, the soldiers, her son-in-law are afraid of her; in her presence their virility seems to disintegrate. She strives to acquire authority, not to take command of the male, but to be self-sufficient, to be other, to lead her own secret life. As beauty is the self, she strives to preserve it, and her fear of aging becomes increasingly obsessive: "While waiting for her creams to be ready, Erzsébet would gaze in her mirror at the intractable set of her forehead, at her sinuous lips, her aquiline nose and her immense black eyes. She was in love with love, she wanted to hear that she was beautiful, the most beautiful of all" (p. 53). Valentine Penrose implicitly refers to Snow White; later she will compare a member of the Bathóry family to Blue Beard, whose original model may have been none other than Gilles de Rais. Erzsébet consults a mirror; the reassuring words of her most loyal servants would be of no avail.

Rather than treat her beauty as a gift to be displayed, she cultivates it in an unusual manner by making herself as artificial as possible. By constantly changing her clothes, she repeatedly disguises herself without ever having to wear a mask. Bored with marriage, with widowhood, with her everyday existence, she lives more and more for her secret performances. The mirror, which plays the key role as she becomes the sole person to see herself, functions as the generative element in her secret stagings. Her beauty leads only to subversion, for she destroys the self to become the other.

Although Countess Bathóry is a noteworthy public figure, prominent in the Hungarian aristocracy, her true fame comes from her secret obsession to kill, to destroy. She acts like a vampire and a sorceress, constantly in touch with supernatural forces. By insisting both on the subversion of the social structure and the interference of occult forces such as witchcraft, vampirism, and alchemy in all spheres of life, Valentine Penrose follows certain trends of surrealist fiction, including translations and illustrations of gothic novels such as *The Monk* or *The Castle of Otronto*.

The author, as we have already stated, prides herself on the reliability of her documentation. She presents the family history of the Bathories, their distinction in warfare, their wealth, their prestige in political life, the various symptoms of their madness. The countess, betrothed at the age of eleven, married at fifteen, has been shaped and determined by these social and political forces at the end of the feudal regime in Hungary. These stable and prescribed structures, these religiously followed traditions are ironically described in the novel. Greatness, rank, precedence, carefully calculated marriage alliances are counteracted by more disturbing historical forces. Warfare waged in all corners causes endless destruction, bloodshed, and poverty. The ideals of the aristocracy, of family heritage are jeopardized by military and political turmoil as well as by vices secretly practiced among the sternest advocates of morality. Moreover, princes and aristocrats in general tend to be afflicted by madness and epilepsy. Sex, crime, and torture have undermined the feudal structure even before Erzsébet's first deeds.

Erzsébet epitomizes these contradictions and paradoxes. She is worthy of the noble lineage of her husband, her father, and her mother; but she is also conditioned by physical and mental crises and trances. After her initial crimes, that might be construed as sacrifices to the universal Mother, she indulges more and more in witchcraft and satanism. Nor is she the only public figure to participate in such practices. Side by side, determinism and individualism live in Bathóry at a time when the feudal system is on the wane and when Renaissance liberation has reached the most remote provinces of Hungary. Determinism provides a partial and distorted explanation of her behavior "To tell the truth, Erzsébet Bathory, when she came into the world was far from being a complete human being" (p. 12). "Je ne sais pas d'où je viens, je ne sais vraiment pas d'où je viens, je suis incapable d'imaginer d'où je viens" (p. 62). ("I don't know where I'm from, I really do not know where I'm from. I am incapable of imagining where I'm from".) Puzzled about her origins, uprooted in her own courts and castles, she will always be exempt from regret, repentance, and guilt feelings. But the heroine will never adhere to any code to which, in spite of early withdrawals, she has been exposed. Gilles de Rais, on the other hand, cries after every deed and with intense remorse returns to Christianity. He rejects his own deeds which he labels as crimes. Countess Bathóry does not bend, she does not accept the aid of a Christian minister, she does not adhere to conventional morality or religion to assess her deeds. She benefits from the relations she has with kings and powerful nobles, yet vainly attempts to poison them in seeking to avoid her trial. She is not burned at the stake as a witch, but condemned to life imprisonment in complete darkness so as to avoid public attention. Erzsébet's actions do not constitute in any way a rebellion. Her actions are dictated by passion, and until death she will stand behind them; she will never forsake herself. She opts for a selfhood which comprises otherness, as Penrose informs her readers.

Bathóry's countless gory deeds stem from her narcissism and self-love. She is the self and the other other as there is no one or nothing else in her life: "Her supreme narcissism, at play in everything she did, held her back from contact with the earth. Maybe the savage music, the incantations in the sorcerer's cabin, filled with the acrid smoke of belladonna leaves and of datura, which was burning there, and her dangerous hunts. . . . maybe all

those things set alight a really living flame in these eyes, which
haunted another world" (p. 24). Her secret life is not spent or
even planned with members of her own class and family, but
with her servants. They act under her orders, they attract young
females for their mistress, they carry out the tortures she prescribes. They constitute a secret society under her orders. Erzsébet compulsively puts beautiful young women in the nude. The
tortures she personally inflicts upon them include aggressive gestures against the breasts and the genitals. She is suddenly overcome with an unquenchable thirst for blood. Desire and passion
motivate these obsessive deeds, the need to practice them in ever
growing numbers. Her lesbianism has always been rumored, her
horoscope, the influence of the Moon and Mercury, are said to
further female sadistic homosexuality. The heroine wants to possess the beauty of young women, but not as images to be contemplated or as objects to be sexually possessed. Her deeds, always
accompanied by ritual incantations, make mutilation and death
indispensable. Erzsébet is a vampire who needs their blood, for
the blood of others has to become her own. Biting young women
is a ritualistic, meaningful gesture. She will bathe in the blood of
young women in order to postpone aging. A blood bath is a
process of rejuvenation. "And every time Erzsébet Bathory wished
to be still whiter, she began once more to bathe in blood" (p. 24).
To promote rejuvenation, she also practices witchcraft, using
philtres, mandragores, and other plants.

Paradox cannot be overlooked, for passions and desire lead an
important member of the aristocracy to sadism and cruelty while
social and political events inscribe their determinism. In addition, lunar and solar forces, prominent at her birth, account partially for her drive toward witchcraft and vampirism as well as
her inclination toward madness. Demons, more pagan than Christian, had taken possession of Erzsébet from the beginning. She is
driven by savage primitive forces which throughout history were
repressed by both religious and secular authorities. Countess
Bathóry's long phalanxes, her sinuously shaped mouth are never
visible in the presence of family and society. Requiring suffering
and not pleasure, she represents the constant need for transgression which becomes imperative for those who follow the impulse

of passion and desire. Contrary to Gilles de Rais, her moral consciousness is beclouded and fogged in. She remains unable to
understand the humiliations inflicted, at the end of her life, upon
a woman of such high lineage.

Valentine Penrose was not the first writer to compare Gilles de
Rais and Erzsébet Bathóry. Shortly before the publication of her
book, Georges Bataille had announced *La Comtesse sanglante* in
his own *Les Larmes d'Eros*.[11] His remarks reveal the fictionality
rather than the reliability of Penrose's documentation. In a few
pages, he opposes Erzsébet Bathóry to Gilles de Rais to whom he
had previously devoted a monograph.[12] The latter is endowed
with unbelievable strength in the presence of his victims, and the
compromise with Christianity does not enter into the picture.
Bataille mentions the pitiless strength of Gilles in watching the
tortured dying: "When at the end the children lay dead, he kissed
them . . . and those who had the most beautiful heads and limbs
were displayed for contemplation, their bodies were cruelly opened
and he delighted in the sight of their internal organs" (p. 162).
The important term here is "contemplation," pointing toward the
inclusion of witnesses and accomplices and linking Gilles de Rais
to Sade. The author of *Les Larmes d'Eros* gives relatively little
information about the countess, but her narcissistic universe (as
represented in *La Comtesse sanglante*) would lack this initiating
and participating ritual. Georges Bataille and Valentine Penrose,
each of whom chose one criminal at the expense of the other,
reveal truths which Christian iconography had often tried to suppress. After the historical Gilles and Erzsébet, Sade increases
our self-awareness by purely imaginary crimes. Penrose further
sharpens this awareness by showing the strength and autonomy
of woman as the other. Roland's portrait of Valentine, abounding
in deviant romanticism, expressed long before *La Comtesse sanglante* the pitfalls of partnership.

But *La Comtesse sanglante* was not Valentine's last book. After
this strong statement of a generic nature she returned to lyric
poetry ten years later. In *Les Magies* (1972), she subordinates,
more than in *Herbe à la lune*, her personal voice to the pursuit of
magic and hermeticism, the everyday to legendary and alchemi-
cal transformation.[13] Seemingly the issue of liberation has be-

come defunct, and any established social order irrelevant. The volume includes a poem devoted to Gilles de Rais. The protagonist, an ivy-clad castle, gives rise to threatening legendary visions converging on archetypal killing. Rather than providing a link to *La Comtesse sanglante* the text is representative of the final stages of Valentine's poetic creation. *Les Magies* appeared almost simultaneously with a "prose-poem" entitled "Tàpies les sources innommées."[14]

We have suggested that the divorce between Valentine and Roland Penrose was not only a matrimonial issue, but that it encompassed their Weltanschauung, their concept of the artist, their attitude toward gender. Yet Valentine did not fully sever her relationship with Roland and especially his second wife, the photographer Lee Miller. She returned to London for visits, but more importantly she shared with Roland an admiration for the Catalan painter Antoni Tàpies to whom the British artist devoted two prologues and later a book.[15] The nature of Valentine's and Roland's homages to Tàpies differ vastly. Roland writes from the perspective of an art critic who situates the painter and wishes to share his admiration with his reader.

Tàpies, as Penrose explains, was in his early stages closely associated with the Surrealists and felt an affinity with their art. He evolved, responding to Oriental philosophy and religion, especially Zen. He related to almost all problems crucial to surrealist theory and practice: the cult of the unconscious and the imagination, persistence in technical experimentation, and the need for the arts to be in the service of liberation. Tàpies, according to Penrose, transformed insignificant and even deteriorated substances, elevating them toward a higher order. His art pertains to a world of paradoxes, made visible through the simultaneous presence of vertical and horizontal directions which encounter each other in the cross. This symbol relates to more than one cult and inscribes both death and rebirth into the work of art. Tàpies aspires toward the transgression of all divisions into order so as to attain the unity of the archetypal.

Even a close reading of "Tàpies, sources innommées" would not reveal any disagreement between Valentine's and Roland's point of view. For Valentine, the evolution from surrealist sympathy to a deep commitment to Oriental philosophy and Western mystics provides a basis for self-identification. These were the paths on which she had traveled, these were the aspirations from which she only occasionally deviated. As Roy Edwards, points out: "because of the writer's committal to the imagery therein discussed it provides, by analogy, a key to her own work and preoccupations" (p. 4). While Roland displays talent as an art critic in his writings on the Catalan painter, Valentine's pages are those of a poet and mystic. Although she points at certain characteristic features of Tàpies' art, making her reader recall the substance, lines, and colors of his canvases, for her these works do not present, as they do for Roland, an end in themselves, but access to a vision, a mediation leading to an archetypal experience, to the principle of life itself. The presence of matter, which she invokes repeatedly, provides a threshold between the animate and the inanimate and bears witness to a continuing reversible process from decay to rebirth, from chaos to order, from void to substance, from silence to voice. Every particle she names brings forth the testimony of a historical process, it alludes to origins, biblical and gnostic. A direction is not merely a line, but a personified sign, surviving or reanimated. Tàpies' universe with its shifting particles and layers moves from matter to spirituality and vice versa. It refers to "scriptures," to their intertextual networks.

Valentine deciphers within these paintings a matriarchical order. Life's principles stem from the feminine essence. From Adam's creation on the sixth day she reaches back to Lilith and forward to Eve: "Life herself, dumb and hidden woman, never inert even in the most confused of her aspects" (p. 197). She invokes the great mother Kali to whom a Hindu temple is dedicated, Atargis, mother Goddess of Asia, the principle of reproduction, but not procreation. Not only is the feminine principle incarnated by mythical and divine figures, but by recurrent signs, shapes, and letters. By its incessant struggle toward unity, it becomes inseparable from the making of texts and images.

Partnership assumes exposure to similar artistic experiences and a presence at the creation of each other's work. Roland's and Valentine's partnership did not follow a linear development. The study of its changing course shows exemplary differences and affinities between a male and a female artist as well as a woman's struggle for alterity within the bounds of surrealism.

Endnotes

1. Xavière Gauthier, *Surréalisme et sexualité* (Paris: Gallimard, 1971); Whitney Chadwick, *Women Artists and the Surrrealist Movement* (Boston: New York Graphic Society, 1985).

2. See Gloria Feman Orenstein, "Towards a Bifocal Vision in Surrealist Aesthetics," *Trivia* (1984), pp. 70–84.

3. Most of these portraits are reproduced in Valentine Penrose, *Poems and Narrations*, Roy Edwards, tr. (London: Carcanet and Elephant Trust, 1977). Translations of Valentine Penrose's texts, when available, are taken from this book.

4. *Roland Penrose* (London: Arts Council of Great Britain, 1980), p. 12.

5. *Herbe à la lune* (Paris: G.L.M., 1935).

6. Roland Penrose, *Scrap Book* (New York: Rizzoli, 1981), p. 53.

7. *Martha's Opera* (Paris: Editions Fontaine, 1945).

8. *Dons des Féminines* (Paris: Aux Pas Perdus, 1951); *Erzsebet Bathory La Comtesse sanglante* (Paris: Mercure de France, 1962); English version: *The Bloody Countess*, Alexander Trocchi, tr. (London: Calder and Boyars, 1970).

9. For further discussion of *Dons des Féminines*, see Whitney Chadwick, *Women Artists*.

10. Sarah Kofman, *L'Enigme de la femme* (Paris: Galilée, 1980), p. 65.

11. Georges Bataille, *Les Larmes d'Eros*. (Paris: Pauvert, 1961).

12. *Procès de Gilles de Rais*, Documents précédés d'une introduction de Georges Bataille (Paris: Club français du livre, 1959).

13. *Les Magies* (Paris: Les Mains Libres, 1972).

14. "Tàpies, les sources innommées," *L'Art vivant* (December 1972–January 1973), no. 35.

15. Roland Penrose, *Prologue to the Catalog of the Tàpies Exhibition at the Institute of Contemporary Arts*, 1965; Presentation of *Poems from the Catalan* (London: Guinness and Button, 1973); and *Tàpies* (Barcelona: La Poligrafa, 1977). After this essay was submitted the following article appeared: Susan Rubin Suleiman, "Reflections on Women Writers and the Avant-Garde in France," *Yale French Studies* no. 75, pp. 148–171.

6

IMAGES OF WOMEN IN AFRICAN TOURIST ART: A CASE STUDY IN CONTINUITY AND CHANGE
Bennetta Jules-Rosette

OVER THE past several years, I have written extensively on women in African religion and on women's work in the informal economic sector in Zaire and Zambia. My studies have included research on women in the arts and crafts. Rather than presenting a study exclusively on one of these topics, however, I should like to reflect on the implications of some of this research by establishing a "counterpoint" between dominant images of women in African tourist art and the socioeconomic status of women. My argument will necessarily entail a few interpretive leaps in order to establish the link between representations of women in African art and their socioeconomic status.

A Definition of Tourist Art

A strong relationship has always existed between the aesthetic and the commercial in various African traditions. In this sense, tourist art, as a system for the production of aesthetic objects to be used for commercial purposes, is not new in Africa. The widespread use of cowrie shells as a form of currency exchange in West and Central Africa is an example. The Islamic bureaucrat Ibn Batutah found cowrie money in the city of Timbuktu in the Malian Empire and further south as early as 1352.[1] By 1497, cowrie money was regularly exchanged with the Portuguese at the Bight of Benin. The cowries themselves were evaluated in aesthetic terms. Beautifully colored and highly polished shells were worth more than plain shells in commercial exchanges.

With Angola's secession from the Kongo kingdom of San Salvador in the fifteenth century, the Portuguese introduced a comprehensive system of taxation. Cowries used for exchange were supplemented by cloth stamped by the royal mint in Lisbon. Stamped cloth "money" was worth four times as much as unstamped cloth in commercial exchanges. Even today in West Africa, the cowrie theme is a common motif on locally made batik and tie-dyed cloth. Popular beliefs exist concerning the magical properties of cowries and their association with wealth, royalty, and power. Hence, the old commercial arts flow into the new arts.

Cut-pile raffia among the Lele and Bushong of southwestern Zaire has a similar history. Raffia was both an object of art and of commerce. The Lele employed raffia for brideprice payments, debt settlement, and cementing alliances. They also used smaller quantities of raffia for mundane purchases such as pottery, arrows, and hoes from neighboring groups. With the advent of colonialism, the Lele assessed the value of Congo francs in terms of raffia cloth exchanges and sold objects very reluctantly for francs and much more readily for raffia. The supply of raffia was controlled by limiting its production. Mary Douglas states: "In frequent conversations about their need to raise raffia cloth, it is a striking act that men think first not of sitting down to weave, but of pursuing any debts and claims outstanding. They hope to meet the demand for raffia by increasing the velocity of circulation rather than by increasing supplies."[2]

In this sense, the old form of commercial art differs radically from the new. Appearing as early as 1914, tourist art made for exchanges to outsiders (chiefly Europeans) has steadily increased in production since the 1950s. The goal of the tourist artist is to glut the market with objects. Production is a form of advertisement. It is also through the "mass" production process of genre and style creation, followed by reproduction, that innovation occurs in tourist art. Elsewhere, I have outlined the system of exchange involved in tourist art.[3] This process involves production by the artists and interpretation and intervention by middlemen, who serve as culture brokers and critics influencing the process of artistic reproduction.

Tourist art objects are visual signs. In combining the artists' and the consumers' views, the tourist art object unites all levels of meaning and expression. As a system of communication, tourist art lacks the specificity of language because of the large range of meanings implied by and perceived in a given object. Artists and consumers attribute different meanings to tourist art objects as signs and as vehicles of symbolic and commodity exchange.

Consequently, tourist art may be analyzed from three distinct perspectives: (1) with reference to its sign value for image-creators and consumers; (2) on the basis of its symbolic exchange value in the communication between artists and their audience; and (3) in terms of its usage and market value. Both the symbolic and socioeconomic values of tourist art have separate meanings for art creators and consumers. Thus, tourist art cannot be evaluated exclusively in terms of its consumption as many art historians claim. The processes of creation and production remain the unexplored dimensions of tourist art. The sign value of a work of art is converted into symbolic exchange value when an artistic genre finds a popular audience. Objects may lose their appeal over time or with excessive reproduction.

Moreover, tourist art is not a sign system that encompasses a unified set of objects or cultural meanings. Instead, the visual marker in tourist art alludes to the sight or exotic experience which is sought by the tourist but is not necessarily a direct representation. Tourist art translates one level of signs into another. Souvenirs are signs of the tourist's journey and proof of travel. They are only secondarily status symbols for consumers. A figurine of a giraffe is important not so much as the representation of an animal but, on another level, as a sign of the place where the animal is found. It also embodies the artist's perception of the object as part of the communication. Therefore, tourist art, like other contemporary art forms, does not imply the holistic sign system that Lévi-Strauss asserts characterizes the "art of primitive societies."[4] It appeals to a mixed audience that cannot read, or chooses to ignore, the subtleties of cultural style. Hence, a fluctuation, or "crisis," in styles is characteristic of tourist art.

The decorative uses of some traditional African art by contemporary consumers are of interest in this context. Recently, Ashanti *akuaba* dolls symbolizing female fertility have been reproduced in the form of decorative ornaments sold as "unisex" costume jewelry in the West. Describing the traditional *akuaba* figure, an art historian emphasizes that the doll's symbolic meaning is based upon "the ideal of perfection of form and beauty desired by the expectant mother for her unborn child."[5] The popular *akuaba* necklace has an exotic appeal, but its primordial connection to female fertility among the Akan is entirely suppressed. The round flat head of the figure and lack of extraneous ornamentation accommodate mass production by modern African artisans who promote its sale to the largest possible audience. Meanwhile, the doll's form has become so simplified that it can be easily fabricated by machine without consulting the original image-creators.

The interactions between the creators, the brokers, and the consumers of art are critical to understanding this chain of events. In the manner of many other African entrepreneurs, the image-creators may lose contact with their market when it extends beyond the local level. Akan craftsmen originally created and produced the *akuaba* dolls. They did not, however, remain the image-creators when the doll had entered the commercial domain.

Images of Women in African Tourist Art

In this paper, I will discuss three key images of women in African tourist art. Although I first located these images in popular Zairian and Zambian paintings, these images may also be found in the form of textiles and wood carvings. They involve images of the woman as: (1) a social persona; (2) a social text or form of discourse; and (3) a visual representation. These three images are: (1) the peasant woman; (2) the "elegant' woman *(l'él-égante)*; and (3) the mermaid or *mami wata*. All of these images involve a tension between continuity and change, and they may be interpreted in various ways.

The peasant woman is usually depicted as stalwart and muscular. She balances a calabash on her head, carries a baby on her back, and often wields a hoe. She is a mother, a good provider, and a loyal and submissive family member. She is both enterprising and obedient, and she poses no threat to her community. Instead, she brings the community honor and nurtures her family. Ilona Szombati-Fabian and Johannes Fabian would classify the peasant woman in their genre category of "things past" for popular Zairian art.[6] I have dealt with this image primarily in the Zambian context (as painted by Zairian artists in Lusaka) and have classified images of women—past, present, and imaginary —as part of a simple subgenre of tourist painting. (Note that one may differentiate between tourist and popular paintings in spite of the overlap between genres and artists.)

The peasant woman is an image that invokes the idyllic past. As such, she resembles the idyllic landscape and the "palm tree and canoe paintings" which are the hallmark of tourist art. There are also variations on these subgenres ("the abandoned house" and "the burning village") which have political overtones while simultaneously invoking an idyllic past for tourist consumption. The peasant woman represents an unambiguous, conventional female role. Yet, ironically, she is often painted with her back toward the viewer, as if her image is fading away, and we no longer know who she is. Such *double entendres* are a typical communicative strategy in tourist art.

The elegant woman (*l'élégante*) stands in direct contrast to the peasant woman. She is dressed in colorful silks, wears expensive jewelry, and assumes a seductive pose. She represents urbanity, wealth, status, and modernity. Although she lures the viewer toward her, she appears alone.

In this sense, she also evokes a feeling of individualism. The artists who painted *l'élégante* told me that she is a dangerous type of woman. She causes men to spend all of their money and then runs away. The elegant woman is often paired with a chief or male elder in sales displays. Thus, she forms a symbolic and visual opposition not only with the peasant woman but also with the older man.

The third image, that of the mermaid or *mami wata* has a long and complex cultural history. Of course, mermaid imagery appears in many cultures. She has been, some believe erroneously, associated with the fish-legged figure in Benin and Yoruba art. This figure appeared in Benin art as early as 1334 and closely resembles the Hellenistic-Etruscan triton. It has two fish tails and appears with either male or female bodies. Fraser states: "Just who or what the fish-legged being represents is a matter of uncertainty."[7] He believes, however, that the being is a god or a deified Oba, and strongly cautions against any association of this figure with the contemporary *mami wata* image. The contemporary image of *mami wata* appears in both Yoruba and Igbo art, often as a female figure surrounded by snakes. The contemporary *mami wata* image on canvas is believed by some to have been influenced by Hindu poster art imported into West Africa during the 1940s.[8] Others find much earlier, independent origins for her,

Figure 6.1. *Mami Wata*. Painting by Mpinda. The *mami wata* is a totalizing symbol in popular Zairian painting.

claiming that the image was copied from Portuguese ship mast-heads.

The *mami wata* bears both foreign and local connotations. She is associated with traditional water spirits of all kinds. In Zaire, she is known as *mambo muntu* or the snake woman because she is frequently accompanied by a snake and is believed to materialize into a snake when angered.

The mermaid has magical powers. She brings wealth and success but at a price. In contemporary popular paintings, she is depicted wearing expensive Western-style jewelry and a watch set to the bewitching hour (2:00 or 3:00 a.m.). Owning her is believed to bring wealth but to require total fidelity. The Nigerian novelist Chinua Achebe has even dedicated a short story to *mami wata*, who chases and haunts a village clerk desirous of becoming a rich man. She finally vanishes, leaving only her long hair behind.

A Socio-Semiotic Analysis of *Mami Wata*

The example of the contemporary *mami wata*, or mermaid paintings serves as a point of departure for making the distinction between the tourist art object as a sign and as a symbolic unit in a larger communicative exchange. The elements found in the painting may be viewed together as a set of signs within an expressive code. Szombati-Fabian and Fabian have referred to the *mami wata* as an artistic genre of popular Zairian painting.[9] On the other hand, I have treated *mami wata* paintings as part of a subgenre of transitional symbols and images of women in Zambian painting. The subgenre includes paintings of idyllic scenes in transition and of modern subjects. The *mami wata* is a multi-vocal, totalizing symbol that connects customary beliefs and imagery with conceptions of the past and future. Within each *mami wata* painting, there are a number of signs and evocative visual markers. The mermaid represents the wealth, power, and danger that accompany change.

Yet, the mermaid is not merely a *passive representation*. Those who purchase her image believe that the mermaid painting has the magical potency to affect their lives. As stated, she is at once an object of desire and a subject of fear.

The interplay of these visual statements makes the mami wata a vibrant, living symbol. Moreover, on the level of painting, the mami wata contains a symbolic response to tourist art. The message content is one of ideological protest. Nevertheless, the form in which the message is presented remains the same as that of tourist art. Resembling tourist painting, the mami wata combines foreign imagery with indigenous beliefs and new conventions of expression. However, unlike other forms of tourist art, the mami wata is intended for active social use by its producers and local consumers. Szombati-Fabian and Fabian point out that the mami wata remains the one painting typical of the social milieu to which most grass-roots artists and local (non-elite) consumers belong.[10]

Interpretation of the mermaid relies upon the contextual uses to which she is put by the artists and their audiences. The mermaid is usually purchased by businessmen and proletarian consumers and is used as a talisman. She is also integrated into the symbolism and practice of urban folk doctoring. At first glance, a tourist who sees such a painting might be offended, fascinated, or perplexed because the foreign consumer does not share the artist's cultural frame of reference for the image. The mami wata represents the allure of wealth and the threat of neocolonialism in the form of a dangerous woman. As stated earlier, after a broken contract, the mermaid is said to materialize as a venomous snake. Both of her manifestations are depicted in the painting, with the deadlier form subordinated to the more appealing, although anomalous, female figure. As a totalizing symbol, the mami wata "has a fan, or spectrum, of referents which are interlinked by a simple mode of association."[11] The mami wata artfully combines multiple layers of meaning. The multivocality of the mami wata image is diagrammed in figure 6.2.

These five levels of interpretation for the mami wata may be used as a vehicle for critically examining the concept of syncretism as it applies to tourist art. Historical antecedents, however, do not explain the uses of the mami wata image. Something more than syncretism is taking place. The mermaid represents the results of immediate contact with outside cultures and values by depicting and idealizing the costs and benefits of "Western" wealth and consumerism. The *mami wata* involves an expanded rather than a restricted system of signification. The expanded system relies on the context of interpretation for its impact. Local consumers "read" new levels of meaning into the *mami wata*, which embodies both icon and act, symbol and process. In this case, tourist art overlaps with the domain of indigenous cultural symbolization.

As in all art, the motives of the tourist artists frequently disappear or are transformed when the art object is received by consumers. The artwork encodes meanings and events on several levels at once. The *mami wata* paintings make sociopolitical statements about the colonial and postcolonial situations in Central Africa as perceived by a contemporary audience. Szombati-Fabian and Fabian apply to Roland Barthes'[12] version of the semiotic model of expression, relation, and content (ERC) as a method for understanding these paintings as communicative acts with meanings that shift in reference to the context in which they appear. This approach uncovers the multivocality of tourist art objects but largely excludes the interpretive role and reception process of consumers in diverse markets.

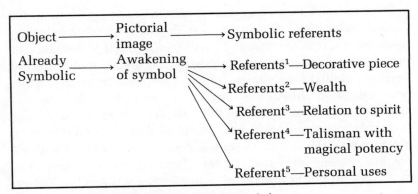

Figure 6.2. The *Mami Wata*—A Totalizing Symbol

Counterpoint: The Socioeconomic Status of Women in Africa

The *mami wata* image represents an ambivalence toward modernity as well as toward new images of women. An old "chicken-and-egg" problem revolves around whether culture reflects or generates social change. Rather than open that "Pandora's box," we may establish a homology between the two processes of change. The reluctance of many African nations to deal with social reforms and legislation concerning women reflects the same sort of fears that the elegant woman and mermaid evoke. Zaire, a major producer of *mami wata* paintings, provides us with interesting social examples that parallel the cultural image.

In Zaire, for example, both the legal system and the national ideology of Authenticity have supported the ideal of the woman as a mother, a domestic figure, and a wife under the direct authority of her husband and kinsmen.[13] Between 1948 and 1960, when Zaire achieved independence, there were few educational facilities for women with "only concerned discussion" by members of the African elite *(évolués)* about formal education for women. Ida Rousseau states: "The *évolués* wanted women who would be properly educated in the Belgian tradition."[14] Their objectives emphasized moral and domestic education for women and a better selection of wives who would not be "an embarrassment to their husbands."

Even today, the ideal woman, if she enters the modern sector through education, remains in female stereotyped positions— teaching, nursing, sewing, and small trades. Legal protections for these women are weak, and are based on a combination of the Belgian colonial laws drawn from the Napoleonic code and the new legislation, which has removed some of the rights customarily held by women. Under the new laws, women need their husbands' permission and signature to work in salaried positions, obtain passports, and open bank accounts. The rights of widows are also poorly protected under Christian, Islamic, and civil marriages. In describing the situation in Zaire, Francille Wilson states:

The combination of the Belgian legal code and "traditional laws" has resulted in a distressing hodgepodge of some of the worst aspects of both in regard to the rights of widows. Not only are many of the Zairian statutes inappropriate for the urban, increasingly nuclear, and ofttimes interethnic Zairian family, but there is abundant evidence that magistrates often ignore the actual ethnic laws and cite statements from the philosophy of *authenticité* when determining cases.[15]

These laws result in the mother's surrender of children to her husband's kin, the loss of inherited property and assets, and the relinquishing of profits from collectively held businesses. Customarily, some of these rights were protected by levirate and other traditional practices that linked the wife and children to her husband's lineage and provided necessary economic and social protections. These mixed legal codes remove customary protections without replacing them with new and clearly enforced inheritance laws. Similar situations exist in Zambia, Kenya, and Cameroon.

Divorced women are victimized by the loss of their property and children, along with the negative images of the status of single women. Often marginalized, separated from their familial support, and pushed out of the labor force, widowed and divorced women in Zaire frequently resort to informal economic sector activities, including prostitution. There is a tendency among both scholars and local politicians in Zaire to confuse independent women *(femmes indépendantes)* and prostitutes, known as *femmes libres*.[16] Divorced women find it difficult to qualify for the family allowances given to male household heads. In order to be eligible, they must prove that their former husbands were guilty of adultery. No consistent enforcement exists for alimony payments, which tend to be inadequate or low. This situation further pushes women, disadvantaged by low education, into marginal or illicit trades.

Ilsa Schuster describes a similar situation for women in urban Zambia. According to Schuster, men do not hesitate to take custody of their children, and women are reluctant to claim the children for economic reasons. In the Zambian context, where several ethnic groups are matrilineal, influential men who are economically much better off than their wives, claim their children regardless of traditional custody practices. Schuster further explains that no alimony is expected for those married under traditional law. Support is left to the good will of the ex-husband.[17] Moreover, young wives, whether married under customary or civil law, are fearful of taking custody payments because this support may give the husband the right to claim the children at a later date. Thus, unemployed women tolerate enormous financial loss and suffering in order to keep their children.

Media and political campaigns have been waged against single women whose lifestyles in urban areas are viewed as deviating from conventional practices. These women resemble the painters' "elegant women" stereotypes. Rhoda Howard cites the political campaigns waged during the early 1970s, and in some cases still continuing, against miniskirts in Zaire, Malawi, Tanzania, and Kenya.[18] Ostensibly, such attire is viewed as an example of Western decadence and a symbolic perpetuation of neocolonialism. These legal and media attacks, however, are also criticisms of the changing socioeconomic role of the independent women wage earners who are entering the white-collar work force in increasing numbers and changing their wardrobes when they do so.

Francille Wilson describes a similar situation in Zaire in which women's status is tied to a "moral hierarchy,"[19] that idealizes marriage and the importance of motherhood. Divorced, single, and independent women are, thus, not only deprived of legal rights but are also morally isolated and socially ostracized by media campaigns.

It is, however, difficult to control symbolic and media campaigns that permeate political and popular culture. Schuster claims that women who do not conform to conventional standards of behavior are treated as "folk devils" by the Zambian media and that such campaigns serve a variety of political purposes.[20] Note that the folk devil is the textual equivalent of the *mami wata* image. "Moral" decline is often blamed on "loose" women whose lifestyles and fashions are viewed as corrupting influences on society. A parallel may be drawn between the folk devil media campaigns and the traditional witchcraft allegations, as well as between the folk devil and the *mami wata*. Witchcraft allegations often resulted in severe social and legal sanctions. The image of the woman as a folk devil operates in a similar way.

Arrests and media campaigns were mounted in Zaire and Zambia during the mid-1970s against young "unaccompanied women" who were labeled as the cause of the decline of the family, the increase in alcoholism, and the rise in urban crime rates. This new class of independent women became the target of repressive measures and symbolic campaigns that stereotyped all women and resulted in limiting their political rights. Upholding the customs and the moral structure of a changing society became the justification for restricting and redefining the rights of an emerging class of women.

This situation extends to the rights of the less-educated women who are forced to support themselves through petty trading and other informal economic activities. Their strategies for survival are labeled as illicit trade, rendering it increasingly difficult for them to escape from a vicious cycle of poverty and ostracism. Women in the petty trades in Zambia have difficulty obtaining sales licenses and official market stalls. Approximately 20 percent of Zambia's urban labor force works in the informal economic sector.[21] For women, petty trading, including vegetable vending, fish mongering, and beer brewing, is a major source of informal sector income. Official preference for the licensing of market stalls is given to men. Women are thereby pushed into informal home trades, which are illegal and subject to frequent police raids.

Legal restrictions limit both the regular clientele of home traders and the profits that they can realize from sales. Beer brewing, the most lucrative form of home trade, is illegal and the brewers are arrested and heavily fined. The illicit nature of home trades reinforces the dependence of women on male breadwinners. Therefore, the divorced or widowed woman who works in the home trades is doubly stigmatized by her marital status and her precarious economic situation. These women are victimized just as the rising class of subelite "independent" women are. They are caught in a vicious cycle of legal restrictions and social and symbolic marginalization. The image of these women as legal and

moral threats deflects serious attention from their actual economic and social situation. The manipulation of cultural images
and beliefs affects the context in which human rights legislation
can be implemented. Current laws related to marriage, inheritance, divorce, widowhood, and access to the labor force often
consist of an ambiguous mixture of colonial legal codes and rein-
terpretations of customary laws. The conditions for the imple-
mentation of these laws are equally ambiguous. They are subject
to political interpretations that reveal a tension between the old
cultural "microcosm" and the universalistic ideals.

Case Studies in Social Change:
Women in the Informal Economic Sector

My case studies of women in Zambia's informal sector indicate
the problems of balancing the "peasant woman" image against
the pressures of modern life in the urban context. The brewing of
home beer along with either vegetable vending or craft sale and
production have become important outlets for women. The association of the home beer trade with prostitution exists among
Zambian law enforcement agencies. A recent survey claims that
70 percent of the home-brewed beer produced in Zambia is connected with prostitution.[22] This finding suggests the importance
of examining the legal as well as social barriers to women's participation in the labor force and requires a broad view of their
informal employment strategies.

Maria Khosa: A Home Beer Trader

For both personal and legal reasons, Maria chose not to brew
stronger illicit beverages. Instead, she worked regularly at brewing a mild South African beer as a daily source of revenue. As her
community reputation grew, she became eligible to enter the legal
beer trade. For the most part, however, she confined her sales to
the home base and did not use middlemen to expand her
clientele.

Hansen provides a case study profile of Maria's trading activities.

Maria Khosa is a 25 year old Sotho from Botswana. She grew up in Johannesburg where she married a Zambian Nsenga by civil marriage five years ago. While in Johannesburg, she worked as a domestic servant. They came to Lusaka three years ago (1970) where the husband, Mr. Elfas Phiri, has worked as a security guard ever since. Mrs. Khosa has attended school for seven years, her husband for eight years. She is a member of the Anglican Church, he of the Dutch Reformed Church. The couple have no living children; all of the four children the wife bore have died.

On their first coming to Lusaka, Mrs. Khosa and Mr. Phiri lived at Mandevu, a squatter settlement where they rented a house. After two years at Mandevu, they moved to Mtendele where they are now building a house of their own, two rooms of which are finished. The house is planned to have six rooms.

Mr. Phiri earns K50 (U.S. $66.00) a month, all of which he hands over to his wife. A good deal of the money is currently being spent on the completion of the house. Further, they send every month K10 (US $13.20) to the husband's matrilineal relatives who live near Petauke. Because of these expenses, Mrs. Khosa started her beer brewing, which she has done for three months. She brews ample supplies of beer every week from Thursday until Sunday. The kind of beer she brews is a South African beer, which she calls "Banba." The beer is consumed in one of the family's two rooms, which is not yet furnished, except for some odd chairs and table which serve to accommodate the clientele. The beer is sold in metal cups for which 10 ngwee (13¢) are charged. Mrs. Khosa reckons to make a profit on her beer sale of K10 ($13.20) every week.

Mr. Phiri did not interfere much with his wife's beer trade. Being a security guard, he was away from the township at work from four p.m. to twelve p.m. and returned to Mtendele on his bike at night conveniently enough to help his wife close down the trade. As the control of illegal beer brewing was becoming very much stricter, Mrs. Khosa was considering domestic work instead.[23]

Mrs. Kave: A Bemba Potter

Mrs. Kave is a forty-five-year-old Bemba widow. She came to Lusaka twelve years prior to her interview in 1975, shortly after the death of her husband. Some years before her migration, she had moved from her small home village in northern Zambia to Ndola to accompany her husband who worked in the mines. Trained as a Bemba ceremonial mistress or *nacimbusa*, Mrs. Kave was already skilled in traditional ceramic work when she came to Ndola. There, she began to experiment with pottery sales combined with home beer brewing.

Mrs. Kave continued beer brewing and was soon joined by several young women apprentices in her neighborhood. Her competent potting skills improved as she taught the members of the "collective" how to make pots for beer parties. Although she monitored her apprentices' brewing and potting activities, Mrs. Kave did not engage in any form of prostitution and did not coordinate their beer or craft sales.

With continued residence in Lusaka, Mrs. Kave gained a sense of the local crafts market, and she learned marketing skills from the men engaged in the local art trade. Mrs. Kave modified the traditional ceremonial figurines used in Bemba initiation rites for commercial sale. The figurines that she produced were rough renderings of fish and animals that were portable and cheap enough to acquire a certain exotic appeal for the tourist consumer audience. The figurines were sold for 50¢ a piece. Two years later, Mrs. Kave had more than tripled her price as she acquired a more accurate sense of the tourist market. Even so, Mrs. Kave and the other potters never sign or mark their work by name. This anonymity is typical of women's craft production as opposed to the individualized commercial arts made and signed by men in Lusaka.

These cases suggest that the struggle of the peasant woman to become an urban woman is more than an idle image in the mind of the artist. Tensions exist at both legal and socioeconomic levels. Tourist art provides a partial commentary on this experience of cultural ambivalence.

Conclusions: Cultural Ambivalence—
Images of Women in Art and Life

The images of women presented in African tourist art outline three parts of the problem of continuity and change: (1) nostalgia for a past life and sense of community with well-defined social roles; (2) the attraction of modernity and its benefits; and (3) the losses accompanying change (neocolonialism, oppression, and individualism). Tourist art, however, remains an indirect form of iconic commentary. As the *mami wata* image as a subgenre suggests, criticism is never direct and is veiled in decorative styles acceptable to a broad audience. A recent example is famine art (Africa's response to "Ethiopian" jokes). Famine art depicts starving famine victims with spindly legs and bloated stomachs. The carvings, which require considerable time and skill, ironically sell for very high prices. On one level, one might view famine art as a crass form of commercial exploitation. Nevertheless, as one begins to untangle the semiotic oppositions, or isotopies, of tourist art, it becomes clear that much of tourist art production plays upon the tension between old and new, past and present and the modern dilemma of choice. The peasant woman's back is turned toward us. The trick is to make the consumer believe that the idyllic past is still alive while conveying to those who can "read" the art the hidden message that the past can be revived but never relived.

Endnotes

1. Karl Polanyi, *Primitive, Archaic, and Modern Economies* (Garden City, N.Y.: Anchor Books, 1968), p. 288.
2. Mary Douglas, "Raffia Cloth Distribution in the Lele Economy," *Africa* (1958), 28:118.
3. Bennetta Jules-Rosette, *The Messages of Tourist Art: An African Semiotic System in Comparative Perspective* (New York: Plenum, 1984), pp. 15–19.
4. G. Charbonnier, ed., *Conversations with Claude Lévi-Strauss*, John Weightman and Dorren Weightman, trs. (London: Jonathan Cape, 1969), p. 62.
5. Paul S. Wingert, *Primitive Art, Its Tradition and Styles* (New York: New American Library, 1962), p. 107.
6. Ilona Szombati-Fabian and Johannes Fabian, "Art, History, and Society:

Popular Art in Shaba, Zaire," *Studies in the Anthropology of Visual Communication* (Spring 1976), 3(4):5.

7. Douglas Fraser, "The Fish-Legged Figure in Benin and Yoruba Art," in Douglas Fraser and Herbert M. Cole, eds., *African Art and Leadership* (Milwaukee: University of Wisconsin Press, 1972), pp. 261–290.

8. Henry Drewal, "The New Faces of African Art: European, Indian, and African Imagery in the Ritual Forms of Mami Wata," Paper presented at the Triennial Symposium on African Art, Washington, D.C., April 16, 1977.

9. Szombati-Fabian and Fabian, "Art, History, and Society," p. 5.

10. *Ibid.*, pp. 5–6.

11. Victor and Edith Turner, *Image and Pilgrimage in Christian Culture: Anthropological Perspectives* (New York: Columbia University Press, 1978), p. 246.

12. Roland Barthes, *Elements of Semiology*, Annette Lavers and Colin Smith, trs. (London: Jonathan Cape, 1967), pp. 48–50.

13. Francille Rusan Wilson, "Reinventing the Past and Circumscribing the Future: Authenticité and the Negative Image of Women's Work in Zaire," in Edna G. Bay, ed., *Women and Work in Africa* (Boulder, Colo.: Westview Press, 1982), p. 162.

14. Ida Faye Rousseau, "African Women: Identity Crisis?" in Ruby Rohrlich-Leavitt, ed., *Women Cross-Culturally* (Chicago: Mouton, 1975), p. 47.

15. Wilson, "Reinventing the Past," p. 164.

16. LaFontaine, Jean. "The Free Women of Kinshasa: Prostitution in a City of Love," in J. Davis, ed., *Choice and Change* (Atlantic Highlands, N.J.: Humanities Press, 1974), pp. 97–98.

17. Ilsa Schuster, *The New Women of Lusaka* (Palo Alto, Calif.: Mayfield, 1979), pp. 105–109, 136–137.

18. Rhoda Howard, "Human Rights and Personal Law: Women in Sub-Saharan Africa," *Issue: A Journal of Africanist Opinion* (Spring-Summer 1982), no. 1–2, p. 49.

19. Wilson, "Reinventing the Past," p. 159.

20. Schuster, *The New Women of Lusaka*, p. 140.

21. Dave Todd and Christopher Shaw, "Education, Employment and the Informal Sector in Zambia," *Urban Community Reports Series*, no. 2 (Lusaka, Zambia: Institute for African Studies, 1979), p. 10.

22. Catherine Mwanamwabwa, "Suggested Income-Generating Activities for Women: A Pilot Study," unpub. report, Lusaka, Zambia, August 1977, p. 42.

23. Karen Tranberg Hansen, "The Work Opportunities of Women in a Periurban Township: An Exploratory Study," dissertation, Arhus University, 1973.

7

THE ELEMENTAL, THE ORNAMENTAL, THE INSTRUMENTAL: *THE BLUE LIGHT* AND NAZI FILM AESTHETICS
Eric Rentschler

In modern fascism, rationality has reached a point at which it is no longer satisfied with simply repressing nature; rationality now exploits nature by incorporating into its own system the rebellious potentialities of nature.

—Max Horkheimer

It never occurred to Goebbels, who was arguably among the least *Völkisch* and the most "modern-minded" of all Nazi leaders, that there might be a contradiction between the type of message he was disseminating (expressing an essentially anti-modern, romanticized belief in age-old habits and customs) and the manner in which it was conveyed (by means of the most popular art form of the first half of the twentieth century).

—David Welch

What the world supplies to myth is an historical reality, defined, even if this goes back quite a while, by the way in which men have produced or used it; and what myth gives in return is a *natural* image of this reality.

—Roland Barthes[1]

EVERY TEXT is an adaptation, a recycling and rethinking of prior conceptions. Artists and entrepreneurs draw on tradition, history,

I am grateful to the University of California Irvine Committee on Research as well as the Focused Research Project in Gender Studies whose generous support provided the means for me to write this essay.

and memory. They do so from a distinct position in time, guided in their resolve by certain intentions. both conscious and unconscious, looking back to the past for certain impulses as they look ahead to their own present creation and its future audiences. For that reason it is clear that every film, no matter how seemingly innovative or avant-garde, is derivative, the product of a number of different discourses which come together in a particular way, imparting to the film a distinct textuality of its own, a multiplicity of voices. Films, therefore, issue as the result of displacement, as appropriations of the given framed by any number of motivations, as borrowings from previous contexts for the purposes of a different present one.[2] Without a doubt, my approach to matters of intertextuality very much insists on accounting for the dynamic and historical terms of the interactions between texts and contexts.

Films, likewise, can only be grasped through a further act of displacement, that of the viewer, who understands works in the framework of his or her own horizon and historical position. I will be discussing a film made in Germany during the early thirties, a highly controversial work by a highly controversial artist, a film viewed by many as a hallmark of Weimar cinema and by others as an artifact derived from a questionable and fateful legacy, a work that comes to us today in a number of forms and versions, varying in running time, clarity of image, and sound track. I write as an American scholar decidedly interested in the larger contours of German film history, as a person whose overriding project involves ferreting out the fascinating and troubling continuities in this legacy of nearly a century. I approach The Blue Light with a number of ambitions, ranging from the quite pragmatic desire to fathom this text's multiple voices to the more general wish to place this film within a larger history while speculating about Nazi cinema. What will become clear, I hope, is that this text can only be appreciated in terms of many other texts, indeed a crucial textuality, matters that will lead us to an understanding of this film's special terms as well as the equally singular terms of Nazi film aesthetics and their place in German film history. Gazing on this cinematic heritage, let me say at the onset, scintillates and horrifies in equal measure, for German films have provided some of the most formally inventive and thematically compelling visions in the medium's history and have likewise demonstrated just how diabolically and systematically the same medium lends itself to abuse. My readings of German film history, therefore, confront a Janus face, a stunning antinomy between a sensitivity for film's creative and constructive possibilities and an attendant knowledge of the medium's powerfully mesmerizing and manipulative potential. Here we will be gazing at the darker side of this countenance.

WE HAVE a double legend to unravel: the legend of Junta related in the film and the legend of the director who made this film.[3] The second image following the film's title reads: "*A Legend of the Mountains by Leni Riefenstahl.*" Already, in these first signs, we find a double falsehood: the film actually derives from a novel by a Swiss writer, not a legend of the mountains; the basis of the tale is the unacknowledged work of Gustav Renker, not the pristine imagination of Leni Riefenstahl. This rather generous notion of authorship and artistic license, we shall see, attributes to the creator a direct access to her source, which in fact has come to her in a mediated fashion. At least the earliest version of the film still lists Béla Balázs as a collaborating scriptwriter; some subsequent ones would not.[4] The title credits, then, come as a dramatic preview of coming attractions, announcing a work that rewrites the past and at the same time attempts to conceal this liberty. A double impulse seems to have framed the film: a wish to sanctify the realm of the elemental and its enchanting powers and, likewise, the resolve to hallow the artistic force who made the film as someone in close touch with this elemental sphere, enjoying an intimacy with the world of nature every bit as unmediated as that of her fictional counterpart, Junta. This legend still circulates among film scholars who view Junta as an embodiment of her creator, someone who "had her own intuitive feelings about nature and was destroyed by her naive disregard of the real world around her, the world she set out to avoid."[5] Riefenstahl has cast herself in the role of the romantic artist, a person whose vision transcends the time-bound and the political, someone whose films reflect a fascination with beauty, strength, and harmony.

Riefenstahl has held onto this self-styled image for over half a century now, despite continuing challenges from critics who claim her visionary powers were compromised in the service of National Socialism, that she enjoyed a privileged status under Hitler which allowed her to produce the definitive Nazi party document, *Triumph of the Will,* the ultimate hagiographical portrait of the Führer and the new order, and anything but the work of an apolitical filmmaker. *The Blue Light,* her debut film as a director, reflects her indebtedness to the romantic legacy from which she derived her artistic persona. The title of course suggests Novalis' blue flower, the quintessential symbol of the romantic quest for the divine and ineffable. Quite strikingly the film blends the iconography of nineteenth-century German landscape painting with the narrative trappings of the *Novelle,* the significant German prose form that flourished in the 1800s, building likewise on the melodramatic constellations of the mountain film of the twenties as well as using the genre's predilection for natural settings and imposing elements. Beyond that, its evocation of landscape and mysterious primal forces reflects a further debt to a darker side of German romanticism, one mined by another of her models, the filmmaker F. W. Murnau. These appropriations deserve closer attention.

A student of art history before she went on to become a dancer and actress, Riefenstahl evidences considerable familiarity with nineteenth-century German landscape painting, above all with the work of Caspar David Friedrich.[6] *The Blue Light* abounds with images redolent of the artist, be it the sweeping unpeopled mountain scapes in general, or single compositions that consciously appear to quote Friedrich, for example, the shot where the painter Vigo stands over the village from the mountain top in the manner of "Traveller Looking over a Sea of Fog" or the morning walk in the mist during the final sequence whose *Stimmung* recalls a host of works by Friedrich. Riefenstahl would speak of her art in terms reminiscent of Friedrich, who once claimed that art was "the language of our feeling, our disposition, indeed, even our devotion and our prayers."[7] *The Blue Light* infuses nature with an arousing power; like Friedrich, Riefenstahl transforms landscapes into emotional spaces, granting to exterior nature an interior resonance. Consistently we encounter a Friedrich-influenced use of silhouetting, where figures shaded in dark contours pose against a luminescent and vague background. Elsewhere we glimpse, as in Friedrich, figures who stand with their backs to us, staring into the distance, small dots against a vast expanse, characters who embody yearning, persons desiring the transcendence that might allow them to merge with the grandeur before them. This wish, to be sure, has a fatalistic manifest destiny: both Riefenstahl and Friedrich are consummate artists of death. To cite one of Friedrich's verses: "Why, the question is often put to me, do you choose so often as a subject for your paintings death, transience and the grave? To live one day eternally, one must give oneself over to death many times."[8] Riefenstahl underlines her debt to the predecessor by introducing a romantic landscape painter into her narrative, an artist not without certain modern leanings hardly typical of Friedrich—ones, though, quite in keeping with Riefenstahl's own impetus as an image-maker.

If the images and the artistic impetus go back to Friedrich's brand of evocative landscape painting, the narrative proper comes equally as a legacy of the nineteenth century. The earliest version of the film couches the story in a form often found in German *Novellen*, i.e., a frame story, *eine Rahmenerzählung*, a legend told to visitors in a modern age of automobiles and tourism.[9] Confronted with trinkets bearing Junta's picture when they drive into Santa Maria, a dapper honeymooning couple from the city enter their hotel room to find a religious painting also with the same image. "Who is this Junta?" asks the young bride. The hotel proprietor, clearly used to such questions, sends for a leather-bound volume with Junta's legend, a text illustrated as well with the mountain girl's countenance. The film will then dissolve from the image on the book cover to a shot of a mist-covered crystal, opening up to a wider view of Junta clasping the rock. The embedded narrative proceeds to explain just who this Junta is and just how her image is linked to the crystals. If anything, the narrative act here duplicates the activity of the painter Vigo, for both provide explanations that explain a seeming mystery, topographies offering routes of access to terrains previously deemed dangerous and perplexing.

The images in the film may speak the overwhelming language of nature worship and the sublime; the narrative in which they are couched, however, bears traces of an intelligence eager to mine nature's secrets, to fathom its mysteries, to transform superstition into knowledge. This endeavor, as we know from German literary history, inheres as an earmark of the nineteenth-century *Novelle*, a genre abounding in similar frame stories couched in terms of the seemingly supernatural which ultimately give way to explanations grounded in the more tangible qualities of human agency, causality, and reason.[10] The narrative trajectory of *The Blue Light* involves the answer to the question, "Who is this Junta?" During the course of the embedded tale, Junta will undergo a marked evolution, changing from a witch and an agent of the uncanny to a martyr and, above all, popular icon.

Romantic images that hallow nature and impart to the elemental a resonance beyond words; a narrative, on the other hand, that casts the marginal and seemingly inexplicable in terms both pragmatic and straightforward. This apparent disjuncture between striking images sanctifying the irrational and the extra-human and a narrative framework couched in decidedly human terms likewise is to be found in the mountain films *(Bergfilme)* of the 1920s, a generic legacy Riefenstahl knew from first-hand, the popular vein in which she received her start as an actress. These Alpine dramas filmed on location amidst majestic peaks featured athletic spirits confronting the elemental forces. Bound by a hearty code, these mountainmen stand above the pedestrian world of restriction and refinement, viewing themselves as individuals in touch with a mightier destiny, the call of the mountains. Sporting visual effects caught in glaciers, rocky peaks, and snowy scapes, Arnold Fanck, the master of this form, built his *Bergfilme* around less imposing narratives, generally romantic melodramas featuring a triangle involving two mountain climbers, usually best friends, and a mutually shared love interest. Siegfried Kracauer appropriately dubbed these films a "mixture of sparkling ice-axes and inflated sentiments."[11]

Clearly the visuals of *The Blue Light* are unthinkable without the work of Franck and his various cameramen. Likewise, Riefenstahl's film contains traces of the romantic triangle in the double pursuit of Junta up Monte Cristallo by Vigo and the innkeeper's son, Tonio. The 1932-film echoes the rhetoric found in *The Sacred Mountain* (1926), the work in which Riefenstahl made her debut as the dancer Diotima. At one point in the film she speaks to Robert, a climber who has just come back from the heights, a scene done in alternating close-ups of earnest and enraptured faces:

Diotima: How wonderful it must be!
Robert: Wonderful and dangerous.
Diotima: What do people look for up on those heights?
Robert: Happiness
Diotima: Is the happiness in beauty, then?

In the two titles, *The Sacred Mountain* and *The Blue Light*, one finds a mixture of natural forces and religiosity, a commingling of the primal power of the elemental and its sway over human emotions.

More crucial for our purposes, though, is the similar role played by Riefenstahl in both films. The character Diotima bears much resemblance to Junta. The initial scenic prologue in *The Sacred Mountain* (a predilection one will encounter in every Riefenstahl film) features the dancer standing by the sea. The editing captures her movements in a way that renders her dance as an emanation of the same spirit that causes the ocean waves to break. A woman as the embodiment of unbridled nature who will become harnessed in the form of image—for we next see her as a picture on a poster advertising her performance, an object of spectacle viewed by a male passerby. In the end, her two lovers having perished in a climbing accident, she returns to the sea, reduced now to stasis, a person who knows no present, someone facing the indifference of the inexorable breaking waves and the sadness of her memories. The conclusion mixes kitsch and death, a very ripe romanticism and the very real presentiment of human transience. Diotima transfigures Vigo and Robert in her own mental projection, the sole substance of her activity now. Woman, then, as a site of projection: either as the image of male fascination which Diotima was in her performances or as the mental screen whose only content is male presence. In either case, Diotima becomes someone without a life of her own, nature harnessed as male fantasy or a woman colonized by fantasies about males, both inhibited and inhabited.

Various critics have also drawn attention to another decisive filmic influence on *The Blue Light,* namely F. W. Murnau's *Nosferatu.* Many have been quick to observe how the approach of the painter to the mountains bears much similarity to Jonathan Harker's entry into the realm of the vampire in the 1921 film.[12] In addition, commentators note how Riefenstahl, like her predecessor, sought to grant natural settings an eerie and ethereal aura, something she, as did Murnau, accomplished through special effects, in her case technical ploys involving time-lapse photography, various filters, smoke machines, and manipulation of the lighting. Still, for all the stress on these similarities, critics have not really established anything more than apparent borrowings, ones without further significance. For them *The Blue Light* exudes at times the "chilly draft from doomsday" atmosphere of *Nosferatu.*[13] The appropriation of Murnau, it would seem, is simply a matter of atmospherics.

Riefenstahl's reliance on Murnau, however, transcends mere questions of atmospherics and special effects. In three ways at least, *The Blue Light* replicates crucial contours of *Nosferatu.* First, both films demonstrate a double perspective bound in images that speak stronger than words and a narrative intelligence whose aim above all is to couch the inexplicable and unsettling in terms of human generality. In *Nosferatu* it remains clear that the visual track takes precedence over the verbal one: Murnau's images show us things that the narrator only partially comprehends and in some cases simply overlooks.[14] In *The Blue Light,* this favoring of image over narrative seems apparent, but will demand further scrutiny. Second, the painter Vigo may arrive from the city in the manner of Jonathan Harker, with doors closing mysteriously in front of him, and a coachman riding away without heeding the traveler's words. Nonetheless, he will in fact come to act like the vampire himself: we will see his greedy and lustful gazes at Junta, we will witness him bending over her at night, enraptured by the sight of her neck and exposed breasts. Likewise, his gaze will virtually suck all vitality from her in the final sequence, translating the body lying before him into a text. Third, and quite important in our context, remains the way in which we encounter women in the two texts. In each case the female figure is framed as image from the very start: the image of Nina at the window when we first see her in *Nosferatu*, the image in the locket that first draws the Count's attention to her. Nina will become the agent of civilization in its battle against the demonic side of nature it feels compelled to repress, the forces embodied by the vampire.[15] Her sacrifice will mean rescue for the plague-ridden city, a sacrifice she willingly takes upon herself after reading *The Book of Vampires*. She knows the terms involved; she makes a conscious choice. The final question left by the film is: civilization at what price? Nina assumes the image of a Christian martyr, denying all worldly aspirations for the sake of saving her husband and the city. *The Blue Light* also casts woman into the role of an image involving a martyrdom. In this case, however, the terms are different. Junta does not understand; she does not grasp Vigo's intentions; she does not have a choice in the matter.[16] If the price of civilization in *Nosferatu* was the sublimation and exorcism of nature's underworld, its more threatening aspect, the price of civilization in *The Blue Light* similarly involves the vitiation of the elemental and the arrest of its forces. And in this process a woman is cast in a fateful image as the unwitting agent of civilization.

I BEGAN by suggesting how this film relies on an interweaving of textual possibilities, an appropriation of a number of impetuses from German tradition. Beyond that, I intimated that this appropriation of primarily romantic legacies, be it landscape painting, literary forms, or filmic prototypes, somehow had a bearing on Nazi cinema, even if the film was made in 1932, before Joseph Goebbels took over control of image production in Germany. We need now to move on to a question posed by the director in a letter to Kevin Brownlow. "What do mysticism and romanticism have to do with Nazism? Isn't Homer's *Iliad* full of mysticism?

How many other works of world literature could also be enumerated?"[17] Riefenstahl has a large throng of apologists, especially in this country, individuals willing to absolve her of sins committed during the Third Reich for the sake of the power of her artistic vision that inheres nonetheless. Others indeed accept the director's claims that she never was anything more than an artist compelled by an aesthetic calling. And even if one has a tough time making this case in the light of *Triumph of the Will* and the *Olympiad*-films, critics have few problems defending *The Blue Light* as something of a psychodrama about a naive and pristine artist. Take, for example, the following observation: "There is more than just a passing, isolated similarity between Riefenstahl's life and the character and experiences of the intuitive mountain girl. They both live for one ideal. For Junta, it is her beautiful crystalline retreat; for Riefenstahl, it is her art."[18]

This kind of generosity and credulity, however, stands at odds with more critical readings of the film and Riefenstahl's canon by Siegfried Kracauer and Susan Sontag, each of which has proved to be equally influential and controversial in popular notions of the artist today.[19] Both writers agree in their castigation of the pre-Nazi mountain films as escapist fare with dangerous implications, works whose high altitudes and lofty attitudes betray a predisposition that would come to rise in National Socialism, a spirit of self-sacrifice and anti-rationalism infused with blind enthusiasm and overwrought pathos. The worship of the clouds and mighty peaks would find more concrete embodiment in the sanctification of the *Führer*. In this sense there is a clear continuity between the choreography of clouds found in the *Bergfilm* and the shots out of the airplane window during the prologue of *Triumph of the Will*, expressions of a resolve to be found throughout the various stations of Riefenstahl's work. According to Sontag, the filmmaker represents "the only major artist who was completely identified with the Nazi era and whose work, not only during the Third Reich but thirty years after its fall, has consistently illustrated many themes of fascist aesthetics."[20]

Drawing a direct line between the mountain cult of the *Bergfilm* and the Hitler cult, Kracauer views Junta as the embodiment of "a political regime which relies on intuition, worships nature and cultivates myths."[21] More recently, the West German journalist Nina Gladitz engaged in a vigorous campaign against Riefenstahl, claiming the director willingly exploited gypsy inmates from a concentration camp during her wartime work on *Tiefland*, promising them help if they cooperated, but in the end leaving them to death in the gas chambers, allegations which the filmmaker passionately denied in an ensuing court battle, a further occasion where Riefenstahl argued that she was an artist, nothing more.[22] For all the persuasiveness of Kracauer and Sontag, there still remains a larger host of commentators ready to defend Riefenstahl, individuals who laud her filmmaking craft and aplomb, the power of her images and editing, people who find no trace of Nazi sentiments or fascist aesthetics in *The Blue Light*.[23] Building on the critiques of Kracauer and Sontag and drawing on another recent approach to Nazi aesthetics, I would like to provide even more conclusive elucidation of how *The Blue Light* essentializes —in a quite literal way—some crucial attributes of films made in the Third Reich.

Speaking of Nazi film aesthetics, however, brings with it a series of problems, quite imposing ones, in fact, which at least must be broached. First of all, as Philip Rosen has argued, the notion of a national cinema cast along temporal lines suggests "an intertextuality to which one attributes a certain historical weight."[24] One assumes, in other words, certain recurrent patternings of meaning in a large body of films, a distinct coherence among movies in a number of different generic veins, as well as a relation between these works and the sociopolitical context from which they issue and the public sphere which they address. Inherent is a connection between the films themselves, the space from which they originate, and the historical nexus they reflect. Such a dynamic notion of intertextuality demands that we talk of Nazi film aesthetics in a manner linking formal and thematic considerations, production- and reception-related concerns, as well as political and historical specificity, a very tall order.

A second stumbling block remains the lack of theoretical approaches to Nazi cinema as well as any real persuasive comprehensive explanation of Nazi film aesthetics. Almost without exception, previous literature on Nazi cinema dwells on sociopolitical considerations, viewing films made in the Third Reich as emanations of the Ministry of Propaganda, concentrating on the blatantly propagandistic productions and the important themes, linking these matters to the evolution of the Nazi state.[25] What one consistently ignores is that the vast majority, about 85 percent of the 1,094 feature films made between 1933 and 1945 in Germany, were entertainment fare, formula productions along clearly codified lines.[26] For all of the insight at hand into the Nazi film economy and the government policies regarding the medium, we have a very limited sense of the formal and stylistic terms of Nazi cinema.[27] In general, critics tend to view Nazi aesthetics as a matter of "auf den Hund gebrachte Kunst," i.e., art gone to the dogs,[28] an art in which content and subject matter dominate over formal and stylistic matters. Speaking of art in the Third Reich in general, Berthold Hinz demonstrates how Nazi politicians eschewed a modernism they deemed degenerate, seeking instead a timeless and immortal German art, one that in reality amounted to a "constant falling back on nineteenth-century art and particularly on what was not the best art of that century . . ."[29] But, as we have seen, all art and every film come about as appropriations of prior traditions. We cannot isolate this penchant for recycling as a dominant earmark only common to Nazi cinema. As we know from Lotte Eisner, Weimar cinema likewise drew heavily on romantic art and literature.[30] Nazi art clearly relied strongly on certain prototypes and in no way forwarded any innovations to the medium film; nonetheless, this derivative predilection alone does not suffice to account for its workings. What is crucial is not only that it drew on the past, but more importantly how it drew on the past, for what reasons, to what effect.

Finally, we have little understanding of the reception dynamics of Nazi cinema—at least nothing approaching the sophistication of the models used today by film theorists to account for the effect of Hollywood films on normal spectators. It has by now become a truism that what film scholars call the "dominant cinema" positions viewers in a way enabling an intense specularity, constructing narratives (through a straightforward flow of events, seamless editing, identification with stars, and closure) that permit total immersion. The spectator becomes a voyeur, a furtive beholder, sitting in the dark, enjoying the pleasure on the screen with only a partial awareness of being privy to what is quite clearly an illicit activity and a solitary pursuit. The most prominent difference between the reception dynamics of the so-called dominant cinema and Nazi cinema is that between a film industry centered on the single viewer's narcissism and a state-run apparatus concerned with collective response. The implied audience of Nazi films, I would speculate, is always a larger community. Quite consistently, Nazi film narratives—and not just the shrilly propagandistic ones—forsake visual pleasure, voyeurism, and female sexuality, the sources of fascination in the classical narrative text, in the name of more compelling categories.

Several previous approaches to Nazi aesthetics allow us some useful ways in which to continue our project. Kracauer's notion of the mass ornament was first expounded in an essay of 1927 and applied in his studies of Weimar and Nazi cinema during the forties. [31] The geometric patterns of thousands of people in *Triumph of the Will*, faceless parts of a gigantic construction, stand as something like everyday expressionism, the creation of the ultimate *metteur-en-scène*, Adolf Hitler, the force who has shaped his vassals in a way according to his designs. Subjects relinquish their political rights for the sake of aesthetic expression; they join in the mass ornament and thus feel themselves part of a larger whole, even if the price of this new identity is relinquishing their thinking persons in a brute demonstration of physical culture. The mass ornament under National Socialism mutes human nature and provides the semblance of mythological immediacy, giving disoriented inhabitants of modernity a sense of belonging and ritual continuity. The mass ornament at once represents a triumph over nature and human nature, a containment of subjectivity and spontaneity, at the same time appealing to the human desire to participate in patterns of organic life and primal community associated with a world not yet violated by the disenchanting forces of modernity.

Susan Sontag builds on this notion in her essay "Fascinating Fascism" (1975). Fascist aesthetics involve for her an inherent sadomasochism, a perverse blend of "egomania and servitude."

The master-slave relations found in fascist art "take the form of a characteristic pageantry: the massings of groups of people; the turning of people into things; the multiplication or replication of things; and the grouping of people/things around an all-powerful, hypnotic leader-figure or force." While fluctuating between constant motion and states of stasis in its choreography, fascist aesthetics above all stresses the containment of the physical, demonstrating a body language bound up in repressing the vital forces and vitiating natural impulses. *Eros* becomes *thanates:* "Fascist art glorifies surrender, it exalts mindlessness, it glamorizes death." Sontag also points out that Nazi art has a decisive misogynistic rhetoric. Women, as the embodiment of the erotic and the physical one is concerned to repress, can only appear as a source of danger and temptation, something that must be overcome if one is to serve one's higher calling. National Socialism, in sum, stands for "the ideal of life as art, the cult of beauty, the fetishism of courage, the dissolution of alienation in ecstatic feelings of community; the repudiation of the intellect; the family of man (under the parenthood of leaders)."[32]

In his recent study, *Reflections of Nazism,* Saul Friedländer argues that the appeal of National Socialism was less ideological than imagistic; its power above all stemmed from the way it worked with emotions, images, and phantasms. The crucial insight in Friedländer's study helps us to understand—more dynamically than has been the case previously—the curious blending of tonalities in Nazi aesthetics, a combination of elements that has continued to fascinate and influence individuals even many decades after the fall of Hitler. Central to Nazi aesthetics is a *frisson,* a response to the collision of two seemingly contradictory elements, the juxtaposition of kitsch and death. The meeting creates an uncanny effect: on the one hand, kitsch, a domesticated romanticism, a sort of art that has been housebroken and rendered safe, a source of harmony and order for the petit bourgeois. On the other hand, though, premonitions of death and destruction, experiences inciting terror, anxiety, and disquiet. Precisely the kitsch element serves to neutralize this border situation, to make the moment of death a less harrowing one, ultimately to sentimentalize it. This "kitsch of death," according to Friedländer, marks "a return to a debased romantic inspiration, to an aesthetic stripped of the force and novelty it had 150 years ago at the dawn of modernity." This reflects National Socialism's penchant for the premodern world as the source of all values, the recourse to prior notions of unspoiled nature, organic communities, and primal directness as antidotes to the ills of the modern world. For Nazi ideology, argues Friedländer, "the model of future society is only a reflection of the past." And this past harbors a romantic fatalism, one dreaming of *Götterdämmerung*, the heroic death, surrender to destiny, "an echo of lost worlds, haunting an imagination invaded by excessive rationality and thus becoming the crystallization point for thrusts of the archaic and of the irrational." [33]

These impulses have direct use value for any interpretation of *The Blue Light*. Kracauer's mass ornament finds concrete expression in the images we see of figures carved into the rocky mountainside, a monument for the youths who perish in their quest for the mystical goal, a structure lingered on by the camera, one that merges elemental nature and human sacrifice in an aesthetic construction. (As he passes the faces etched in stone, Vigo will ask, "What are those figures?" a question that echoes the bride's query about Junta. The connection, we shall see, is not fortuitous.) Similarly, following Sontag, we find in the film a transformation of Junta's potential threat and erotic attraction (witness the way in which she—through no fault of her own—sexually excites Tonio and is the object of lustful stares and the manner in which the editing connects her with animals) into a source of local pride and worship. This transformation mirrors most strikingly the "kitsch of death" discussed by Friedländer: as Junta dies, we see her face freeze into a crystal-studded image as the frame dissolves into the portrait adorning the book with her legend. This same image will likewise become a kitsch object offered by children to newly arrived tourists, the picture of someone whose afterlife as a commodity, legend, and fetish clearly has much bearing on the Alpine community's welfare. Without a doubt, the citizens of Santa Maria have become consummate recyclers of native tradi-

tion, every bit as resourceful in their instrumentalization of images and women as the National Socialists. Both hark back to a
romantic past while pursuing distinct present purposes.

FOR ALL the help Kracauer, Sontag, and Friedländer offer in
understanding *The Blue Light*, two important issues still remain
unresolved, ones central to the film and Nazi aesthetics in general, considerations that are inextricably bound. First of all: women,
as Sontag points out, represent something Nazi aesthetics inevitably wants to overcome for the sake of more important male
goals, those of sacrifice, duty, and surrender to a larger destiny.
This clearly obtains in *The Blue Light*: in order for the village to
thrive, Junta must die. What is overlooked, though, is that she
does not totally disappear after her death, in fact she becomes
much more present in death than she was in life, previously a
source of scorn and persecution, presently one of meaning and
reverence. Her fate, likewise is that of the nature she embodies;
the film collapses the violation of nature and the intrusion into
her intimate sphere, quite expressively so. The *mise en scène* of
Vigo's entry into Junta's cave involves shots that link the painter's
gaze to that of the camera, voyeuristic trespasses into her private
space. The mining of the grotto becomes the plundering of a
womb.[34] The process described—and to a degree valorized—
here involves a mix of rape and necrophilia, where Junta is forced
into a certain image, one definitely not of her own making, one
that is preyed upon and worshipped by the community.

Second, and related: the film clearly champions the mountain
community and presents its inhabitants as a viable culture in
touch with archaic impulses, a healthy body. One may sense, as
Kracauer points out, a certain sorrow and nostalgia after Junta's
demise, but this is not the sole response engendered by the film.
His formulation touches on another voice present in the film's
conclusion: "To be sure, at the end the village rejoices in its
fortune and the myth seems defeated, but this rational solution is
treated in such a summary way that it enhances rather than
reduces Junta's significance."[35]

The film pictures the celebration of the townspeople after the
exploitation of the mine as an ecstatic moment, one not without

disquieting overtones, especially in the shot of spilled wine glasses whose traces on the table suggest blood-letting. But the title introducing the film heralds the townsfolk as a people untouched by modern malaise. I quote from the original prologue:

> We, the people of the Dolomites, far from the strife and turmoil of the outside world, dwell primitively in the rugged wilderness and magnificance of the Italian Tyrol. We are a simple peasant folk and strange legends have come down to us through the centuries casting shadows on the peace of our lives.
>
> Above all do we cherish the legend of Junta, the Mountain Girl, whose story we have reverently engraved for future generations.

The premier Nazi film historian of the thirties praised the racial hardiness of their physiognomies, the features of people who decended from the Visogoths, faces captured in loving close-ups by Riefenstahl's camera.[36] What is so readily overlooked by previous commentators is the manner in which the text of Junta's legend reflects the same intelligence that mines the grotto. Clearly, the inscribed text as well as the film in general reflect a perspective both wise to the ways of nature *and* modernity, a town that traffics with legends purchased at a bloody price, a price involving as Kracauer put it, a "rational solution," one that rids the people of someone they perceived as a threat and a nuisance and at the same time leaves them the heirs of a considerable material legacy—something all too reminiscent of the "final solution" enacted on individuals viewed by the state as outsiders a few years later in Nazi Germany.

These two points demand further scrutiny and a more dynamic approach. I would like to suggest a paradigm, a triadic relationship whose terms are the elemental, the ornamental, and the instrumental, a constellation quite graphically present in *The Blue Light*, one that inheres in much of Nazi fantasy production. Put simply, what happens in these films is a transformation, a rendering of the elemental as ornament. One takes recourse to a world of myth, nature, and primacy, reshaping this world in new structures—a process, however, informed by larger designs, an overriding instrumental rationality. It is precisely this third term, though, the instrumental, which becomes elided and to a great degree invisible. For Nazism, as we know from Ernst Bloch, well recognized the mighty appeal of nonsynchronous sensibilities, thoughts out of keeping with modern realities, especially a romantic anti-capitalism fueled by a discontent with contemporary civilization. One turned to an evocative past of peasants, blood and soil, and idyllic retreats, utilizing "gothic dreams against proletarian realities," "needs and elements from past ages,"[37] ones of decisive value in the state's coordinated effort to capture the imaginations of its citizenry, to colonize their fantasy life. It is here where one confronts the double face of the Third Reich. For all its romantic ideals and images of a transfigured past, German fascism was decidedly involved in the material domination over nature through a vast technology, one that stretched from the rationalized way in which an entire country was organized by an elaborate bureaucratic mechanism to the military machine and the world war and ultimately the death camps, vast factories that recycled human bodies, pressing out of them every possible material gain before disposing of them.

This double face marks *The Blue Light* as well. On the one hand, a seemingly romantic sentimentality and strident anti-modernism; on the other, when we look more closely, the virulent and self-legitimating use of instrumental rationality, both as a continuing mining of the crystals and an elaborate ideological construction that justifies it, erecting Junta as a saint who led to the valuable minerals. The film displays a certain melancholy at the death of Junta and the loss of enchantment, at least on the surface. (Nowhere, though, do we find images of mourning, except for the pained face of the innkeeper who grieves for Tonio while the village rejoices.) One uses the tools of modern technology, the cinematic apparatus, to present this narrative and further couches the putative legend in terms more in keeping with modernity, transforming Junta from a source of enigma ("Who is this Junta?") into the site of value and signification, shifting her from the space of mythical primacy to that of present-day legend. What we have here is a mercenary impulse that mines the elemental, places it in a pleasing ornamental design, all the while seeking to erase the traces of one's governing instrumentality. National Socialist cinema demonstrated little onscreen self-reflexivity even though its productions—from inception to performance—remained under the close scrutiny of a state apparatus highly conscious of its ideological mission. In *The Blue Light*, what happens to nature happens to the female body as well; both submit to a powerful instrumental rationality that uses them as a source of meaning and makes them the site of worship, at the same time, however, forsaking them in the name of more compelling designs.

The key to many Nazi feature films, I would like to suggest, is the way in which these productions functionalize the female body. It is well known that Nazi Germany reduced women to the status of an appendage, at best of use in the household and as the bearer of future soldiers, significant only in their service to the male order.[38] The natural state posited in Nazi cinema is the male bond; its heroes invariably rise to overcome obstacles to perform their duty to their nation, people, and leader. Eroticism in these films more often than not comes from homophilic attachments; it rarely issues from the relations between the sexes, but rather involves the intoxicating sensation of joining one's comrades in a larger cause.[39] Crucially and consistently, the projected weak images of women form the basis of signification for many Nazi films, reflecting a vulnerable and ultimately paranoid male order. Put in other terms: women act as a negative image without which no positive one can exist, the basis of signification for much of the fascist imaginary, that definitive triumph of male fantasy production. Nazi cinema goes far beyond the institutionalized sexism of Hollywood movies and the way in which the classical narrative recuperates even the strongest women in the male discourse. Nazi cinema does not leave it at simple recuperation, though; women are to be overcome, indeed sacrificed.

Some examples are in order before we return to *The Blue Light*. Nazi propagandists regularly projected attributes of themselves they did not want to acknowledge or have recognized onto others, be they Jews, communists, or foreigners. In this sense, these "others" act as doubles, understandable only as mirror reflections. Women, likewise, figure as a stand-in for a frenzied phallic order unsure of its status and fearful of any threat. In Hans Steinhoff's *The Old and the Young King* (1935), the young Frederick the Great must transcend the part of himself that bears feminine traits. So that he can rule and—quite literally—assume the gaze of the father in the male realm of the state, Frederick must witness the execution of Katte, his homoerotic love interest. Women in the film act as disturbances, individuals who protest the incursions of the military world and are identified with foreign signifiers: gambling, fashion, effete manners, narcissism, extravagance, treachery. A sequence in Herbert Selpin's *Water for Canitoga* (1939) essentializes quite strikingly the way in which women have no substance of their own; they only signify in relation to male orders. We view four women performing at a New Year's celebration in a saloon, each with a number on her chest, 1-9-0-6. They are signifiers, meaningless in and of themselves, significant only in their place in a larger construction, one shaped by a master of ceremonies—just as the hero of the film (played by Hans Albers) brags about using women at his will, taking them whenever he wants. Interestingly enough, though, his main love interest, one he will of course forsake, bears the name "Winnie." Earlier in the film when he is at his worst and most diminished, he refers to himself as "Winnetou," indicating how the male projection of a dependent woman has quite a bit to do with his own self-doubts. The German revue-film of the period, as Karsten Witte argues, similarly "has a certain predilection for showing men with deficient ego-strength, who subsequently need to develop their identity all the more aggressively against women."[40] The protagonist Friedemann Bach in Traugott Müller's 1940-film of the same name never leaves the world of woman to assume the mighty gaze of his father and his place in the male community. He will die, "the too weak son of a too strong father," someone whose nomadic ways mirror a nonpresence bound in an identification with women.

The Blue Light functionalizes the female body in a similar way, already in 1932. Even in the case of one of the epoch's few female directors, a filmmaker who consciously fashioned herself as an artist standing beyond all temporal constraints, we find this fatal proclivity, perhaps more unabashedly than anywhere else in Nazi cinema. A director ostensibly fascinated by the elemental and the mystical in nature, Riefenstahl crafted her debut film in a way that for all its apparent environmentalism and pantheism in fact will vindicate the violation of Monte Cristallo. The final shot of the original version shows the honeymooning couple looking at the mountain which appears no worse for the wear, retaining its evocative powers despite the incursions of the villagers, who still profit from the crystals. An artist who took ready recourse to the legacy of German Romanticism, Riefenstahl, so we have seen, recycled this heritage in a way quite in keeping with subsequent National Socialist praxis. Harnessing nature through a cinematic apparatus, Riefenstahl acts like the painter Vigo who captures landscape images on canvases, likewise imaging the child of nature Junta.

The terms of Junta's transformation into an icon deserve another look. Junta, we recall, falls from the mountain to her death, a victim of despair. Vigo stands over the deceased in a morning light that transfigures her. In a subjective shot that aligns the camera's gaze with that of the onscreen artist, we see how the male look virtually metamorphizes Junta's countenance. Vigo's regard transposes her image, changing the dead woman in front of him into the living presence of legend, a face framed by crystals which illustrates the cover of the village narrative. The look and its transformative powers are paralleled by the cinematic apparatus which enables this process to be visualized in a dissolve from the dead body to the living legend. Junta in this way has to be denuded of life, rendered as ornament, in order to find further existence. The elemental becomes the ornamental and this transformation clearly has an instrumental background. As we come to the conclusion of the legend, a hand closes the text, but whose we cannot see. No doubt the intelligence framing the narrative is a heavy-handed one, hardly as innocent and naive as Riefenstahl and her defenders would have us believe.

EARLIER I said that we were dealing with a double legend, that of *The Blue Light* and that of Leni Riefenstahl. In retrospect the director has repeatedly spoken of this film as something akin to a life's script:

In making this very romantic film by instinct, without knowing exactly where I wanted to go, I also found myself charting the path I would follow later. For, in a certain fashion, it
was my own destiny of which I had had a presentiment and
to which I had given form. [41]

If the film represents any future course of events, I have argued, it
above all presages the way in which Nazi cinema appropriated
various texts, ranging from an idealized past to romantic legacies
to the female body, draining them of content, stripping away
history, and casting them in different forms meant to legitimate
the present designs of a misogynistic state controlled by a mighty
machinery. Riefenstahl has talked about her work, frequently and
consistently, over the years resolutely averring that if she served
any cause, it was that of beauty and harmony, not National Socialism. Her major fault, she claims, was her innocence, something she shares with the heroine of her first film.

   If one looks over the facts offered by Riefenstahl regarding *The
Blue Light*, one reaches quite different conclusions. Indeed, for
all of Riefenstahl's ostensibly noble intentions, one encounters an
overwhelming instrumentalism at work in this film, from the very
inception of the project, through all the stages of its production
and repeated exhibition, up to the very present. Let us first turn
to the source itself: Riefenstahl, until very recently, maintained
that she had based the film on a peasant legend of the Alps,
something reflected in the film's collective prologue ("We, the
people of the Dolomites . . ."). Later, though, she changed her
story, claiming now that the film came from her own imagination
and not local legend. The fabrication, she submitted, was due to
the anxieties of a young filmmaker:

I was afraid. It was my first film. I was afraid if I said it was
my own, the critics would say that it's no good. I was lying
a little bit. I said the story all came from the Sarn Valley. But
every character, everything that happened came from my
head. I wrote it like a legend . . . but it was my own idea. [42]

This, we would find out, was also a fiction. *The Blue Light* stemmed
in fact from a novel she had read by Gustav Renker, a Swiss
author well known to Arnold Fanck with whom she had worked.

Hardly a local legend or her own vision, the film amounted to an adaptation of Renker's 1930 book, *Crystal Mountain*. [43]

This rather cavalier attitude toward one's sources indicates just how ardently Riefenstahl has endeavored to uphold the popular myth of herself as an instinctive and direct filmmaker rather than the calculating and resourceful figure documented by historical fact. She is a resilient soul ever ready to rewrite the past, be it in her different accounts of the source of *The Blue Light*, be it her steady denial that she knew anything other than her artistic calling. Interestingly enough, descriptions of her relationship to the mountain peasants, how she entered the village and worked to win their trust, parallel almost exactly the manner in which Vigo wins the confidence of Junta. [44] If Riefenstahl bears a striking resemblance to anyone in the film, it is that of her onscreen enunciator, the romantic artist from the big city who appropriates landscapes and people with a marked regard for controlling and containing images.

Although often hailed as a masterpiece of German film history, *The Blue Light* did not do well at the German box office nor did it fare well in the press. Riefenstahl attributed the negative response to the Jewish assessment of her work. According to her friend Harry Sokal, she was furious after reading the pans of the film:

> When the first bad reviews appeared, I was as mad about them as Leni Riefenstahl. . . . Leni came to me *extremely* upset and said, "What do these Jewish critics understand about our mentality? They have no right to criticize our work?"
> . . . Leni was *convinced* that the failure of *Blue Light* in Germany was because of the bad reviews. . . . She told me, "After we come to power, the Jewish newspapermen will not be allowed to print anything in German. They will have to write in Hebrew because we don't want too many people to understand what they write. . . ." [45]

Riefenstahl, obsessed by the film, had it rereleased in 1938 in a version expunging all the names of Jewish coworkers, including Béla Balázs and Carl Mayer, two of the scriptwriters. After World War II, she reassembled outtakes of the film, the original negative

having been lost, added a new score, deleted the framing passages, redubbed the voices, and once again rereleased *The Blue
Light*, this time likewise receiving a lukewarm response in Germany. She later had plans to redo the material as a ballet. For
some time in 1960 she contemplated remaking the film with
British backing, a project which in the end fell through.[46]

If we are to read *The Blue Light* as a document reflecting the
career of Leni Riefenstahl, we can do so along lines quite different
from the ones privileged by the filmmaker. I say this knowing
well that she enjoys a very strong following in the United States,
among avant-garde adherents, enthusiastic cineastes, among some
(but in no way all) feminists, individuals willing to champion her
as an artist and to underplay her political past. *The Blue Light* is
a film that shows how a woman and a mountain grotto are sacrificed for the sake of a community, a community that mines both
as raw material, recognizing their considerable exchange value.
Leni Riefenstahl likewise mined the stuff of nature and the romantic past in making this film, repeatedly avowing that she was
guided by intuition and vision, rather than any sociopolitical
calling. The terms of these appropriations have a lot in common
with the way in which National Socialism worked over the past.
The Third Reich practiced what Jeffrey Herf has spoken of as a
"reactionary modernism," an instrumentalism that blended the
cultural system of the romantic past with the rationality of modern technology.[47] Riefenstahl, hardly the innocent, on many occasions returned to *The Blue Light* in an attempt to remine its
treasures, unconvincingly justifying herself with the jargon of
authenticity while bearing out, in a much more persuasive way,
the dialectic of enlightenment.

Endnotes

1. Horkheimer, *The Eclipse of Reason* (New York: Oxford University Press,
1947), p. 101; Welch, *Propaganda and the German Cinema 1933–1945* (Oxford:
Clarendon, 1983), pp. 97–98; and Barthes, *Mythologies*, Annette Lavers, tr. (New
York: Hill and Wang, 1972), p. 142.
2. See Dudley Andrew, *Concepts in Film Theory* (Oxford/New York: Oxford
University Press, 1984), p. 97.

3. Riefenstahl insisted on playing the mountain girl "according to her own vision," claims Renata Berg-Pan in *Leni Riefenstahl* (Boston: Twayne, 1980), p. 72. "She wanted to play in a film where *the woman* is the most important figure —not *the mountain* as had been the case in all the Fanck-directed films in which she had acted. In Fanck's films the woman had always been in the background. 'I wanted a good part, and since I did not get it, I had to write it myself,' Riefenstahl also confessed."

4. For an account of the various versions of the film and critical response to *The Blue Light*, see Peggy Ann Wallace, "An Historical Study of the Career of Leni Riefenstahl from 1923 to 1933," diss. University of Southern California, 1975, pp. 392ff. The names of Jewish co-workers do not appear in the 1938 rerelease version.

5. Richard Meran Barsam, *Filmguide to Triumph of the Will* (Bloomington/London: Indiana University Press, 1975), p. 9.

6. See Ruby Rich, "Leni Riefenstahl: The Deceptive Myth," in *Sexual Strategems: The World of Women in Film*, Patricia Erens, ed., (New York: Horizon, 1979), pp. 202–209, where the author uses insights from Robert Rosenblum's *Modern Painting and the Northern Romantic Tradition* to elucidate the visual strategies in *Triumph of the Will*.

7. Quoted as rendered in William Vaughan, *German Romantic Painting* (New Haven: Yale University Press, 1980), p. 74.

8. *Ibid.*, p. 76.

9. The first release version apparently no longer exists in a definitive form. The 1951-version came in the wake of the apparent loss of the original negative during World War II. This contains outtakes and unused material Riefenstahl had retained from the production. It must be noted that the 1951-production differs markedly from the 1932 film, above all in its eradication of the framing passage. For a reconstruction of the original film, see Wallace, pp. 287–298.

10. See Martin Swales, *The German Novelle* (Princeton: Princeton University Press, 1977), p. 28: "I would argue that the mainspring of much novelle writing is the contact between an ordered and reliably interpreted human universe on the one hand and an experience or set of experiences that would appear to conflict utterly with any notion of order or manageable interpretation on the other. Hence, the novelle derives its peculiar and insistent energy from what one can best describe as a hermeneutic gamble, as a shock confrontation with marginal events. Implicitly, the attempt to make an ordered statement of that which by definition resists the ordering intention is one of the central undertakings within the narrative universe of the novelle."

11. Kracauer, *From Caligari to Hitler: A Psychological History of the German Film* (Princeton: Princeton University Press, 1947), p. 111.

12. See, among others, Peggy A. Wallace, "The Most Important Factor Was the 'Spirit': Leni Riefenstahl During the Filming of *The Blue Light*," *Image* (March 1974), 17(1): 26–28; and Frieda Grafe, "Leni Riefenstahl: Falsche Bauern, falsche Soldaten und was für ein Volk," in *Beschriebener Film 1974–1985*, special issue of *Die Republik* (January 25, 1985), nos. 72–75, p. 41.

13. Wallace, *Image*, p. 26.

14. See Robin Wood's reading of *Nosferatu*, "F. W. Murnau," *Film Comment* (May–June 1976), 12(3): 7–8.

15. See Wood, p. 8: "One is tempted toward a straight-psychoanalytical interpretation: Nosferatu is the symbol of neurosis resulting from repressed sexuality (repressed *nature*); when the neurosis is revealed to the light of day it is exorcised, but the process of its emergence and recognition has been so terrible that positive life (Nina) is destroyed with it."

16. Kracauer, curiously, speaks of Junta as "a sort of gypsy girl" (p. 258). She speaks only Italian and does not understand the German of her would-be benefactor from Vienna, the painter Vigo.

17. Quoted in Wallace's dissertation, p. 307.

18. Wallace, *ibid.*, p. 300. See also Berg-Pan, p. 79: " 'The story of the girl and that village,' Riefenstahl confessed to another interviewer, 'is nearly the story of my life, but I didn't know that until later.' "

19. Sontag's article appeared as "Fascinating Fascism," in *The New York Review of Books* (February 6, 1975), vol. 32, no. 1. It will be quoted according to the reprinted version in Susan Sontag, *Under the Sign of Saturn* (New York: Vintage, 1981), pp. 71–105. Cf. Andrew Sarris' critique of the piece, "Notes on the Fascination of Fascism," *Village Voice*, January 30, 1978, p. 33: Sontag "quotes from the few film historians who support her position, and ignores or insults the rest. Siegfried Kracauer's very questionable *From Caligari to Hitler* is trotted out as if it were holy writ, its mandate for 20–20 hindsight renewed. Still, the problem with either a prosecution or a defense of Riefenstahl is that so much of the evidence has disappeared in the rubble of the Third Reich that we can never be quite sure whether Leni was Little Eva (as she claims) or Lucretia Borgia (as Sontag suggests) or (more likely) an opportunistic artist who has been both immortalized and imprisoned by the horror of history."

20. Sontag, "Fascinating Fascism," p. 90.

21. Kracauer, *From Caligari to Hitler*, p. 259.

22. See Wolfgang Rumpf, "Infame Lügen?" *Tip*, December 14, 1984, pp. 56–57; and Ulrich Enzensberger, "KZ-Zigeuner tanz' mit mir," *Konkret*, February 1985, pp. 12–17.

23. See, for instance, Berg-Pan, p. 80: "There is no mention of any political regime in *The Blue Light*; and although intuition does, indeed, play an important part in the film, that alone certainly would not make it a Fascist work."

24. Rosen, "History, Textuality, Nation: Kracauer, Burch, and Some Problems in the Study of National Cinemas," *Iris* (1984), 2(2): 69.

25. Among many examples, see Erwin Leiser, *Nazi Cinema*, Gertrud Mander and David Wilson, trs. (New York: Collier, 1975); Julian Petley, *Capital and Culture: German Cinema 1933–45* (London: British Film Institute, 1979); and David Welch, *Propaganda and the German Cinema*.

26. See Gerd Albrecht, *Nationalsozialistische Filmpolitik. Eine soziologische Untersuchung über die Spielfilme des Dritten Reiches* (Stuttgart: Enke, 1969). Albrecht distinguishes between films "with latent political function" and those "with manifest political function."

27. A marked exception here is the work of Karsten Witte, especially his article, "Visual Pleasure Inhibited: Aspects of the German Revue Film," J. D. Steakley and Gabriele Hoover, trs., *New German Critique* (Fall/Winter 1981–82), nos. 24–25, pp. 238–263.

28. Grafe, "Leni Riefenstahl," p. 44.

29. Hinz, *Art in the Third Reich*, Robert and Rita Kimber, trs. (New York: Pantheon, 1979), p. 21.

30. Eisner, *The Haunted Screen*, Roger Greaves, tr. (Berkeley/Los Angeles: University of California Press, 1969), p. 17: It was in the "mysterious world" of Romanticism, claims the author, "attractive and repugnant at the same time, that the German cinema found its true nature."

31. Kracauer, "The Mass Ornament," Barbara Correll and Jack Zipes, trs., *New German Critique* (Spring 1975), no. 5, pp. 67–76.

32. Sontag, *Under the Sign of Saturn*, pp. 91 and 96.

33. Friedländer, *Reflections of Nazism: An Essay on Kitsch and Death*, Thomas Weyr, tr. (New York: Harper & Row, 1984), pp. 30, 49.

34. This is Frieda Grafe's phrase, "Leni Riefenstahl," p. 48: "Es ist nicht der Gipfel, der die Männer magisch anzieht, es ist eine Höhle im Gipfel. Da wird ein Schoss geplündert."

35. Kracauer, *From Caligari to Hitler*, p. 259.

36. Oskar Kalbus, *Vom Werden deutscher Filmkunst* (Altona-Bahrenfeld: Cigaretten Bilderdienst, 1935), 2:66. If there is any undeniable influence of Béla Balázs on the production, this expressive use of the human physiognomy would seem to be the most prominent one.

37. Ernst Bloch, "Nonsynchronism and the Obligation to Its Dialectics," Mark Ritter, tr., *New German Critique* (Spring 1977), no. 11, pp. 27, 30.

38. Take, for example, utterances of Rudolf Hess in 1936 at a meeting of women's organizations: "We grant the rest of the world the ideal type of woman that it wishes for itself, but the rest of the world should kindly grant us the woman which is most suitable to us. Not that 'Gretchen type' which foreigners imagine as being a somewhat limited, indeed unintellectual creature, but a woman who is capable of intellectually standing at her husband's side in his interests, in his struggle for existence, who makes the world more beautiful and richer in content for him. This is the ideal woman of the German man of today. She is a woman who, above all, is also able to be a mother." Quoted in *Nazi Culture*, George L. Mosse, ed. (New York: Schocken, 1966), p. 42. See also Renate Wiggershaus, *Frauen unterm Nationalsozialismus* (Wuppertal: Hammer, 1984); and Rita Thalmann, *Frausein im Dritten Reich* (Munich: Hanser, 1984).

39. See Gertrud Koch, "Der höhere Befehl der Frau ist ihr niederer Instinkt: Frauenhass und Männer-Mythos in Filmen über Preussen," in *Preussen im Film*, Axel Marquardt and Heinz Rathsack, eds. (Reinbek: Rowohlt, 1981), pp. 219–233.

40. Witte, "Visual Pleasure Inhibited," p. 252.

41. Quoted in Wallace's dissertation, p. 403.

42. *Ibid.*, p. 285.

43. For a close comparison between *The Blue Light* and Renker's *Bergkristall*, see Appendix B of Wallace's dissertation.

44. See Berg-Pan, p. 77: "The initial interior scenes involving the local peasants were taken at Runkelstein Castle. The peasants were allegedly descendants of the Visigoths, and Riefenstahl liked the stark and clear lines of their faces and their proud bearing. In the beginning the peasants refused to be photographed. Diplomatic skill, tact, and small bribes were necessary to win their confidence, and this provided a good lesson for Riefenstahl, who put to good use what she had learned

about winning reticent people when she made her film about the Nuba several decades later."

45. Quoted in Wallace, p. 394.

46. *Ibid.*, p. 402.

47. See Herf, *Reactionary Modernism: Technology, Culture, and Politics in Weimar and the Third Reich* (Cambridge: Cambridge University Press, 1984).

III
LOSSES AND GAINS

8

THE TWO COUNTRIES OF WRITING: THEATER AND POETICAL FICTION
Hélène Cixous

I ONLY know about what my life experience has taught me, what my life and my body have taught me, but it's really subject to all kinds of questioning. I thought I would tell you about an adventure in writing and what it has made me discover: I have been writing for a long time with my right hand, and now I am writing with two hands. With my right hand I have been writing a lot of poetical fiction and now I'm using my left hand in order to write plays.

And why do I say that I write with my left hand? It's a metaphor. I write with my right hand. But it's my right-left hand that I use. That is, I use a hand which is very awkward. I have great difficulties in writing for the theater, whereas I feel I have less difficulty in writing poetical fiction. It has really caused all kinds of questioning because I didn't know I would ever write with my "left" hand. I didn't even know I could do it. And at the same time, when I started doing it, I realized it was entirely different from my poetical writing in every way. There's not one single feature of my theatrical writing which is identical with my poetical writing.

It's not really contradictory; in a way, it's a complement. How-

Presented to the Focused Research Program in Gender and Women's Studies, UCI, May 1988. This lecture was given directly in English, which is not my native tongue.

ever, it makes me travel all the time between two countries and
remark again on differences. I'm following only one way, my own
way, but I consider it as an example because on the way I encounter all kinds of writers who I'm sure have had the same kinds of
adventures and surprises as I have had. On the way to a piece of
work there will always be crossings, encounterings, and inter-
weavings.

Now it all begins for me with Paradise Lost. That is, with
paradise and loss, with both types of experiences, with utter bliss
and utter despair. And I'm going to dedicate that first part of my
reflection to writers who spring from that strange couple, paradise
and loss. So I dedicate this to Karen Blixen, who started writing
only after having lost the whole continent of Africa. I dedicate
that to Clarice Lispector, a Brazilian writer, our contemporary,
and for me she is the greatest writer of the century. I consider her
a kind of female Kafka. She was of Russian origin. She was
brought to Brazil when she was a couple of months old, and
inscribed in her whole vision of the world is that first unlived
event, the loss of mother or father country. She doesn't write
about that, but it is really something that has shaped her strength.
As with Tzvetaeva, the great Russian poet who died early in 1941
after having lost and regained paradise several times; the first
time through the Russian Revolution, and afterward through many
different exiles within her own country and outside. And when
she died it was really because she had no earth left under her
feet. Nothing to eat and nothing to stand on,[1] so she just hanged
herself from a tree. She was forty-nine. And nothing left on that
dire Russian earth but bare tree and air.

Now these writers have really shaped and re-created the country they have lost into "the other country." Of course "country"
is a metaphor for something else, for the maternal body. Losing
and rewinning, regaining and reconquering—for me these go
together. I realize that I, in my own life, have benefited from such
a loss. I was born in Paradise Lost. And this paradise was Algeria,
a country in Africa which was a French colony. When I was very
small, perhaps two or three, I clearly remember knowing that it
was already lost. It wasn't mine; it was the others'. And that was
right. I had no longing. And no belonging. No sense of belonging.

Now my writing was born in Algeria. No. I should say out of Algeria; out of a lost country, out of a lost father and of a foreign mother. All of these little traits which might appear as unsatisfactory were very fertile for me. I've had that luck to know first foreignness, exile, war, the phantom memory of peace, mourning. And actually I learned about hatred, when I was three, in a large garden full of flowers. I suddenly knew that uprooting existed and that human roots know no borders, no nationality. And that under the earth, at the very bottom of the ladder of the world, the heart is beating.

At the same time I had the luck to be surrounded by different tongues, by different languages. My mother was German. My father was of Spanish origin. One spoke French in my home, and German, Spanish, Arabic, etc., around. I could also speak hen with the hens around me. And I was born in the city that was called Oran. When I was very small, I used to get lost in Oran. I was nearsighted, so Oran appeared to me like a kind of veiled woman, a beautiful veiled woman. I was always lost in her womb. I immediately realized that Oran was the signifier, though, of course I did not know that word "signifier" but I knew the word Oran. It was the key to the other country.

And with *Oran*, I had absolutely everything.

Of course, I had it in French and in other languages. In French "or" is gold, and "an" (*year*) so I already had the golden year in my city. And I added, naturally, the first pronoun in French—"je" —and I had an "orange." I realized that by adding myself to my maternal city, I would get the fruit. Again I heard Oran say *hors, en*, which means outside and inside so that both outside and inside were inside. Now through the name Oran I entered the secret of language. I discovered that my city meant fruit. It was a fruit. But a fruit was a word and the word was a fruit. In the word, the fruit.

Then I lost it. The city, not the word. I've never come back to Oran, but it comes back to me all the time—in writing. Actually when it started coming back in writing I didn't realize it. All my books were full of *or* or *an*. My unconscious was inscribing my lost country. It was in Oran that my father introduced me to the noble mysteries of language. That he gave me, he taught me very remarkable words. For instance, he taught me the word "extraordinary." Now the word "extraordinary" is extraordinary. I always kept thinking when I was a child how extraordinary it was that what was extraordinary should have an extraordinary signifier, not just a tiny little signifier, but really a large extraordinary one.

My father was a stork. That is, he used to be called "Stork" as he was a scout, and he was surrounded with men who all had animal names and when I was very small I didn't realize that these were pseudonyms. I thought that they were real. Afterwards, I forgot about that and the stork came back with all kinds of birds in my books—until I realized that my father was a stork. And I realized that I used to wonder what the sex of the stork is, or what the sex of my father is. Now it is very difficult to decide and this indecisiveness of sex and of role is fundamental for me.

I was so happy when I was small that I thought I was going to pay for that, knowing from my surroundings that mankind is not born for happiness. This was very wise, because we have to pay. So I imagined that I would have to sacrifice my mother, as Abraham his son, that she was going to die, my mother-son, and I was already mourning my mother when my father died. In the end, I just wondered who was who. My father became a little my mother by disappearing. And when I wrote my first book—my first real book—it was called *Inside* and it grew directly outside the grave of my father. But when I wrote it I was still rather young. I didn't understand what I was doing, it just came. My father was the source, the origin, and I just wrote what he dictated to me.

What happens when you have exile for earth? When you are a citizen of Exile. What happens when you're trekking out of your Egypt? You go into the desert and God provides manna. The definition and etymology of manna are beautiful. First of all, about the substance of it: the Bible reports very precisely what kind of food it is. It is a kind of coriander seed, it tastes like honey, it's like corn flakes. One might suspect that it is solid, but it may also be a kind of maternal milk. When it appeared, the Hebrews kept asking "Man- hou?" which means, "But what is that?" Now manna is a "what-is-that?" And it is again a kind of orange, it's again food and word. As Milton said, "His tongue dropped manna and could make the worse appear the better reason."

My latest book is called *Manne*. It's dedicated to the Mandelas and the Mandelstams and it tells their two intertwined stories. Actually, I started by writing on the Mandelas, then came the Mandelstams, who were inhabiting my dreaming memory. And suddenly toward the end of writing the book I realized that it was called *Manna* and it had to do with manna.

Mandelstam is my favorite Russian poet, an immense poet, and he was condemned for poetry and sentenced to deportation to Siberia, where he died in 1938. And his story, the story of his courage, of his weakness, of his power, of his inventing another world is for me quite comparable to that of the Mandelas, except that one is a poetic epic and the other is a political epic. But they evince just the same type of heroism and resistance to exile.

The Genesis of a Piece of Writing

There is a seed, and the seed of a work of art is a stroke: you get hit by something, and then that's the beginning of a writing. I can be started on my way by a stroke of poem: that was what happened when I read some of Mandelstam's poems. You can be hit by a voice, by something mysterious in a voice, which of course is the essence of the body—an accent. Or by a sentence. One of my books was initiated by one sentence. It was a sentence of Kafka. But actually, it wasn't of the writer Kafka. It was of the man Kafka. When he was near death and breathless with pain, he couldn't speak, so he would scribble little sentences on scraps of paper. Fortunately for us they've been preserved, all these wonderful little sentences that say almost nothing. These nothings are extraordinary. One of these sentences runs, "*Limonade, es war alles so grenzenlos*" which means "Lemonade everything was so limitless."

For me, it was really the summing up of the whole experience of life. I dreamt on that sentence for a long time and finally came out with a book of 250 pages, which is entitled *Limonade, tout est si infini*. But why did I write 250 pages on one sentence? I did that because I am alive, and I just couldn't get myself to write a book that has only one sentence. But I think that one should come to the point where that becomes possible. I still hope I'll do it. Once. Actually, it happens to me sometimes when I write for the theater. I have to write things that are that size, whereas my drive would be to write a whole book on that small thing. Which means that I sometimes feel I am on the verge of death when writing for the theater.

And again you can get the stroke from a person, either a legendary person or a real person. And once I got hit by a hat. I was watching on television a documentary on South Africa. I saw a large demonstration taking place in Soweto and there were all those little black kids, who were dancing their way—toward death, actually—and shouting, singing, and floating around on that huge crowd was a huge black hat. On that huge black hat there was a huge plume of ostrich feathers. And under that hat there was a black orange, smiling. That was beautiful Winnie Mandela. And I was awed and full of admiration, because of that feat of imagination and insolence, that wearing of a huge black hat, as a kind of future flag of South Africa, in the middle of that sea of kids, dancing and mourning. I never forgot that and it started me actually wanting to write something on the secret of the Mandelas, how they survive and how they live—actually how they enjoy, how they make love, whereas they are separated by an eternity sentence.

Of course there were other things that prompted me to write. For instance, the theme of exile, which has always been with me, which is a kind of earthly condition. I do not consider it as unhappy, I consider it as having to be lived through and corrected. For me, a writer in the French language, "l'exil fait taire" /"l'exil fait terre": which means both that exile prevents you from speaking, makes you breathless and at the same time it makes for earth.

As you probably know, Mandela's word has not been heard for twenty-six years. His voice has disappeared completely, it's forbidden. He is condemned to be buried under silence. Yet at the same time, everybody in South Africa hears his voice symbolically. He is heard. So all this made me want to write in book form that dancing-mourning I had seen; that Woman Mandela who is both a mother and a daughter; this huge movement. She is both completely womanly, she always seems to be big with child because she is so very round, she seems always on the point of giving birth, and she does, she gives birth to the genius of Africa, and at the same time she is phallic, with all her feathers, this woman/mother who has to give birth to her own man.

But it was not enough for me. I had that second story coming to feed the first one, and be fed by the first one. I had to have that kind of intertextuality which for me is the basis of every text I write. It's not a theory, it's just a need. And everything was written in this way by addition and multiplication: East and West, North and South, White and Black, History and Poetry, Russia and Africa, Man and Woman, Heat and Ice.

For me, all texts are composed beings. They grow all the time and out of intertextuality. One text makes love with another text and gives birth to another text within a book. We are composed beings, exactly as a text, composed of many people. According to the persons who compose you, you're a different person and you may even be of a different—I should say sexes, but this is not a real mistake, I'm doing it on purpose. I myself, for instance, I realize, I'm mostly composed of "women"—quite by chance. I have no trace of my grandfathers except as being wiped out of life. And neither of my grandmothers had traces of grandfathers. My grandmothers also remembered their own grandmothers. So I am mostly peopled with "women." And it's probably made me write the way I write. I might have been composed of "men," and I would have written differently. But then, what are "men" or "women" composed of?

Now the poetical text is an ideal medium to inscribe that sort of haunting, of being composed of different instances, of different parents or brothers and sisters or utter strangers. The weaving of signifiers allows everything. But what happens with that when you write for the theater? Well, you can't do it. Theater is action —I mean the way I do it, anyway—it asks for a lot of characters to come on the stage. You can't just weave each character, you don't have all the time and space on the stage you have when you write a book.

And yet there is that multiplicity. What happens with it? What happens on the stage with all those characters who belong to the regions of our unconscious? Actually, the vision, composition, the ambivalence of the subject are distributed into different characters. On the stage you will have five different characters to express one struggle, one conflict of the self. Whereas in the text one conflict of the self has five voices that intermingle into one. And it's very strange to be led to that sudden separation of what is one voice into several.

To finish with my signifiers, they are of course, intertextual; they are also inter-linguistic. Mandela's name contains the word "Mandel." In German, *Mandel* is almond. With my German ear, I heard that Mandela contained an almond. As regards Mandelstam, his name actually means an almond tree. "*Mandela, Mandelstam, deux amandes dans la pointrine du monde.*"[2]

History has gratified me again with another fruit, *Mandel/*almond.

Now I could go on and on opening my fruit, and finding other fruit in my fruit: until I find "Dante" in "Mandelstam." Actually Mandelstam has written on Dante. Probably also because this Russian explorer of Inferno was full of Dante's letters. Indeed, language itself is a sort of supernation. It is de-nationalized, which is a blessing. Poets like Mandelstam and Tzvetaeva have written in several languages,[3] and with equal power, because they knew they had to do away with frontiers and limits. Everything was theirs that they could write.

Coming back to what I want to do when I write poetical fiction. I want to write *almost-nothings*. That is, I want to write what seems to mean almost nothing in our normal lives, but to me is the essence of life. I want to write what is almost impossible to write. I want to write at the very extremity of writing. I'm not alone in having that kind of wish. Celan, the German-writing poet says that nowadays poems have the tendency to be written just on the edge of the abyss and it's true and that's what I am interested in.

I want to write stories that both tell us all the secrets of life and death and are also almost imperceptible. I love a story of Akhmatova. In the terrible years of Yegov, she was queuing up in front of a Leningrad prison as she had been queuing up for months and months because her son had been deported. And the queue was very long. Suddenly, a woman turned back, and this woman was faceless. That is, her face had been worn out by waiting and by history. And the woman said to Akhmatova, with a toneless voice, "Could you describe that?" That was indescribable. And Akhmatova said, "Yes."

That is the honor of a poet, to dare say, "Yes, I can describe this indescribable." Unfortunately, usually the thing that is indescribable is such because it is fatal. It is: *the worst*. I want to describe the worst. I even want to feel the worst. (But the best, the very, very best, is just as difficult to describe.) I had a problem when I wrote *Manne* because I had to describe Steve Biko's death, and it was really beyond my reach. It took me a long time, and finally I discovered that I had to change my writing entirely to make it really almost breathless. I had to write poems. To set poems in the sea of prose.

Writing must out-write itself. It must go as far as possible from our limits and the limits of writing. And yet, of course, it remains words. I'm interested in that very flamboyant moment at the door of life or death, when the narrative suddenly breaks like a sob, when it becomes extremely difficult to remain alive. When Kafka can only write a book in one sentence. When you've got to struggle in order to be where you are to inhabit yourself. When Mandelstam couldn't write the poem that was singing in him because everything was forbidding it and even his hands could not hear the word.

That is actually the position of Dostoevsky in *The Idiot*. While the novel tells the story of the Prince, one theme recurs again and again, and it's the famous scene of the man who is going to be beheaded. This is Dostoevsky's primitive scene. He was about to be put to death, but he got his release at the very last moment. And that started his whole reflection on life in writing. It was at the moment that he thought, "I won't be of this world anymore," that he discovered everything in life. In the *Idiot* he tells us twenty different stories of all kinds of people who are about to die and at that very moment they understand and they feel.

In front of death you've got to hurry to live. But we, the lazy, when we hurry we bustle around instead of being in a hurry toward life. Death does awaken us. But we don't always need death to be awakened. Clarice Lispector, for instance, didn't have to be threatened by death to make every single instant a kind of revelation.

What I'm interested in is what I call the precarious. Something which is almost on the verge of disappearance, which we have to pray to keep alive. We who forget the most present, our mother just behind us, our maid (we've often had maids), all types of mothers, and our close friends.

Or even turtles. At one point in one book, Clarice Lispector suddenly strikes a chord and says, "But what about the turtles? I haven't thought about them for a century!" Of course, you might study these turtles as if they were human beings. When I wrote *Vivre l'orange*[4] I was paying homage to Clarice Lispector, a writer who cares for us *and* for turtles . . . .

Now what about the theater? What do I do with tiny little things when I write a play? What do I do with those kinds of insights Joyce would have called epiphanies, with small anecdotes, moments that are emblematic of something great? Well, those little scenes I use in the theater. For me they are the secret kernel of a whole play. I try to find a small detail that is not artificial. A concrete yet sublime detail. I can force a detail to come in a scene, but as long as I don't hear that tiny little heart beat in a scene I know that it doesn't work.

When I was writing *L'Histoire terrible . . . de Sihanouk,* I remember that at one point I was very happy because I felt that something was circulating around me in the playhouse, in the imaginary playhouse. I knew it was a metaphor and I couldn't grasp it. I told you I'm nearsighted but when I write I'm blind, and it's very important for a writer to be blind. So I didn't see it; I felt it. And finally I saw it coming with my blind eyes and it was a very old bike that has been used throughout the ages and yet is always there, still here "today." And it's used by a dead king, the dead king of Cambodia, who actually might be my father. (I didn't realize when he came on my inner stage that he might have been my father, he, the strange survivor of Cambodia.) He survives because he's dead. And he travels across the whole of Southeast Asia up to Peking on that old bike.

Bikes become exquisitely poetical things when they turn into metaphors.

But then there's something I want to do with writing for the theater. I want to write about fate. My type of writing for the theater one might situate in the line of Shakespearean historical plays. I've always loved them, I've always read them, but I've never considered these plays as giving me a political message. And I'm sure it did not carry one either in the time of Elizabeth. Politics were the pretext. History is the daylight or stagelight in which human beings are steeped.

I want to tell the epic of the heart. Actually I started at a very modest level when I wrote the *Portrait of Dora*, I only put three or four characters on the stage. Yet already it was something that had to do with modern fate. Maybe I should not use that word. In French, the word is *destin*, and I think it's less marked than fate. Destiny—it belongs to the vocabulary of tragedy or epic. I think that we have *destins*. We have fates. Usually we consider ourselves as ordinary citizens and we forget that we are characters in a legendary narrative. Bataille wrote all his novels in that perspective. He said that writing was only worthwhile if we make the narrative of something apparently quite ordinary appear as something extraordinary.

Now what interests me in the theater is the story of one person, of a people, reaching the fatal point when things might turn differently. For instance, there is that time when Sihanouk was in Paris and there was turmoil in Phnom Penh, a rebellion being prepared to dethrone him. He is warned, but doesn't take the warning seriously and changes his mind several times. We all shudder, we spectators, and all shout as if we were looking at a puppet show: "You should go back to Cambodia!" And he keeps telling us, "Yes, I will go back to Cambodia." And then he goes to Moscow and he loses his country and not only his country but his people as well. And that's the beginning of a quarter century of despair. There's no explanation except the unconscious. The unconscious of a man and of a people and of history and of the planet.

I am particularly interested in that mystery of our not knowing yet what we already know. And if I don't know it myself, my other self knows it. But *I* don't want to know it. It's the scene of our blindness. We're blind and we act as if we weren't, but it's our blindness that leads us. This was the case with Freud, in *Portrait of Dora*. Actually, although I didn't do it on purpose, because I'm a really and truly blind person, I realize now, when I open my eyes, that it is a story of blindness.

On the stage I show what I like to call the "eve of the battle." One of the greatest plays of Shakespeare is *Henry V*, to me. It's not that I cherish *Henry V* above other Shakespeare plays, but I'm moved by the eve of the battle. I'm moved that someone has dared to make a play on the eve of the battle, because nothing happens. Everything *will* happen. Everything is going to happen. Now that "is going" is important and the eve of the battle is actually, I think, our human condition. To me, for instance, every time I'm going to give a lecture it's the eve of the battle. I know a lot about the eve of the battle.

Eve. She is our mother, of course, and not only is Eve our universal mother, but also my mother, my own mother is called Eve. So it's the eve of the battle. It's before we know anything, before we are born, and life is going to happen to us. I like that imminence, which for me is the very metaphor of our life, when it is active.

The Creation of Characters

I've never written novels. I've never been able to write a novel. Sometimes, I used to regret I hadn't been born a century earlier: I would have liked to write like Dostoevsky. But it's too late. You can't write like that any more. Why can't we, why can't I? The time of "representation" and "expression" is past. I belong to the epoch of inscription. I can't write a novel; I can't create characters within the scope of fiction. I have discovered I can create characters on the stage, but not in a modern novel, because I use my body to write, my complete body to write a fiction.

I write as a woman. As a woman I can write of women. As a woman, I can use my body to inscribe the body of a woman. But I can't do that for a man. If I wrote a novel, I would have, on the one hand complete women and on the other hand semi-real men. This I can't do.

What about the stage? There are plenty of men in my plays. But that is because the theater is not the scene of sexual pleasure. You don't describe sexual pleasure in a play. Romeo and Juliet love each other, but do not make love, not in front of us—although we know they do elsewhere. They sing love, and in the theater it's the heart that sings. And the human heart has no sex. That's how we communicate. Sexually, I cannot identify with a male character. Yet the heart feels the same way in a man's breast as in a woman's. Which does not mean that my characters are demi-creatures and that they stop at the belt. They lack nothing. They have breasts, penises, everything. But I don't have to *write* it. Those who write it are the actors and the actresses. They provide for the whole body, I don't have to invent, and that's why writing for the stage is so pleasant for somebody who's always felt the limit that springs from difference.

On the stage everybody is not-me, and yet they all say "I." All those "I's" who are almost entirely different from me are yet born from my first person. The "I" must admit that there is one point, one intimate, secret point, where I and this I, this other I, speak with the same breath—this "I" that is you and that "you" who is me and is not me.

This becomes remarkable when I feel that the characters I create could never be me. I could never be them and not only that, I reject them. I could hate them, and they are hateable in front of the whole world. Murderers, villains, who say "I."

Now how do I do that, how can it be? First of all, sometimes I don't succeed. When they are really too far away, when I have absolutely no grain in common with them then it doesn't work. They become like puppets.

So there is a mystery that is not a mystery: we experience it. For instance, all of us here who do not know one another except that we are all together, have that little grain in common that helps us communicate. Maybe that does not go very far, but in the theater it goes very, very far. Actually when you write for the theater you come to a point when you are completely dispossessed of yourself. You can't just give yourself an order. It comes about. By and by you're invaded by the characters and you may even not realize that your self is growing lower and lower. Eventually the self disappears. And at one point in writing, I fainted. I thought it was because I was exhausted, but then, I realized it happened every time I was writing a scene that was so intense that I really identified with every character. That was particularly dramatic and there was no room left for me, that is all. And so I accepted my being burnt down, or driven out of the scene of which I was the living stage.

Don't believe that it's pleasant; it's unpleasant. It's frightening. That is really a strange phenomenon of possession and dispossession. Yet it's the secret way the writer and the actor must accept to go, in order for characters to emerge. This extreme receptivity, this expulsion of the self.

It is a feminine feature of that strange work of giving birth to others. And from my experience, when I see actors and actresses become others—they *do* become others—I'm sure that it's a kind of death that they've experienced. They *do* abandon something of themselves completely. I have been a witness of this sacrifice in the Théâtre du Soleil. They give up their selves. It's such a powerful trance that when they have become the characters you cannot speak to the actors at all. You can speak to the characters. You can have a conversation with Pandit Nehru. Not with the actor. Which means that you too are changed into a kind of theater person, although you are yourself. But you have to use a foreign language, the other's language. Now, it's really a form of detachment, which for the actors is so ascetic that it is almost sainthood. I'm not a saint at all, I never reach that detachment. Or I do that in my room when I write, and I become fifty persons; that is, I lose one self, but in exchange, I get fifty characters. But the actor loses himself/herself and gets only one character in exchange.

The question of the jouissance of that kind of position raises itself immediately. Because, as I said, it's not always a pleasure. It's more of an anguish than of a pleasure. And can one write without pleasure? The pleasure comes later. The pleasure is a motherly one: It comes when you suddenly see all those characters coming to life and enjoying that. That miracle makes you not regret all your efforts.

I sometimes write about themes—for instance in the *Indiade*, I wrote on a theme which for me would require ten volumes of analysis, i.e., on the theme of love and separation and all the paradoxes of separation within love. Of love as having to go along with separation, as paradise goes along with loss. All the themes I could teach a seminar on for a whole year I had to condense in one small scene between Gandhi and Jinnah. I must say I could not have written it at one stroke. I wrote it too long at first and too philosophically. I then had to proceed by "translating" my thought into action and condensing and condensing. I'm not really skillful with very concise works. But I have to be tense and dense on the stage. And when I compel myself to tighten my breath I sometimes think that I'm learning, I'm going my way toward that ultimate book which will be only one sentence long. But of course I can't go there before I've written all the large books I feel like writing.

I know that some people who know my work have started wondering whether I would abandon my "right" hand for the "left" hand. But no. Of course, I know that I've got to use the two of them. And they don't fight. There's that little fable in Kafka about his two hands. His two hands are at war and the left hand is trying to kill the right hand. I don't think my hands are at war. I think that they help each other.

That's what happened with *Manne*, which is the first text with characters I've ever written. Now those people are real people. Of course, I've "invented" them or reinvented them, but their origin is reality. I hope they come to life. And at the same time, since it's not a play, it's written in the third person. This I had never done. Characters on the stage speak in the first person. Now what do I do with that third person? Actually I have difficulties with the third person. There comes a time when I feel at one point it carries me very far away from the first person, from myself, from that "I" which I trust. I trust I. It's not that I trust myself in a narcissistic way, but I, me, I, the first person that is rooted in my own flesh, doesn't lie.

I can of course be deceived. I can make mistakes, but I don't lie. Whereas the third person—I don't know: it's so far. I can't check with my own flesh and feelings. So this I cannot bear. Where the third person becomes too much of a stranger and I can't control the language of the third person with my own body I've been obliged to come back to the first person. Actually, in *Manne,* although the heroes are strangers to me I've come back now and then to "myself" when I felt it was absolutely necessary in order to be truthful.

So I have written "I" even in the name of Nelson Mandela. In the name of Winnie Mandela it's not difficult: she's a woman. In the name of Mandelstam, it was not too difficult because he was a poet, and he's got a poetic body with which I can communicate at the level of language and the unconscious. For Nelson Mandela it was a problem. Because he's a typically manly man. He needs his body, he needs his man's body in order to survive, and he entertains this body, he keeps it alive, he practices sports. Now how did I deal with that "foreign" body? Actually, I tried to "translate" it as honestly as I could, so there are several different scenes which inscribe Mandela's body. The sportsman's body I didn't want to identify with, I can't anyway, so I've only pictured it through the eyes of Winnie Mandela, and this is not very difficult to do. A woman watching a man exercising. It might be Molly Bloom . . .

But what about the lover's body? the erotic body? It's not utterly impossible. I don't think I can write it completely. But there is part of a man's body which surrenders to a woman's body in the act of love. When one really loves, one is invaded by the other, man or woman, as the land is invaded by the sea and this I could try and feel. Since I have experienced the familiar otherness of a woman's body. The discovery of a new continent. Sea and land have a shore in common. They translate into each other. This, of course, is only a part of the experience. But what I could do as a human being was to imagine what the loss of a body is. Mine. Thine. The world my body. What happened to Mandela.

What happened to Mandelstam. Particularly what happened to Mandela when he was suddenly caged in walls. What happens to a human body when suddenly you cut everything away from it. It's not that you're only deprived of space; of freedom. Space is your body. Ways are your legs. The axe works in every way, cuts your eyes, your ears, the air from your lips. It's a hundred deaths.

This you can figure out. Of course it's very difficult, as suffering hasn't happened to you directly, but it can happen in dream and in love. See how Milton has written of the agony of separation that Samson suffered. So this is only to point out that I really can't do without the first person. That is why I'll never be able to write a classical novel. The first person will always come back. Everything else of course is silence.

Now I have my two "hands" writing in two different genres, completely different, completely opposed, in their economies. When you write fiction you have all the time in the world, you have eternity. But on the stage you have no time. Instead of time you have urgency. You only have a minute. Twelve minutes. Nine minutes. You write by the clock. You have almost no self. And you have mortality because everybody who works in a theater group knows that though the theater is an eternal genre, it's mortal. It's going to end. It's going to end at the end of the performance. It's going to end at the end of the year. It's going to be wiped out of the earth. And be buried only in memories.

And that is a lesson in humility. One has to live with the theater exactly as Dostoevsky in front of death. One has to live passionately and immediately. And the author also has to learn that she's not the only author, she isn't the only person that's creating the play. She is only a demi-author. The other part has to be fulfilled by the others.

Writing for the theater is like writing the soul and waiting for the body to clothe this soul. And then one has to be on the way to write a book of four lines. As I told you I think it's the dream of every writer to come to the day of writing a very small book of three words. Sometimes I dream about them. Of course, they will be different from what I have dreamt. But what I also know is that whatever I write at the end of my life won't be a play. It will necessarily be on the side of poetic fiction. I need my self to die. I

do need myself to die. I can't be without myself to die. So I think
I shall write my last sentence with my right hand.

References for the Works Cited:

Fiction:
Limonade tout était si infini. Paris: Des femmes, 1981.
Manne aux Mandelstams aux Mandelas. Paris: Des femmes, 1988.
Theater:
L'Histoire terrible mais inachevée de Norodom Sihanouk Roi du Cambodge.
Paris: Théâtre du Soleil, 1985.
L'Indiade ou L'Inde de Leurs Rêves. Paris: Théâtre du Soleil, 1987.
1. And no one to whom to address a poem.
2. "Mandela, Mandelstam two almonds in the world's breast."
3. Russian, French, Italian, German and . . . Angelic.
4. [Recall Cixous's earlier play on the word; during the lecture she wrote the
word "l'orange" to illustrate the rupture, the breaking up of the signifiers *or*,
Oran, je.—ed.]

9

THE MULTIPLE LIVES OF ADDIE BUNDREN'S DEAD BODY: ON WILLIAM FAULKNER'S *AS I LAY DYING*
Gabriele Schwab

I could just remember how my father used to say that the reason for living was to get ready to stay dead a long time.

Addie, in *As I Lay Dying* (p. 134)

The Grotesque Body in Carnivalesque Literature

WILLIAM FAULKNER'S *As I Lay Dying*[1] is, on one of its multiple levels, a novel about the grotesque life of a dead body. It is not so much, as the title might suggest, about the process of Addie Bundren's dying but about the bizarre forms of an extension of her life beyond death. Just as her dead body becomes a haunting protagonist of the carnivalesque funeral procession of the Bundrens to Jefferson, so her phantasmatic body,[2] created in the minds of her sons, becomes the dominating protagonist of a drama that stages the internalized mother as a complex and ambivalent way of mourning.

On the surface, both the plot and imagery of Faulkner's novel, and especially its portrayal of the grotesque body of the dead mother and the offensive transgressions of cultural taboos during her funeral procession, are indebted to the carnivalesque tradition. According to Bakhtin,[3] carnivalesque literature creates its grotesque bodies as universal and cosmic bodies. In this context, the grotesque body of the dead mother evokes the archaic fear of the mother with her overwhelming powers and the mysteries of her reproductive functions. On a more general level, the carnival of the dead body of the "great mother"[4] reveals a dark form of dealing culturally with fears of the female body and with the threatening aspects of femininity.

Faulkner's spectacle of the dead mother's grotesque body pushes beyond the boundaries of pure carnival and exposes such fears through a poetic language designed to externalize internal images of the mother and the maternal body. As will be shown, the language of As I Lay Dying relates in a specific way to the body. It evokes grotesque images of the body that resemble the grotesque bodies of carnivalesque literature. Faulkner's text, however, establishes a crucial difference in perspective. Instead of an external view of a spectator who beholds a grotesque body in its deviations from the cultural norm, the characters in As I Lay Dying obliterate this otherness of the grotesque body because they create the deviations and distortions of bodily images as internal images of the body. This phantasmatic distortion becomes especially meaningful where it expresses the characters' internal image of the mother.

There is a whole range of literature that presents the grotesque female body as the other of male desire. The grotesque dead body of the mother can be understood as one of the most radical cases of this cultural symbolization of the female body. In twentieth-century literature, grotesque representations of the dead maternal body represent the cultural coding of a phantasmatic body whose opposite is represented by the "exquisite cadaver"[5] of young girls or brides. Their dead body functions as a symbolic object for a necrophilic male economy displayed in a whole canon of romanticizing literary forms, the most radical of which is the gothic novel. In contrast to this romantization of the dead body of young heroines, the carnivalization of the dead body of the mother can be read as a specific cultural representation of the maternal body. Following Bakhtin, one would be inclined to see this carnivalization as a subversion of the official cultural coding of the maternal body. But the subversive character of the carnivalesque dead body of the mother is ambivalent: as long as it is represented as a grotesque body it is staged as socially obsolete. The status of the marginal, the irregular, the violation of the norm is preserved in the carnivalizing literary form.

In Faulkner's text the presentation of the grotesque body of the dead mother becomes even more ambiguous because it is embedded in a series of highly stylized inner voices of different characters incorporating diverse and often conflictive perspectives. This "polyphony of voices"[6] evokes the grotesque body of the dead mother not only as a product of the culture of the depraved white farmers of Mississippi. On a different level of abstraction, this body is also a product of a literary culture of the early twentieth century which experiments with the inner speech of literary characters as a way of exploring the boundaries of a fictional mind. In *As I Lay Dying* this experiment culminates in evoking the extensions of Addie Bundren's, that is, a dead character's mind through a multiplicity of voices. This interest of the experimental literature of the time in inner speech is paralleled by a simultaneous interest in the boundaries of the body and its literary presentation. The characters in *As I Lay Dying* perceive the dead body of Addie Bundren as a transgressive body. Very much like the grotesque bodies in carnivalesque literature the mother's dead body is presented in multiple forms of dissolution, fragmentation, mutilation, metamorphosis, decay, and putrification. The fact, however, that these processes are viewed from internal rather than external perspectives lifts the staging of the grotesque body from within the generic form of pure carnivalization into a space beyond parody where the carnival turns into a verbal equivalent of what Artaud termed "theater of cruelty."

The grotesque body in this theater of cruelty appears as the effect of Faulkner's attempt to create a poetic language capable of rendering an aesthetic expression of the unsublimated body. This project, of course, constitutes an aesthetic paradox because any literary or dramatic presentation which aims at representing the unsublimated body has to face the problem that its very mode of presentation—be it theatrical performance as in the case of Artaud's theater of cruelty or a speech performance as in the case of Faulkner's novel—necessarily entails a form of sublimation on a higher level of abstraction. I will try to show how in *As I Lay*

Dying Faulkner's way of dealing with the aesthetic paradox of the sublimation of the unsublimated body forms one of the major achievements of his use of poetic language. Faulkner's verbal theater of cruelty collapses the distance of an outside perspective on the grotesque body of the dead mother because this body is created by inner voices that give expression to a "grotesque soul,"[7] which, in turn, is the creator and beholder of the grotesque body. Instead of portraying the grotesque body and the grotesque soul in isolation from each other, *As I Lay Dying* grasps them in their interaction and reveals how they engender each other. The reader is never granted the distance of a spectator with an unbroken exterior perspective because the inner voices assimilate him or her to the internal drama of the grotesque souls of the Bundrens, who produce the effects of the grotesque body of the dead mother because her death has unleashed a process of desublimation which affects the boundaries of the body as much as the boundaries of mind, perception, and speech.[8]

The Carnivalesque Funeral Procession

Addie Bundren's dead body is the main protagonist of a carnivalesque funeral procession to Jefferson. The longer she is dead, the more active her corpse becomes—not only through the purely biological process of decomposition but also through an increasing power of the dead body over the other protagonists. The longer this body is dead, the more difficult it becomes to bury it, to simply get rid of it, or even to destroy it. The longer it is dead, the more it affects the bodies of the other characters, too, the more it melts them into a collective body in a closed entropic system with its own order of space and time. And the longer it is dead, the more it changes into a macabre transitional object used by the members of the family to act out a black symbiosis in death, the regressive dynamic of which expresses itself in a somatic grief and prepares the final separation from the mother. Whatever seems like a carnivalization from the distance of characters outside the family or from the distance of the overall textual perspective, corresponds, in the internal dynamic of the Bundrens, to a process in which, for the family, the biological body of the mother disappears to the extent to which its decomposition requires an obsessive if not obscene presence. Unable to bury it, the characters let it disappear behind the diverse phantasmatic bodies which they create, or else they have its very existence swallowed up by actions which are aimed at preparing the funeral while, in fact, they delay it endlessly. Like prisoners of a collective system of madness, the Bundrens become blind to the reality of the decomposing body of the mother.

At the beginning of the novel, Addie Bundren is seen as dying, her head bedded on a pile of pillows from which she can survey her eldest son Cash working on her coffin. The whole family awaits the death of the mother in a kind of suspense, each of them mistrusting the others. Anse Bundren, the father, cherishes the fantasy of using the funeral trip to the city to buy himself new teeth after fifteen years of a toothless existence. Dewey Dell, the daughter who is pregnant from a secret love affair, waits for her mother's death in order to "buy" an abortion in the city. She is so absorbed by her unwanted pregnancy that she can experience the grief for her mother only in a hysterical fit "beside herself," throwing herself onto the emaciated body of the mother which is said to resemble "a bundle of rotten sticks" (p. 37). In fact, she literally buries that body under her own sensual corporeality. In this image mother and daughter melt into a dark version of a grotesque "pregnant death," with the only difference that this image does not, like the carnivalesque "pregnant death," exhibit life in death but instead inverts the process by drawing the unborn life into death. Thus, the image even mirrors Addie's philosophy according to which life itself is only a preparation for a long death. The daughter and the father, however, are more successful than the sons in escaping the swallowing presence of the dead body. Dewey Dell, because she does not want, like the others, to get rid of Addie's dead body but of the living body of her unborn child, and Anse, because he focuses all the libidinal energies left in his inertial state of mind onto the aquisition of new teeth and a new wife.

The sons' cathexis of the mother's body has a deeper and more encompassing meaning in the text. Cash, the pragmatist in the family, loses himself in his maniacal hammering on his mother's coffin. The obsessive concentration with which he works toward its absolute perfection reveals his tendency of making a fetish of the coffin—a cathexis which, during the process of events, the other characters begin to share when they experience the coffin as intermingled with the body of the mother. Darl and Jewel, the two antagonistic brothers, steal away from their dying mother for a three-dollar business—only to return with that fateful delay which turns the journey to Jefferson into the carnivalesque spectacle of an endlessly delayed funeral. Thus begins the grotesque life of Addie's dying, dead, and finally decomposing body, the catastrophic odyssey to Jefferson with the coffin in a wagon, followed by an increasing number of buzzards.

Addie herself has prepared the staging of the carnivalesque funeral procession in an act of aggressive distancing from her family, following her unwanted pregnancy with Darl. Thus the journey to Jefferson becomes a last manifestation of Addie's power over the family beyond death.

> Then I found that I had Darl. At first I would not believe it. Then I believed that I would kill Anse. It was as though he had tricked me, hidden within a word like within a paper screen and struck me in the back through it. But then I realized that I had been tricked by words older than Anse or love, and that the same word had tricked Anse too, and that my revenge would be that he would never know I was taking revenge. And when Darl was born I asked Anse to promise to take me back to Jefferson when I died. (pp. 136 ff.)

This motif of an aggressive maternal power endows the activity of the dead body as protagonist of the odyssey to Jefferson with a specific significance. Addie's dead body is turned into a symbol of the negative, overpowering, and devouring mother. It seems as if her body grows into the bodies of her family in order to work on their endangerment or mutilation from the inside. On the concrete level of plot Addie's body affects the others through body experiences and mutilations which afflict them under the extreme conditions of the journey, especially during the various adventurous attempts to save the coffin from water or fire. Cash, for example, who nearly dies after recovering the coffin from the violent river, is finally bedded with a broken leg on his mother's coffin in the wagon. This spectacle is all the more grotesque as Cash has turned the coffin into a fetish of the dead mother. Lying on it in his fever, he now tries to spare it from every stain by compulsively polishing it over and over again in the middle of total chaos. Jewel, who recovers the coffin from the river and, after Darl's arson, also from the burning barn, continues the journey covered with blisters and open wounds. They recall those other wounds which Addie had earlier inflicted on him during the cruel ritualistic whippings with which she wanted to tie him back to her own body acting upon the magic fantasy "that only through the blows of the switch could my blood and their blood flow as one stream" (p. 136). Darl and Vardaman, the two sons who share Addie's oversensitive state of mind, transform Addie's dead body in their fantasies in such an intense way that they live on the verge of psychotic breakdown.

The transformation of the spectacles of the characters' bodies into a carnivalesque spectacle is grounded in different textual strategies which place the grotesque body in relation to the grotesque soul. First of all, there is no real outside perspective of a narrator but a kaleidoscope of inner perspectives which orchestrate closeness and distance and which could be described as a strategy of wandering gazes. The voices of characters outside the family incorporate, of course, a more distanced gaze, one which, as in the case of Samson or Armstid, represents the external perspective of the community on the obscene, insane, and grotesque spectacle of the funeral procession. More importantly, shifting perspectives within the characters' perspectives reveal acts of grief or of defense against grief, the denial of emotions or the breakdown of the boundaries of the self. The spectrum of those shifting perspectives reaches from a decidedly distanced spectator's role, which could be called an "interior outside perspective," to an absolute loss of distance or even to the breakdown of the capacity of semiotic articulation. Especially Darl, whose voice occupies by far the most sections, juggles artistically with shifting perspectives—all the more so as his capacity for extrasensory perception allows him even to describe events which take place in his absence.

This orchestration of distances both draws and transgresses the boundaries of the novel's own process of textual carnivalization. The more distanced the perspective, the more space is granted for a carnivalization that shows the spectacles of body and soul in a grotesque light. Yet the breakdown of distance in the characters' voices simultaneously crumbles all those comic or grotesque effects which stem from the inadequacy of the Bundrens' social behavior. Carnivalization in fact fulfills a distancing function in Faulkner's text, and whenever the characters obliterate that distance through the effects of their inner voices, they also overstep the bounds of a carnivalesque presentation and pull the reader into the interiority of their perspectives. On the other hand, the carnivalizing strategies fulfill their own function in the presentation of the grotesque soul. They could be seen as the aesthetic equivalent of a displaced, denied, or temporarily suspended grief. This, however, does not preclude the possibility that even the carnivalization of death itself achieves a specific work of mourning. But in the latter case it would be a form of sublimation which turns the actual emotion into its opposite. Darl's fit of laughter at the foot of the coffin, for example, emerges on the boundary between a hysterical dissolution of the self and a reflective carnevalesque mocking of death.

The carnivalization of bodies, mainly achieved through that distancing perspective which I have called an "interior outside perspective," belongs to a more general textual strategy which mediates outer and inner events through a precise description of bodily expressions. This form of representation of the body can still be understood in the tradition of an "unconscious realism." [9] If Faulkner's bodies appear fantastic or overdimensional, it is not because a parodistic gaze exposes their weaknesses in grotesque distortions, but because a relentless naturalism approaches the characters through their bodies and reads all deviations of the norm as signs. If Darl says about Peabody "He has pussel-gutted himself eating cold greens. With the rope they will haul him up the path, balloon-like up the sulphurous air" (p. 34), the sharpness of his dissecting observation not only reveals Peabody's personality through the signs of his body but also grasps the whole culture which has produced this body. The characters' and especially Darl's gaze, and, mediated through him, the textual perspective pierce through the surface of codified bodies. Or, more precisely, the gaze that is stylized in the text observes what a gaze on the body which is filtered by cultural habit normally excludes: the uncodifiable, the bizarre, the eccentric, or obscene, in short, all those dimensions which transgress the social body. Concrete bodies are seen with their deformations, exuberances, or mutilations, as, for example, Anse's missing toenails or his toothless face which is explicitly described as a carnivalesque farce:

" 'Why don't you go on to the house, out of the rain?' Cash says. Pa looks at him, his face streaming slowly. It is as though upon a face carved by a savage caricaturist a monstrous burlesque of all bereavement flowed." (p. 63)

Darl's remark about his father's face reveals a more general feature of the ways in which he grasps the world. His observations of the body have become so hypersensitive, obsessive, or even fantastic, that all bodies appear to him as grotesque bodies. In addition, Darl's observation can be read as a comment upon one of the most central devices of the text whose "savage caricatures and monstrous burlesques" focus primarily upon those aspects of the body which escape social codification. This very device is used to engage the paradox of a carnivalesque sublimation of the unsublimated body, a paradox that is mainly expressed in the perspective of Darl, whose gaze tears off the conventional veils of the bodies in order to read them as signs in which the grotesque soul is reflected in its "abject nakedness." Darl turns, in fact, into an opponent of Addie by revealing what she tried to conceal with her relentless pride, her "furious desire to hide that abject nakedness" (p. 39).

The nakedness of the unsublimated body in Faulkner's text exposes the abject of the human condition with a gaze which seems all the more compelling because it is itself implied in the abjection, is itself naked and unprotected. It is not the cold exterior gaze, but the passionate interior gaze which exposes the abject not as other but as the innermost core of the self. The grotesque that appears in the abject is, at the same time, the most human because Faulkner's grotesque bodies emerge in that domain where the archaic life of the biological body maintains itself against all helpless attempts to conceal or sublimate it.

As seen from the outside, during the funeral procession the family gradually loses all sense of reality and piety conventionally required when dealing with the dead body of a close person. In the experience of the characters the mother's body in the coffin loses its organic reality to the extent to which they either abstract from it pragmatically or transform it phantasmatically. It is true that throughout the trip the family continues to pursue the aim to bury Addie's body in Jefferson. However, this aim becomes an empty telos in a system of action governed by different laws. To the extent to which the characters deny the organic reality of the dead body, that is, its decomposition, the body itself turns into the obscene protagonist of the insane odyssey. With its bulkiness, its chemical processes of decomposition, its stench, its obstinate burdensome presence, and the necessity to get it under ground, it ultimately asserts itself against all attempts to ignore it. At the same time, however, the family can only get through all the catastrophes if they succeed in at least partially denying the penetrating reality of the dead body. This denial becomes a condition for their being able to continue the journey against all rules to avoid causing public offence, and unperturbed by the ordeals of nature or the disapproving gaze of the townspeople who see in the funeral procession an undignified and obscene spectacle and who try to flee the smell of the corpse.

This collision of the Bundrens' temporarily autonomous system of order with the social order of the community not only contributes to the carnivalization of the text, but also to the psychological portrayal of the characters. The psychosocial economy of the family [10] is mediated by a system of signs which constitutes itself on the cutting line between two contrary systems of order and which realizes itself by continually transgressing that line on one or the other side: the Bundrens act temporarily from inside a closed system of madness in which the habitual orders and behaviors fall prey to increasing entropy. Even the notion and experience of time is affected. While the decay of the corpse is tied to historical time or, if one likes, to the Bakhtinian "little time," the characters seem to act in an arrested "here and now" which denies the "little time" along with the temporality of the mother's dead body. This denial, however, which, on a practical level, allows for the endless delay of the funeral, reveals, on a psychological level, the insistent but ambivalent tie of the Bundrens to the mother. The sheer incapacity to separate the dead body of the mother from the familial body appears as if an unacknowledged mourning with all its ambivalences has been displaced onto the body. The characters' emotions remain bound to the life of the bodies and can be read as signs of a somatic mourning which replaces the emotional mourning and practices rather the denial of death than a carnivalesque laughter at death. Not only the grim adventures on the journey but even Vardaman's or Jewel's flight into the imaginary life of a phantasmatic maternal body can thus be seen as the spectacle of an unachieved or displaced mourning or of the internalization of the mother in fantastic shapes.

The end of the text, on the other hand, thematizes the externalization of the mother from the family. When, after an eight-days-long journey, the Bundrens' outrageous parade arrives in town, their funeral wagon has a macabre resemblance to a circus wagon —with the only difference that the coffin is not the prop of a clownery but carries the mother's corpse.

> It was Albert told me about the rest of it. He said the wagon stopped in front of Grummet's hardware store, with the ladies all scattering up and down the street with handkerchiefs to their noses ... It must have been like a piece of rotten cheese coming into an ant-hill, in that ramshackle wagon that Albert said folks were scared would fall all to pieces before they could get it out of town, with that home-made box and another fellow with a broken leg lying on a quilt on top of it, and the father and a little boy sitting on the seat and the marshal trying to make them get out of town. (p. 161).

The parade with the coffin reveals the abject dimension of Faulkner's carnivalization. Different from Bakhtin's grotesque bodies who celebrate their corporeality in lustful excesses, Faulkner's bodies are grotesque because life has turned them into grotesque forms or mutilated them. Similarly, Addie Bundren's dead body is grotesque because the decay of the body, death, and decomposition seem obscene to those who do not—like the members of the family—avert or censor their gaze. In fact, the apparent aim of the journey, the funeral, gets lost more and more until the actual burial finally seems like an anticlimactic coda. The funeral procession has been overgrown with such bizarre events that the Bundrens become not only oblivious of the time constraints regarding the burial of a dead body but hardly even think any more of mentioning the mother's funeral in their reports: "Let's take Cash to the doctor first," Darl said. "She'll wait. She's already waited nine days" (p. 186). All cultural or ritual significance of the funeral has vanished. Addie's burial is reduced to the raw act of digging her body under the earth. By the end it gets mentioned only in a subclause in Cash's report about the actual event, Darl's arrest: "But when we got it filled and covered and drove out the gate and turned into the lane where them fellows was waiting, when they came out and come on him, and he jerked back, it was Dewey Dell that was on him before even Jewel could get at him" (p. 188).

The desacralization of the mother's funeral which follows the nine days of humiliating treatment of her dead body reveals how the Bundrens have literally and figuratively done away with the body of the mother. From this perspective their odyssey resembles a macabre ritual of liberation. At the end, after the mother's image is repressed along with her body and her death, the terror is contained and everyday life can return—if only on a brittle surface level. Cash is treated by a doctor, Dewey Dell fails in getting an abortion, Anse buys new teeth with the money for the abortion, stolen from Dewey Dell, and instead of Addie he takes a new Mrs. Bundren back home.

Even this lamentable spectacle of a return to a fragile "normality" is mediated through images of the grotesque body. Cash describes the appearance of the new couple as a carnivalesque parade. Anse, with a guilty "hangdog face" appears with his new teeth in grotesque metamorphosis while his new bride follows him, "a duck-shaped woman all dressed up, with them kind of hard-looking pop eyes" (p. 208), with her "graphophone," the technological object of desire from the big world, which Cash will henceforth invest with nearly the same intense interest he had invested in his mother's coffin.

> Pa was coming along with that kind of daresome and hang-dog look all at once like when he has been up to something he knows ma ain't going to like, carrying a grip in his hand and Jewel says.
> "Who's that?"
> Then we see it wasn't the grip that made him look different; it was his face, and Jewel says, "He got them teeth." It was a fact. It made him look a foot taller, kind of holding his head up, hangdog and proud too, and then we see her behind him, carrying the other grip—a kind of duck-shaped woman all dressed up, with them kind of hard-looking pop eyes like she was daring ere a man to say nothing. (pp. 207 ff.)

This condensed final image of the text is paradigmatic for the way in which Faulkner links the spectacle of the grotesque body with that of the grotesque soul. The parade of grotesque bodies and the phantasmatic cathexis of objects like the new teeth or the new gramophone reveal not only what the characters observe but also what they try to hide from themselves and others. The image shows the new normality of the Bundrens to be a spectacle of repressions and displacements, of guilt and hypocrisy, and at the same time as the expression of a familial economy, in which the women are as exchangeable as the objects which can be invested with fantasies and desires.

The Phantasmatic Body

The strongest expression of the spectacle of the grotesque soul on the familial stage of the Bundrens is found in the fantasies which transform the body of the mother. They belong to the spectacle of the grotesque body, too, with the difference that they don't stage the living body but the internalized body. The latter, in turn, not only founds the internal image of the maternal body, but also the characters' own body image that helps to mark the boundaries of the self.

Jewel's and Vardaman's phantasmatic representations of the
mother as horse or as fish are the best examples. Since Jewel's
displacement of the internal representation of the mother on a
horse is unconscious, it is mediated in the text through Darl's
voice. Darl, who not only has access to the events which take
place in his absence but also to the inner dramas which remain
hidden to the protagonists themselves, tries in an obstinate and
rather ambivalent way to confront Jewel with the death of the
mother. Jewel refuses to answer the reiterated question "Do you
know she is going to die, Jewel?" (p. 34). But when Darl insists
"It's not your horse that's dead, Jewel," he hurls a desparately
angered "Goddam you" (p. 75), at him. If Darl ends this exchange
by simply stating with absolute certitude his inner perception
that "Jewel's mother is a horse" (p. 75), the reader's attention is
drawn to the phantasmatic aspects of Jewel's obsessive fixation
on his horse, a detail which retrospectively overdetermines the
meaning of all scenes with Jewel's horse. The most compelling
image in this context is again attributed to Darl's perception when
he describes how Jewel rides through the flames on the coffin of
his mother. "This time Jewel is riding upon it, clinging to it, until
it crashes down and flings him forward and clear and Mack leaps
forward into a thin smell of scorching meat and slaps at widening
crimson-edged holes that bloom like flowers in his undershirt."
(p. 176)

On a psychological level, all these scenes act out the hidden
oedipal desires in a displaced way. Instead of being made ex-
plicit, the oedipal connection is grasped where it is unconsciously acted out: on the stage of inner dramas and through
displaced images and objects. This process overdetermines the
imagery of the whole text. The visuality of the interior voices
functions not only as a purely poetic device. Visual metaphors
correspond, at the same time, to concrete fantasies and allow thus
for a poetic stylization of a character's unconscious.

In addition, the phantasms of the body form part of the dynamic of textual carnivalization. This occurs not only at the level
of an analogy between these phantasms and the images of the
grotesque body, but is also expressed in how the characters act
on the basis of those phantasms in their social world. The Bun-

drens' social behavior during their funeral trip to Jefferson draws its carnivalesque effects from a collision of the social order with the order of the unconscious. Vardaman's dealing with the body of the fish shows the uncannily grotesque dimensions of this collision because it results in the actual mutilation of the dead body of the mother. Vardaman condenses the dead maternal body with the body of a fish which he cuts up and carries, full of blood, into the house in order to have Dewey Dell cook and serve it to the whole family. Thus Vardaman takes part in a totemistic familial meal at which the dead body of the mother which he has himself cut up is devoured. Regarding the distribution of power in the family, it is relevant that the totemistic meal is not a patriarchal but a matriarchal one where the body of the archaic "great mother" is incorporated. But like the patriarchal totemistic meal, the matriarchal one, too, is an excess, one of archaic guilt and of an affirmation of immortality.[11] One could even say that on the unconscious scene of the phantasmatic body, Vardaman stages the maternal archaic-oedipal variation of the Freudian totem meal.

In his dispersed and fragmented monologues, Vardaman dissolves the boundaries of Addie's body in order to recreate it in a world in which I and Not-I, inner and outer space, human and animal body are melted together to form an undifferentiated whole. At times, Vardaman's fantasized mother leaves her dying body and reemerges in new bodies like that of a rabbit, of a horse, or of a fish. At one time, Vardaman sees the old shell of her body inhabited by an other, strange women. Then he can conclude that it is not the mother who is nailed into Cash's coffin but the other woman. The feverishly shifting transformations of the moldable body of the mother ward off the terror of her death:

> It was not her. I was there, looking. I saw. I thought it was her, but it was not. It was not my mother. She went away when the other one laid down in her bed and drew the quilt up. (p. 54)

> And so if Cash nails the box up, she is not a rabbit. And so if she is not a rabbit I couldn't breathe in the crib and Cash is going to nail it up. And so if she lets him it is not

her. I know. I was there. I saw it when it did not be her. I
saw. They think it is and Cash is going to nail it up.

It was not her because it was lying right yonder in the
dirt. And now it's all chopped up. I chopped it up. It's lying
in the kitchen in the bleeding pan, waiting to be cooked and
et. Then it wasn't and she was, and now it is and she wasn't.
And tomorrow it will be cooked and et and she will be him
and pa and Cash and Dewey Dell and there won't be anything in the box and so she can breathe. (p. 55).

Vardaman's fantastic metamorphosis of his mother's dead body
aims at preserving the internal image of the mother. However, the
freeing of the mother from her bodily existence, symbolized in
the cutting up of the fish body, is only partially successful. Fantasies that Addie slips into other bodies, including the bodies of
her own family, cannot totally repress the obstinate presence of
the real dead body in Cash's coffin. While, from an outside perspective, the phantasmatic bodies create a conflictive polarity
with the "real" dead body, on a textual level and, correspondingly, on the level of the fictional world of the characters, this
polarity is effaced along with the boundaries between their conscious social and their unconscious phantasmatic perceptions.
Even the fact that after the totemistic fish meal Vardaman holds
the mother to be in the bodies of the other family members does
not prevent him from poking holes into the lid of the coffin and
thereby mutilating the face of his dead mother. This desparate act
reveals the complex contradictions of Vardaman's imaginary world
along with a subliminal aggressivity toward the dead mother.
Similar to the cutting up of the fish, the poking of holes into the
coffin releases the mother from her dead body into other bodies:

But Jewel's mother is a horse. My mother is a fish. Darl says
that when we come to the water again I might see her and
Dewey Dell said, She's in the box; how could she have got
out? She got through the holes I bored, into the water I said,
and when we come to the water again I am going to see her.
My mother is not in the box. My mother does not smell like
that. My mother is a fish. (p. 155)

The very same act can achieve both: a liberation from death
and a mutilation. The mutilation, however, can only take place

in conjunction with a fantasy of liberation. By cutting up the fish as well as by boring holes into the coffin Vardaman acts out phantasms of the fragmented body.[12] Both actions show how Vardaman attempts to ground his threatened sense of self in a phantasmatic attachment to the dead body of the mother. By condensing it with other bodies, by transforming and mutilating it, or by having it devoured, Vardaman turns the body of the mother into the space where he enacts the drama of his own internalized mother.

The Phantasmatic Body as Stage for the Grotesque Soul

Faulkner's theme of the phantasmatic body gains a specific relevance in the context of carnivalesque literature. By staging a spectacle of the phantasmatic body, the text also grasps "the spectacle of the grotesque soul." On the one hand, the *grotesque* bodies in Faulkner's text are used to express psychic or social deformations of the characters. On the other hand, however, the *phantasmatic* bodies can be read as the unconscious subtext of the familial drama. The inner dramas of the characters are not only reflected in their actual body language and through their grotesque bodies, but also in the imagery of the internalized bodies which they use as props.

Vardaman's phantasm of the mother as fish, for example, reveals the affinity of the grotesque body in carnivalesque literature to the psychological phantasms of the fragmented body. Since body phantasms are produced unconsciously they can be understood as a special expression of the unsublimated body. Vardaman's unsublimated body phantasms express the abject ground of the carnivalesque images of the grotesque body. These images, however, have already domesticated the abject whereas Vardaman's phantasms retain it in its latent horror. What appears as raw material in the phantasms of the fragmented body is formed and molded in the literary images of the grotesque body. These images are ambivalent: it is true that the grotesque body in carnivalesque literature exposes that which tries to transgress, protrude from, or destroy the boundaries of the body, including death as the most extreme case. The comic aspect of the images of the grotesque body, however, integrates and neutralizes the abject formally. The aesthetics of the "other body" is subversive only insofar as it is opposed to the official body images of a specific culture. This subversion, however, reaches its limits where those bodies are exposed as the "other body," that is, where they are still seen as deviant from the cultural norms.

Vardaman's raw phantasms of the fragmented body undermine this dynamic between a cultural norm and a deviant carnivalesque image. Instead of sublimating the terror of the other body in a carnivalesque grotesque, Vardaman's phantasms bring the terror to the surface of the literary presentation. This device goes to the core of Faulkner's way of radicalizing grotesque images of the body. Though inspired by the literary tradition of grotesque realism and the carnivalization of the grotesque body, *As I Lay Dying* goes beyond the specific kind of aesthetic sublimation which founds that tradition. While carnivalesque literature in the narrow sense presents the grotesque body from an outside perspective, Faulkner shifts the presentation into the consciousness or even the unconscious of literary characters. For them, the dead body of the mother turns factually into a grotesque body because they can neither face the terror of the mother's death nor the reality of her decaying body. A defense against death is thus at work in both cases. But while the participants in carnival see the grotesque body, and mediated through it death, from the outside and while they create distance with their laughter at death, the Bundrens produce the grotesque body themselves, be it through their endlessly delaying Addie's funeral or be it through Vardaman's performing his imaginary transformations of Addie's body, followed by its real mutilation. Instead of distancing the dead body in a carnivalesque ritual, the Bundrens are overpowered by the insistence of the dead body with its decay, its stench, or even the pure fact that it is always there because they are unable to bury it.

In the context of this theme of the phantasmatic body as scene for the grotesque soul, Darl's voice gains a special function. It is characterized by a high level of self-reflexivity and by his artful shifting of distances. These features culminate at a breaking point when Darl splits into two personalities and talks in an interior monologue about the "other Darl" who has been taken to an insane asylum in Jackson. Darl's arrest is a consequence of his putting fire to the barn with the mother's coffin. With this ambivalent act he not only wanted to terminate the undignified situation with the rotting corpse but also to break out of the Bundren's closed system of collective madness. Darl's desparate act fails because of Jewel's intervention, and the relative restabilization of the familial system is achieved at the price of Darl's exclusion. To confine Darl, whom Addie herself had never accepted and with whose birth she planned her dying, to an insane asylum is, within the familial system, an act supposed to guarantee the family's normality. At the same time, Darl's expulsion is like a belated affirmation of Addie's secret rejection. From the perspective of the familial system, however, both Darl and Addie are excluded at the end because the hospitalization of Darl is concommitant with Addie's burial. Just as Addie exerts more and more power as a dead character and Darl exerts more and more power as a dominant voice they become more and more removed from the family and ultimately forgotten. Darl's expulsion is thus a symbolic act which stands for and covers up the more important one: the final expulsion of Addie from the familial system and the liberation from the terror of her devouring dead body. From his outside perspective, Darl is now able to perceive the familial madness as a carnivalesque spectacle in which all the family members played their part. "Beside himself," he breaks into an unbounded archaic laughter which, as the only semiotic sign available to him grasps the situation somatically. This laughter is comic and tragic at the same time, but it is not parodistic because it includes himself without any distance. It is not cathartic either because it does not provide relief. The others misunderstand this archaic laughter in stupified horror, whereas Darl finally smothers it in an animalistic foaming. In his last monologue, in which he sees and describes himself as other, he hurls an endlessly desperate "yes" against the system of denial and repression which founds the family's madness.

"What are you laughing at?" I said.
"Yes yes yes yes yes." (p. 202)

Our brother Darl in a cage in Jackson where, his grimed hands lying light in the quiet interstices, looking out he foams.
"Yes yes yes yes yes yes yes yes." (p. 202)

As much as Darl's actions fail in the social context of his fictional world, as effective they become in counterbalancing the other perspectives. Cash voices a notion of the fragile boundaries between madness and sanity, a fragility which marks the whole text and gives the theme of the grotesque soul its sociocritical dimension: "But I ain't so sho that ere a man has the right to say what is crazy and what ain't. It's like there was a fellow in every man that's done a-past the sanity or insanity, that watches the sane and the insane doings of that man with the same horror and the same astonishment" (p. 189).

In the splitting from himself through an outside perspective, Darl stages himself on the scene of the two colliding systems of order which mark the text and found its carnivalesque dimension. Darl's performance goes beyond a carnivalesque self parody because it plays on different levels at once and synthesizes his capacity to dwell simultaneously at different places and in different minds. The ambivalence underlying his arson, for example, can be understood fully only when one considers it as an action on two levels simultaneously: on the level of a social order where Darl, recognizing the obsolescence of the funeral procession, wants to end it violently, and on the level of the temporarily effective inner order of the family's collective madness, where Darl sees the events according to the inner logic of the familial economy. On this level, the spectacle stages the Bundrens as "grotesque souls." Addie Bundren's dead body is phantasmatically invested or transformed according to each protagonist's position and status in the familial system. In this process her body assumes the quasimythical dimensions of the archetypal "great mother," in whose presence the protagonists of the familial drama regress to a level of archaic emotions.

On that level, Darl reacts with his arson against the devouring

"Great Mother" who uses even her decaying body to assert her power beyond death. Intuitively Darl thus also grasps the motif of revenge with which Addie had planned her funeral in Jefferson long ago. Darl's arson was supposed to mark both the real and the imaginary mother's death as an annihilation, as a transformation of her body into ashes, and as an expulsion from the center of the family. At the same time, he takes revenge for Addie's refusal to ever admit him to that center. The fact that it is Jewel, Addie's favorite, who recovers the coffin from the flames, adds to the overdetermination of the whole scene.

It is important to understand why Darl acts directly and un-mediatedly against the imaginary mother while the other sons transform her body phantasmatically: Cash with fetishizing the coffin, Jewel with shifting the inner representation of the mother on a horse, and Vardaman with his phantasm of a fish-mother. Darl is the only son who consciously renounces any phantasmatic representation of the mother. Her death is no more representable for him than its denial. With his radical insistence on the empiri-cal dead body, however, he tries to abandon any image that could provide an inner representation of his mother. She is for him neither in a fantasized shape nor in her dead body. Darl literally obliterates her existence because he does not create any internal image of the dead mother.

> "Then what is your ma, Darl?" I said.
> "I haven't got ere one," Darl said. "Because if I had one,
> it is *was*. And if it was, it can't be *is*. Can it?"
> "No," I said.
> "Then I am not," Darl said. "Am I?" (p. 79)

Both Vardaman's or Jewel's fantasies of a horse or a fish and Darl's refusal to create an inner representation of the dead mother disconnect the internal mother from her dead body. Both atti-tudes turn the dead body into the Other of the mother. But Darl's ambivalent game with the phrase "if I had one" and the surpris-ing conclusion "Then I am not" reveals that his refusal to create an inner representation of the mother is itself overdetermined. If Darl "is not" because the mother is not, then this must not only be understood in the simple sense that *her* death annihilates *him*.

On a more complex level, Darl also plays with the fact that his mother has never given birth to him completely in the sense of a psychological birth which presupposes the recognition and acceptance of a child. In that respect, his mother was a phantom for him even during her lifetime, an everpresent absence. In a way she only gains an uncanny presence through her death. The dead body stands for the mother who refuses him an existence. Like an uncanny transitional object which extorts a never lived symbiosis in death, the dead body simultaneously is and is not the mother. To expose this body to the flames in order to free himself from its tyranny would seem like a cathartic self-creation from her ashes. When this fails, Darl splits himself into the one who, like a sacrificial victim, takes over the role of madness, and the one who now perceives himself from the outside with his old clairvoyance.

The privileging of Darl's perspective breaks the carnivalesque form of the text in multiple ways. For Darl, the spectacle of the grotesque body cannot be separated from the spectacle of the grotesque soul because he reads the others and speaks himself in the language of the body. He had developed his own "somatic semiotic" on the basis of which he not only understands and regulates "the exchanges between body and world, but also those between inner and outer world, I and we, identity and alterity."[13] Darl's "somatic semiotics," however, appears like the inverse of Bakhtin's because it does not celebrate the joyful eccentricity of the body which ecstatically overflows the world with its inside or with the ecstatic laughter of the grotesque soul. Darl's laughter is an act of destitution. Behind the carnivalesque masks of socially coded bodies it grasps the grotesque bodies and souls in their "abject nakedness." Darl's gaze desublimates the bodies for the gaze of the reader. Desublimated bodies, however, appear as grotesque because they violate the internalized social gaze on the body. At the same time, and therein lies the paradox, desublimated bodies are, in the strict sense, not representable in a text without gaining a secondary form of sublimation. Addie Bundren's rotting corpse, for example, affects the reader always on two levels. Darl's perspective transmits the horror both of concrete organic decay and of the raw phantasms of the body which work in the characters' unconscious beyond sublimation. His perspective evokes thus the two different forms which the unsublimated body can assume: the organic and the phantasmatic embodiment. As a literary character who carries a specific textual perspective, Darl also creates an aesthetically sublimated body of the mother which can be situated on the boundary between the literary tradition of a carnivalesque presentation of the grotesque body and a verbal "theater of cruelty," which tries to evoke the horror of the unsublimated body within aesthetic sublimation.

Forms of Sublimation in the Carnivalesque Text

The paradox of an aesthetic presentation of the unsublimated body determines the status of the grotesque body in Faulkner's text. Instead of the deliberate distortions and exaggerations of universalized bodies in an archaic ritual of carnival, Faulkner's "realism" externalizes the bizarre performances of the unsublimated or desublimated body. In this context, it is decisive that the grotesque body in the center of the text is the body of the mother. This body of the mother is the cultural body which forms the basis not only for the body- and self-images of the children, but also for the first forms of symbolizing the female realm. The prohibitions and taboos, the mysteries and mythologies which turn the body of the mother into a symbolic object for the cultural formation of subjects require ever new forms of sublimation which control the archaic desire directed toward this body.

The mother's body is both the real and the imaginary object of that primal symbiotic stage which Addie, in her monologue, opposes to the empty world of false words. It is precisely because the maternal body dominates the primordial realm of archaic emotions that it has to be symbolized and acculturated in an endless chain of imaginary displacements and transformations. The culturally internalized maternal body which differs from, doubles, replaces, or obliterates the equally cultural body of the "real" mother is the phantasmatic body of the Great Mother. As an imaginary space where the most archaic desire coincides with the most abject horror, this imaginary body not only creates the Other of the real body of the mother but Otherness as such.

The rotting corpse of the mother radicalizes the horror of the phantasmatic Great Mother. As I Lay Dying sublimates this horror by exposing the old myth and making it the object of a potentially transforming aesthetic experience. Without the relieving function of a literary carnivalization, the rotting, smelling, and mutilated body of the dead mother in Faulkner's text would be the apotheosis of abject horror. It is significant for the economy of an oedipal family structure[14] that it is the sons who evoke the body of the mother in their monologues by describing how they exert real or fantasized violence toward it. In these monologues Addie's dead body is, for her sons, less a symbol for the death of the mother than an incorporation of the "other," the archaic "great mother."

The deeper power of Addie Bundren's dead body lies here. The power bestowed on it in the minds and emotions of the other characters even makes it appear as if Addie were able to use her dead body in order to recreate her primordial fixation to the sons as a grotesque farce because her dead body can draw them into a regressive fusion. For the sons, the dead body of the mother is full of resonances of the devouring and overpowering aspects of this fusion, but also full of resonances of the violence of separation from the maternal body. It is the culturally "significant" body of the mother, the untouchable, impossible, absent, tabooized body that dies by giving birth in death to its negative Other: a raw, dead female body who, with the drama of its decomposition and the imaginary horror which it inspires, threatens the life, the body, and the self-boundaries of those to whom it has given birth. This is why the decomposing body of the mother ceases more and more to represent the dead mother in order to represent instead the deadly female principle of the negative archaic mother, the mother who devours her children, or death that infects life.

By presenting a carnivalesque epos of this cultural body of the negative "great mother," Faulkner's text creates a form of sublimation of the abject which reactualizes an archetypal fantasy of the female in a modernist form. In the fight about and with the dead maternal body, in its imaginary transformations and its real mutilations, the sons react, among other things, against their fear of the archaic mother. The decidedly flat ending of the text shows the rotten corpse and along with it the dead mother finally defeated, neutralized, and buried. The abject is under control; everyday life regains its force. The weird normality of the Bundrens at the end of the novel, however, shows the inseparable link between that normality and the forceful expulsion of the abject from the social realm. From this perspective, the abject gains the status of a "cultural unconscious" which Faulkner's text enacts in the creation of a phantasmatically overdetermined fictional world.

For the reader, of course, this control of the abject is effective from the very beginning and throughout the whole text, for the text as a whole sublimates the archaic mother as a grotesque character. There is a certain irony in this: the text evokes a phantasmatic cathexis of bodies by penetrating through the skin of cultural notions of the body and by presenting the unsublimated or desublimated body. At the same time, however, the neutralizing fictional presentation of the sublimated body has to be understood as a sublimation of the archaic mother which also allows the reader to act out, in the reading process, ambivalences toward this internalized image of the mother. The text thus plays the role of a third party which, according to Julia Kristeva's conception of the abject, helps to carry through the fight against the archaic mother. "In such close combat, the symbolic light that a third party, eventually the father, can contribute helps the future subject, the more so if it happens to be endowed with a robust supply of drive energy, in pursuing a reluctant struggle against what, having been the mother, will turn into an abject.[15]

By carnivalizing the grotesque dead body of the mother, Faulkner's text provides a cultural form of sublimating the dead maternal body. The archaic fight for and with that body recreates and exposes the taboos, fears, and ambivalences which form the basis of the mother's cultural and phantasmatic body. This recreation, in turn, mediates a specific cultural sublimation of the maternal body as an aesthetic experience which is open to interpretation and thus ultimately works toward a cultural change of the underlying patterns.

Carnivalesque Epos and Theater of Cruelty

Carnival and death, involuntary comedy and displaced mourning, the real drama and the phantasmatic spectacle of death which
doubles the real drama—those are the emotional poles of tension
in Faulkner's text, which, through their interaction, guide the
reader's response. The history of reception reveals a striking tendency to solve this tension through an isolation of both realms.
The question if *As I Lay Dying* should be read as grotesque farce
or as heroic epos misses the point because both tendencies are
inseparable in the text and fulfill their function only in their
fusion. This tension determines the atmosphere of the textual
world as much as the status of the grotesque bodies.

The epic structure of the long funeral procession is as evident
as its carnivalization. Since Valéry Larbaud, in his preface to the
French edition of the novel, has emphasized affinities with the
funeral procession of the Homeric queen,[16] the epic character has
over and again been emphasized by critics. The epos, more precisely, the eleventh book of Homer's *Odyssey*, also provides the
source for Faulkner's title: "As I lay dying the woman with the
dog's eyes would not close my eyelids for me as I descended into
Hades."[17] But the novel gains its specific relevance as a narrative
text of the twentieth century through the explosion of the epic
frame, that is, through the carnivalization and theatricalization of
the epic material. In her analysis of Bakhtin's theory of carnivalesque literature, Julia Kristeva argues that the epic structure is
monological, dominated by the totalizing perspective of a narrator who articulates the specific in the general. The carnivalesque
principle, on the other hand, is seen as dialogical, polyphonous,
dionysian, and antirationalistic.[18] According to Kristeva, carnivalesque literature draws upon the language of the body and the
language of dreams, creating homologies between linguistic structures and structures of desire.

If one assumes with Bakhtin and Kristeva that the epic and the
carnivalesque are the two basic currents which form the tradition
of narrative, then one would argue that Faulkner's text joins these
tow currents in one flow. The eruptive force of the carnivalesque
explodes the epos from within, drawing it into an archaic swirl

bordering on the fantastic and phantasmatic, and flooding the boundaries which ideally guarantee the identity, substance, causality, and definiteness of the epic. The voices of Faulkner's characters show all the basic features of the carnivalesque. The characters think analogically and inclusively, their perspectives relativize each other if not themselves, their fantasies and phantasmatic actions are excessive and transgressive. The epic structure remains there as a wrapping unable to contain what protrudes from inside—not unlike the grotesque bodies in carnivalesque literature, or Addie's dead body, can or do no longer want to contain what protrudes from them.

The closeness of Faulkner's carnivalesque voices to the body and the dream, their primordiality and visuality, their performance as a glee of inner dialogues and monologues creates another closeness, too, which is as important to the status of the text as the carnivalization itself. It is the closeness to the theater. It was again Larbaud who first stressed the affinities of *As I Lay Dying* to the theater. Carnival and theater both have their roots in the archaic forms of festival. The roots of representation itself reach back to an originary theater without representation from which the tradition of theater has inherited an insistent longing to efface the traces of representation.[19] A similar longing is voiced in Addie's monologue, both in her deep mistrust of language and in the theater of cruelty which she stages again and again in her violent rituals with the children.

Addie's monologue, inserted after two thirds of the novel, polarizes the world of the text. Her voice provides a central perspective because it has a privileged position in the polyphony of voices. While the other monologues direct their perspective toward Addie's dying, her death, and the drama of her dead body, the focus of Addie's monologue lies on her life and the roots of her planned death in this life. Addie is the only one who projects her life as a story with a narrative structure. This is as important for the status of her monologue as for the image that one gains of Addie from the totality of monologues. While the other monologues complement, relativize, or contradict each other and add to an oscillatingly overdetermined and principally open, continuable whole, Addie's inner perspective reaches from a different level into the perspectives of the other characters. The latter carry strikingly few memories of Addie. The overwhelming reality of Addie's dead body overshadows the memories of her life. Instead of consciously controlled memories, the stream of consciousness brings rather unconscious representations and fantasies of the mother to the surface. Those images, however, with their archaic shapes, their elementary passions, and their uncensored unconventionality, are, in a way, closer to Addie's self-image as conscious memories could ever be, closer even than the form of expression used in her own monologue, because they penetrate into those archaic domains which are more primary but also more abject than the world of verbal shapes which Addie rejects as false and alien.

The world which Addie opposes to the world of verbal shapes is characterized by an archaic solitude and by the desire for a symbiotic primordial unity in which the sheer separation of bodies is already a torture. In violent rituals she injures the children's bodies in order to recreate forcibly an aggressive form of primary undifferentiation. Her passionate rejection of the empty speech of coded words makes her regress to a form of body language which does not express itself through gestures but instead marks the body of the other directly. Addie rejects language in its function of separation and differentiation because she sees it as founding the separation of bodies. This attitude is rooted in a romantic idealization of the archaic and the primordial. For Addie, language founds the death of body and soul by substituting actions through empty sounds and by turning people like Anse into echos of their words. The sadistic rituals with the children are Addie's privately staged "theater of cruelty" in the strong Artaudian sense of a theater which rebels against representation. As the simple act of naming is already too much for Addie, she tries in the dark of the night to regain the lost unity with her children by a repudiation of their names: "And then I would think *Cash* and *Darl* that way until their names would die and solidify into a shape and then fade away, I would say, All right. It doesn't matter. It doesn't matter what they call them" (p. 137). With the same passion with which Addie dreams of abandoning herself to the wordlessness of nature and the body, she refuses herself to the symbolic order of the world with its words, separate bodies, sublimated socialities, and intimacies.

And yet, in her social world, Addie, the former schoolteacher, is far from living the form of archaic femininity which she cherishes in her fantasies. Her monologue, self-reflexive and self-confident, reveals a relatively high rhetorical articulation. Her cutting criticism of the mindless empty world of Anses and Tulls is a cogent social criticism, voiced in "inner words" which cannot live the primordial dream but only conjure it verbally. Yet it is precisely in the face of the inner contradiction in Addie, which she herself consciously lives and articulates, that the funeral procession gains its deeper significance not only for the psychology of the Bundrens but also for the aesthetic status of Faulkner's text.

Addie's voicing her passionate desire for the archaic and primordial as a sharply self-reflexive and verbally articulated criticism of language opens up a perspective on two polar forms of expression which the text constantly plays off against each other: the empty speech of characters like Anse Bundren, Cora Tull, or the minister Whitfield on the one hand, and the archaic language of the body or of phantasms which expresses itself in Addie's whippings of the children, in Vardaman's phantasmatic fragmentation of the body of the fish/mother, or even in Cash's and Jewel's forgetfulness of the body in pain. Those forms of bodily expression are, of course, themselves voiced verbally and thematized on the abstract level of literary articulation. The text itself as a form of literary speech stages these forms of bodily expression in the polyphony of different voices as a performance on the boundaries of carnival and verbal theater of cruelty.

The resonance of Artaud's "theater of cruelty" in Faulkner's text has not remained unnoticed in its history of reception. Five years after the publication of the novel, none other than Jean-Louis Barrault, who celebrated Faulkner as one of the writers with the greatest influence on his generation, staged the text's first theatrical adaptation inspired by Artaud. Based on the language of the body, *Autour d'une mère* unfolded itself as a "drama in its primitive stage,"[20] as a form of pantomime around the grotesque body of the dead and totemistic mother who, with a mask and an oversized black wig, owns the only voice in the text and speaks two lyrical monologues. Artaud himself, fascinated by Faulkner's text and Barrault's adaptation, mentions them in his writings as an attempt to revitalize drama in its magic and ritual forms.

The question is, then, what the metaphor of a "theater of cruelty" or, more precisely, a carnivalesque theater of cruelty means when used to characterize a narrative text—a text which has only language available as a means of expression, while Artaud has conceived his "theater of cruelty" against the "tyranny of the word?" "The signifier is the death of the festival," writes Derrida in his analysis of Rousseau in *Of Grammatology*.[21] The word sublimates the greed for living, the cosmic relentlessness, the utter necessity, and the painful corporeality for which Artaud chooses the metaphor of cruelty.[22] Artaud problematizes the relationship of language to the body or, more precisely, the separation of language from the body, with the aim to subvert the power of language on the theatrical stage. Faulkner, on the other hand, stages the language of the body within poetic language and on the basis of a narrative structure. The language of the characters is centered in the body and expresses itself over and again as a breakdown of the semiotic. The characters read themselves and their world because they know how to read bodies—their own, the bodies of others, and the bodies of the objects in their world.

This is also the context in which I understand a problem that has been discussed so insistently in Faulkner criticism, namely, that the verbal articulateness of the characters by far exceeds the likely capacity of articulation in persons of a similar social background. This is only a problem if one reads the monologues as realistic inner monologues. It seems more appropriate, however, to read the monologues partly as poetic abstractions of inner experiences. The monologues are understood, then, as the linguistic equivalents for something that is usually not articulated or cannot be articulated in a social context but which expresses itself socially in the drama of the body, especially the drama of the unsublimated and uncivilized, the undomesticated and uncodable body which violates the boundaries of social conventions and taboos. Like Artaud in his "theater of cruelty," Faulkner, too, grasps the body in extreme situations such as death or decay, in situations that is, in which they are threatened by desublimation and which releases unconscious energies and fantasies in those who assist the drama of those bodies. This is why the carnivalesque spectacle in Faulkner unfolds itself toward its vanishing point in a theater of cruelty. The carnivalesque in Faulkner's text is more archaic, undomesticated, and "cruel" than the "sublimated carnival" of parodistic or satirical carnival rituals or, for that matter, of carnivalesque language games. Like Darl's laughter, the laughter provoked by Faulkner's text, is not parodistic but archaic, murderous, and dead serious. It does not ridicule the civilized and coded body in parodistic exaggerations; it is rather the expression of the unsublimated, the "other" body in the face of death. The fact that Faulkner stages this "theater of cruelty" as a purely verbal theater of inner voices even overcomes partially the antagonistic polarization of language and archaic desire which Artaud's conception presupposes. Faulkner's text shows how the unconscious already expresses itself in images of the grotesque body which his protagonists transform into phantasmatically staged "stories." The drama of the grotesque body and the grotesque soul appears in this process as an undividable unity.

Endnotes

1. William Faulkner, *As I Lay Dying* (Harmondsworth: Penguin, 1963). All future references are to this edition and are cited in my text. An earlier version of this article in German appeared in Walter Haug and Rainer Warning, eds., *Das Fest in der Literatur*, Poetik und Hermeneutik XIV, (Munich: Fink Verlag, 1989).

2. I use the term phantasmatic in the psychoanalytic sense of an unconscious fantasy that underlies and partly determines the experience and actions of a person or, in this case, a literary character. The phantasmatic body is an internalized image of the body where the body is transformed according to the cathexis of the person in question. In extreme cases this phantasmatic body can be experienced as real and replace the image of the organic body.

3. For the references to Bakhtin's theory of carnivalesque literature and his conception of the grotesque body see Mikhail Bakhtin, *Rabelais and His World*, Helene Iswolsky, tr. (Bloomington: Indiana University Press, 1984); *The Dialogic Imagination*, Michael Holquist, ed.; Caryl Emerson and Michael Holquist, trs. (Austin: University of Texas Press, 1981); *Speech Genres and Other Late Essays*, Caryl Emerson and Michael Holquist, eds., Vern W. McGee, tr. (Austin: University of Texas Press, 1986).

4. See Erich Neumann, *The Great Mother: An Analysis of the Archetype*, Ralph Manheim, tr. (Princeton University Press, 1970).

5. I owe the analysis of the "exquisite cadaver" to Judith Pike, "The Spectacle of the Heroine's Death," dissertation, University of California, Irvine, 1988.

6. For a more detailed analysis of intertextuality in Faulkner's novels, see John T. Matthews, *The Play of Faulkner's Language* (Ithaca: Cornell University Press, 1982); Michel Gresset and Noel Polk, *Intertextuality in Faulkner* (Jackson: University of Mississippi Press, 1985).

7. On the concept of the "grotesque soul," see Renate Lachmann, "Die Schwellensituation. Skandal und Fest bei Dostoevskij," in Walter Haug and Rainer Warning, eds., *Das Fest in der Literatur*, pp. 322–325.

8. The history of the reception of Faulkner's *As I Lay Dying* shows how unsettling these shifting inner perspectives and the loss of distance is for critics who try to determine the presence of an authoritative perspective. An interesting example is Eric Sundquist's attempt to grasp Faulkner's own presence in the text which, ironically, he ends up locating in the hovering buzzards. See Eric J. Sundquist, *Faulkner: The House Divided* (Baltimore: Johns Hopkins University Press, 1983).

9. See Gabriele Schwab, *Entgrenzungen und Entgrenzungsmythen. Zur Subjektivitaet im modernen Roman* (Stuttgart: Franz Steiner Verlag, 1987), pp. 63–75, on the concept of "unconscious realism."

10. The term "economy" in this context condenses the Freudian notion of the economy of the psychic apparatus with the notion of a cultural economy of a system of signs with exchange value.

11. On the relevance of the totem feast see Sigmund Freud, *Totem and Taboo*, A. A. Brill, tr. (New York: Vintage Books, 1918). See also Renate Lachmann's article "Die Schwellensituation," as well as Bakhtin's introduction to *Rabelais and His World*.

12. See Jacques Lacan, "The Mirror Stage," in *Ecrits*, Alan Sheridan, tr. (New York: Norton, 1977), pp. 4–5, on the phantasm of the fragmented body. For a Lacanian analysis of *As I Lay Dying*, see also Wesley Morris, "The Irrepressible Real: Jacques Lacan and Poststructuralism," in Ira Konigsberg, ed., *American Criticism in the Poststructuralist Age* (Ann Arbor: University of Michigan Press, 1981), pp. 116–134. Morris, however, does not discuss Lacan's concept of phantasms of the body, but rather the relationship between the real, the symbolic, and the imaginary.

13. For a discussion of the "somatic semiotic," see Renate Lachmann, "Die Schwellensituation," and Mikhail Bakhtin's introduction to *Rabelais and His World*.

14. See John T. Irwin, *Doubling and Incest/Repetition and Revenge: A Speculative Reading of Faulkner* (Baltimore: John Hopkins University Press, 1975) for a psychoanalytic reading of oedipal motifs in Faulkner's work.

15. Julia Kristeva, *Powers of Horror: An Essay on Abjection*, Leon S. Roudiez, tr. (New York: Columbia University Press, 1982).

16. Valéry Larbaud, "Preface," to *Tandis que j'agonise* (Paris: Gallimard, 1934), p. i.

17. See Mary Jane Dickerson, "*As I Lay Dying* and *The Waste Land*: Some Relationships," in Diane L. Cox, ed., *William Faulkner's As I Lay Dying: A Critical Casebook* (New York: Garland, 1985), p. 189.

18. See Julia Kristeva's comparison of the carnivalistic with the epic in *Semeiotike: Recherches pour une semanalyse* (Paris: Gallimard, 1969), pp. 143–173.

19. See Jacques Derrida. "The Theater of Cruelty and the Closure of Representation," in *Writing and Difference*, Alan Bass, tr. (Chicago: University of Chicago Press, 1978), pp. 232–250; Gabriele Schwab, "Die Provokation Artauds oder Grenze der Repraesentation und Sprachkrise im modernen Theater," in *Samuel Becketts Endspiel mit der Subjektivitaet. Entwurf einer Psychoaesthetik des modernen Theaters* (Stuttgart: Metzler Verlag, 1981), pp. 14–35.

20. Jean-Louis Barrault, *Reflections on the Theatre*, Barbara Wall, tr. (London: Rockliff, 1951).

21. See Jacques Derrida, *Of Grammatology*, Gayatri Chakravorty Spivak, tr. (Baltimore: Johns Hopkins University Press, 1976).

22. See Antonin Artaud, *The Theater and its Double*, Mary Caroline Richards, tr. (New York: Grove Press, 1958).

10

ETHIOPIA AS A LOST IMAGINARY SPACE: THE ROLE OF ETHIOPIAN JEWISH WOMEN IN PRODUCING THE ETHNIC IDENTITY OF THEIR IMMIGRANT GROUP IN ISRAEL
Tsili Doleve-Gandelman

IMMIGRATION IS a story of change. It is a story of new opportunities, the transformation of old structures, the creation of new ethnic identities out of new social boundaries, the longing for the country of origin—what has now become an imaginary space. Yet, while every immigrant undergoes these changes, the experience differs according to age and gender.

The following is an attempt to describe some of the "woman's perspectives" in the integration of a specific immigrant group into Israel—the Jews of Ethiopia, also known as the Beta Israel or the Falashas,[1] who number about 15,000, the majority of whom immigrated in the 1980s. Though some observations presented herein may be relevant for other cases of immigration, the paper does not profess to be a comparative study or a "typology" of immigrations, but rather endeavors to document the concrete experience of the women we met.

The present study is part of a broader research of the integration of the newcomers into the Israeli educational system. This research pursued the general question of the construction of a new identity and the transmission of culture under circumstances of recent immigration. The fieldwork was carried out in a town of 24,000 inhabitants, among them more than 1,000 Ethiopian Jews. Some of these had just arrived in the country and were studying in the Ulpan; others had come several years before and were settled in their permanent lodgings.

The study focused on the role of the Ethiopian Jewish woman in producing the ethnic identity of her group vis-à-vis Israeli society, on the one hand, and the younger generation of Ethiopians, on the other.[2] The context of the analysis was essentially a familial one; the mother was important for us both as a role and as an informant, though we were not specifically interested in her as a "woman." We did not interview in depth any woman who was not also a mother. Nevertheless, the data we gathered revealed a differential immigration process for men and women.

The Adult School as a Locus for Interpreting the Differential Roles of Man and Woman

The changing role of Ethiopian Jewish women must be seen against the background of the "womanized" environment of adult education (Ulpan classes) in Israel. For a period of ten months, Ethiopian immigrants attend these Hebrew classes for five hours a morning, six days a week (Sabbath excepted), within Absorption Centers in which most of the immigrants reside for varying periods of time.[3] During this transitional stage ("between and betwixt," to use V. Turner's terminology),[4] when the group is not yet integrated into a specific social setting, the "Ulpan student" is the first significant role that the new immigrant performs.

Although the Ulpan is the formal setting in which the newcomers are supposed to learn Hebrew, it is also a tool for passing on the dominant ideology and culture.[5] By definition, the Ulpan teacher is given a great deal of freedom as a "cultural broker." The Ulpan claims to be more than a mere language school ("We are not Berlitz") and functions as an introduction to Israeli history and culture. In Israel in general and with the immigrants of Ethiopia in particular, the boundary between public and private life is blurred and we often find the teacher interpreting the private life of the student. Hence, the Ulpan is extremely important for integration, and its teachers are predisposed to discuss and interpret what may appear to an outside observer as personal matters.

The great majority of Ulpan teachers are young women who are active interpreters of the division of labor between men and women as it exists or should exist in modern society—an interpretation about which there is little consensus between the many segments of Israeli society and which is a subject of negotiation between spouses in the best of cases. One observed teacher emphasized a belief in sharing work between males and females within the household. This attitude was expressed within the context of a story of a fictive immigrant family. A certain episode in this story tells of a father who gets up during the night to give a bottle to a crying baby. The following is a transcription of classroom occurrences as the story was being told to the immigrants:

> Teacher: "Does Moshe [the father] want to get up in the middle of the night?"
> Male student: "No, he wants to sleep."
> Teacher: "He must get up. Moshe wants to rest. He is tired. But Uzi [the baby] is crying. The baby wants to eat. Moshe has to get up. The child is crying. Who gets up in the home? Father gets up."
> Male student: "Yes, *your* husband gets up." (Someone translates the sentence into Amharic and the class bursts into laughter.)
> Female student: "My child cries, my husband gets up."
> Teacher: "In Ethiopia child cries, father gets up?"
> All students together: "No! No!"

The principal of the Ulpan related an incident in which one of the female students attempted to apply the "Israeli way of life" as this was expounded in the Ulpan. She insisted that her husband get up at night to feed the baby. The following morning the woman appeared with a black eye.

This approach to the division of labor, however, was contrasted by free class discussions in which the teacher tended to focus upon the woman's role of housewife. Apparently, the role of the woman who kept up a household was much clearer and more familiar to the teacher than that of the man. She could relate with more understanding to her female students concerning their traditional work, as is illustrated in the following interchanges:

> Teacher: "Have you done the laundry yet? Have you put your laundry into the machine?"
> Female student: "Yes."
> Teacher: "Have you washed the laundry?"
> Student: "Not yet."
> Teacher: "Not yet?"
> Student: "I have not done my laundry yet."
> Teacher (addressing a female student who entered class late): "It is almost eleven. Where have you been?"
> Student: "Work at home."
> Teacher: "I also have to prepare food. I also have to take care of my children, but I am in class on time."

The teacher did not find equivalent topics of conversation with men.

The officials and social workers who deal with the everyday affairs of the immigrants are also women. Some of the social workers organized a conversation group with the women in which they too apparently offered a new interpretation of the female role. One of the grievances voiced by the male immigrants in seminars on the integration of the Ethiopian Jews attended by the latter, some professors, and some civil servants was that the Israelis were giving strange ideas to their women, a fact which caused family troubles.

It is difficult to evaluate the influence of this "womanized environment." In my own fieldwork, I have not observed dramatic changes in the families. However, new perspectives concerning "woman's work" and "man's work" were evident.

Household Work and the Transmission of Culture

As a result of their immigration, the working habits of the Ethiopian Jews have undergone a complete change. In rural

Ethiopia, whence most of our informants came, the master of the household regulated the work of the men (mainly in agriculture but supplemented in some measure by the practice of some crafts) while the mistress regulated that of the women. Moreover, the household was autonomous and depended only partially on a cash economy. Upon their arrival in Israel, however, the livelihood of the families came to depend upon the relation of its members with some external organization, be it a factory, a hospital, or a welfare agency. The household as a locus for economic production has therefore shrunk to the point that it has become exclusively the woman's domain. In contrast, the "home," the female domain in the former household in Ethiopia, has kept its relative autonomy although it has also been subject to dramatic changes. The complete disappearance of "men's work" in the home is consequently crucial to understanding the gender-differential transmission of culture within the family.

Whereas in Ethiopia the fathers used to teach their sons to till the soil, work the iron, or weave cloth, they have ceased to do so in their present circumstances. In contrast, mothers who used to weave baskets, cook specific dishes and embroider their dresses are continuing to teach these crafts to their daughters, though they have abandoned one of their occupations, namely the making and marketing of pottery.[6]

The male immigrants are no longer autonomous farmers or ironsmiths, but have become inserted in the modern process of production. The only traditional occupation that very few of the older men maintain in their homes is the weaving of cloth, mainly for the traditional *natala* (the "toga" worn by the men);[7] however, in our fieldwork we did not meet a single son who had learned the occupation in Israel.

The differential role of the parents in transmitting the culture in Ethiopia is evident from the response of one informant, an old man who was the father of married sons and of an elementary school girl:

In Ethiopia the father teaches his children. The mother looks after the children. The father plows the earth, sows, harvests. If a male child reaches a certain age, I can teach him to plow. I can even send my daughter to learn [at school].[8] The mother, for her part, teaches the daughter to make the bread, the *injera*, to embroider and to weave the traditional basketwork receptacle, the *safet*.

According to this same respondent, the father also taught his sons to honor adults, to be faithful to friends, to avoid stealing and breaking the law, while the mother taught her daughters to make coffee, to welcome a visitor, to cook, and to spin.

When asked whether Ethiopian parents were teaching their children the same things in Israel, he answered that he was only teaching them "the generations," that is, the genealogy of the family which determines possible marital partners. It was the government who "looked after the children"; he was not even working. To the specific question as to whether the mothers (his wife, for instance) were teaching the daughters to prepare the *injera* or to weave the *safet*, his answer was affirmative. Interviews with female informants and schoolchildren confirmed that the girls continued to learn from their mothers the skills and crafts necessary to produce a part of the material culture, just as they had done in Ethiopia. On the other hand, both male and female children indicated that their father remained the source for learning the code of behavior, e.g., to "honor the elderly" and "not to quarrel with other children." Nevertheless, the changes in cultural transmission brought about by immigration seem to have been somewhat less dramatic for females than for males.

The Home: A Place of Tradition and Transformation

While the Israeli "home," in concrete material terms, enabled the women to recreate and transmit some of the traditions and culture into which they had been born, it nevertheless was vastly different from the physical home in Ethiopia. As one can well imagine, there is quite a gap between the hut in rural Ethiopia and the apartment building—even if only a few stories high—in Israel. The difference is not only in the material environment but also in the way one functions in that environment (how one washes, cooks, heats the stove, disposes of the garbage). The products used for everyday life are not the same and one does not obtain them in the same way. Many informants underlined the fact that in Ethiopia a family grew virtually everything it needed to subsist, although certain commodities were bought in the marketplace, while in Israel one had to run everyday to the store and pay endless bills for gas, electricity, water, and the rent.

Indeed, the gap between the two ways of life was the cause of great concern to the officials and civil servants who worked with the immigrants and whose job it was to facilitate their adjustment and final integration. Paraprofessional social workers (actually assistants to the social workers themselves) entered the home of every Ethiopian family during the beginning of its stay in the Absorption Centers (which the immigrants entered upon arrival in the country) in order to explain the functioning of this particular kind of housing. They explained cooking with the unfamiliar ingredients (and even did some cooking), and they demonstrated how to take care of infants according to the Israeli norm, how to clean the apartment, and how to arrange the closets. It is thus clear that the first impact of life in the new country was felt by the women—indeed, brought to them—in the intimate domain that is their homes, even though this learning process was never very intensive and was restricted to a short period. Moreover, there is no doubt that the material environment and the new economic structure based on the exchange of money for goods dictated all kinds of changes in the work of the woman and the functioning of the home.

I shall elaborate on one essential aspect of the continuity and change within the home: the preparation of food and the making of "identity through food." The preparation of food made up an essential part of women's work in Ethiopia: it entailed carrying water from the river, grinding cereals to make flour, kneading the dough and then baking the daily *injera* (prepared with flour from a cereal called *tef*). One had to grind the red pepper to make the hot sauce *(berbera)*, brew the Ethiopian beer *(tellah)*, grind the coffee beans for the traditional *bouna*, and till the vegetable garden situated close to the kitchen area. In contrast to the great deal of time off from work enjoyed by the men in Ethiopia and regulated by the agricultural calendar, the work of the women was hard and continuous with no seasonal breaks. In fact, the woman's "time off" was regulated by her biological function of menstruation and birth (see below).

In comparison with the routine described above, there is no doubt that the preparation of food in Israel is much less demanding. Each apartment has running water, beer can be bought rather than brewed at home, as can readymade flour, and many homes have an electric coffee grinder. On the other hand, the women have the new chore of shopping at the local store and of traveling once or twice a week by bus to the central market. It should be noted that this type of work is also done by men and that the daily shopping at the local store for fresh commodities such as dairy products and bread is mainly done by the children, boys and girls alike.

The preparation of food by the woman is more than a mere "chore" and its consumption by her children and husband is more than a mere life necessity; they are also the continued affirmation of a specific culture and tradition—sometimes the sole surviving element of a lost culture—and a daily revival of the relationship between nourisher and nourished. Whereas in Ethiopia, the mother, aided by daughters and daughters-in-law, was the *direct* nourisher, in Israel, this is no longer the case. Now the woman has to compete with processed food which she does not know how to prepare.

The homemade staple of the Ethiopian Jews is the *injera*, made, as noted above, from the protein-rich *tef* cereal. A liquid dough is prepared and fermented without the help of yeast, then let to stay for several days. The dough is subsequently poured on a ceramic plate and put in the open fire. The end product is a spongy cake with a sour taste. The *berbera*, the hot sauce, and *wot*, the meat sauce, are spread upon the *injera*, which is then eaten with the hands. For the Sabbath, the *dabu*, a special bread-cake, is prepared.

These dishes were prepared by the women in all the households I visited, even in families which had been in Israel for several years. Though the making of the *injera* has had to be adjusted to the lack of *tef* and to the changed baking methods, it continues to be prepared and to be part of the daily diet. Along with their *injera* the families regularly buy bread in the shops, mostly for the consumption of children. The adults, however, prefer their traditional product.

We asked the children who attend school as to their preference for bread or *injera* and in most cases they chose the former. A twelve-year-old girl even "reasoned" that bread was less fattening. Though the children sometimes eat *injera* in the home and though the girls are taught its preparation by their mothers, it is rarely brought to school. Many a time a child will buy a roll as a snack on the way to school instead of carrying the homemade ethnic bread. Furthermore, the children place continual pressure on the mothers to obtain money for ice cream and other modern sweets. In some families the sweets seem to have actually taken the place of real food. The mothers do not yet know how to prepare any of the sweets which the children crave. One of our informants reported: "If I buy biscuits and cookies [for her five-year-old], she eats only this all the time!" It thus seems that the food prepared by the mother is partly rejected by her children, who adjust rapidly to their new environment.

The women also appear to be ignorant of the relative nutritional value of the new food. One mother—and this was not an isolated case—who gave her baby a very sweet, commercially prepared dessert as a staple (in a bottle with an enlarged hole in the nipple that allowed the pudding to seep through), confessed she did not know that this rather expensive gourmandise had little nutritional value.[9] Another example of the new "inadequateness" of the woman as the provider of meals may be found in the story of a young man who invited his army comrades to join his relatives and friends in a feast celebrating the name-giving of his child. The food prepared by his wife and other women in the community was "Ethiopian." At the last minute the young man almost panicked, not knowing what food to serve the "Israeli" guests. Finally, he asked to go with one of our team to the market in order to buy the "appropriate Israeli" food for the occasion.

All these examples show that the women—at this stage of their integration in the new environment—have not yet acquired the basic codes underlying the commercially processed "Israeli" food.

Consequently, the immigrant mother is constantly forced to face the fact that she is no longer the only mediator and interpreter of the food domain.

Woman-Made Artifacts as Markers of Group Ethnicity

Like Jews the world over, the Beta Israel have developed strategies to keep their boundaries as a distinctive group intact.[10] They and the officials responsible for their integration, as well as the Israeli elites (especially in the political sphere and the media), have tended to emphasize the common Jewish heritage, particularly upon the arrival of the Beta Israel in the country. At the same time, however, these same officials have recognized the value of certain parts of specific ethnic cultures as a result of the lesson learned from the "errors of the 1950s," a coded phrase referring to certain failures in the integration of immigrants brought about by the "melting-pot" policy of that period[11]—i.e., during the first years of Israel's existence.

Essentially, immigration leads to a reversing of identities. An immigrant who was "a Jew" in his country of origin becomes an "Ethiopian" or an "American" in Israel. In other words, the country of origin becomes the new ethnicity.[12] In this new ethnicity, women play an important role as producers of artifacts and "ethnic" food.

In every Ethiopian home I have visited, I have seen in the living room a decorative basketwork object made with stems of plants swathed in threads. This object, the *safet*, is the product of the traditional handiwork of Ethiopian Jewish women. In Ethiopia, it was used as a vessel or tray to contain the *injera*.

The tradition of making the *safet* has been retained in Israel, although the use to which the object is put, as well as the material from which it is made, have changed. The basket is now made of stems gathered by the women in the open spaces near their homes and swathed in synthetic wool (often obtained from the unravelling of second-hand sweaters received as gifts) rather than straw or raffia. Though this change implies a range of new possibilities

in combining colors, it also makes the *safet* unsuitable as a receptacle for the *injera;* instead, it is hung on the wall.

One can now say that the *safet* has become "framed," almost
in a Goffmanian sense;[13] once an everyday practical object, it has
now become a symbolic object invested with new meaning. In
some respects it has become an icon for the new ethnic identity.
A young woman, pointing to the *safet* on the wall remarked, "It
is a good object for memory [i.e., remembering]." Indeed, in its
new function the *safet* serves as a bridge between past and present. It stands for the changes which the Beta Israel have undergone—just as its fabrication and structure have changed. It has
become an object of display with a primarily decorative function
within the new space in which the immigrants now live.

For the Israeli, and to some extent for the immigrants, too, the
safet, placed in its new context, has become an iconic synonym
for the Ethiopian ethnic identity, a marker of the Ethiopian ethnic
group. For the civil servants working toward the "absorption" of
the new immigrants, a home in which a *safet* is displayed is
immediately identified as that of an Ethiopian Jew. The word
safet itself—an Amharic word—is used by the people working
with the new immigrants. Through this positive attitude toward
the *safet,* the Israelis express their selective support for the culture of the immigrants. This shows that the Israelis are trying not
to repeat the "error of the 1950s." In this sense, the *safet* is also a
marker of the new attitude of the absorbers.

The immigrants themselves—at least the women—also recognize the *safet* as a marker distinguishing their own culture from
the "Israeli" one. Thus, it is precisely this artifact which is given
as a gift to people outside of their ethnic group. I have seen *safets*
hanging in the offices of social workers, and one of the field-
workers in this research was given one as a present.

One of the reasons that the *safet* functions so well as an icon
for the ethnicity of the Ethiopian Jews is that it has undergone
transformation. Thus, 'it is and it is not,"[14] at one and the same
time, an object of Beta Israel culture in its diasporan Ethiopian
context. In some respects, it has become an icon of metamorphosis. This transformation and even "displacement" parallels that

which every ethnic group has to and is expected to undergo in its integration in Israel.

The special role played by the "universally accepted" *safet* is not assumed by another synonym-object produced by the immigrant women—the *injera*. While the people who deal with the integration of the newcomers recognize this bread as a marker of "Ethiopian" ethnicity (for instance, the Ulpan teacher will ask: "Have you cooked for the Sabbath? Have you baked the *injera*?), they react to it negatively. Nobody likes it; everybody has stories to tell about its sour taste. The principal of an adult school told me that the immigrants have learned that teachers, when invited, have to be served Israeli food.[15]

Thus, the women are producing markers of their ethnicity: one which is accepted and displayed and one which, in the eyes of the "Israelis," emphasizes the ethnic difference in its original force and is therefore rejected.

The latter statement, however, must be somewhat qualified. In more relaxed relations between the "new immigrants" and the "Israelis," the ethnic food sometimes becomes a positive marker and an expression of the new Ethiopian ethnicity. For instance, one of the informants began to serve *injera* to a member of the team who used to visit her regularly. Understanding that this bread was not exactly to the liking of her guest, the woman prepared a less sour version of it for the following visits. The women also urge the visitors to drink *bouna*, the Ethiopian coffee, saying, as I heard many time "This is ours." At other times, we were given "Israeli" instant coffee.

The Lost Space

Of all the changes that the Ethiopian Jewish immigrants, and the women in particular, have undergone, the most profound seems to be the transformation in spatial terms.

The new immigrants build the perception of their daily life through constant comparison between their present and the constantly changing image they have of their past. Invariably, when asked about their daily routine in Ethiopia, they compared it to their new life (and vice versa). Their country of origin has become an "imaginary space," the more so as there is no hope of being allowed by the Ethiopian government to visit it in the foreseeable future or of having the financial means to do so.

However, there was one specific space in Ethiopia that lacks a parallel in the Israeli context; it is a space which seems lost forever.[16] The reference is to the "impurity hut"—the *yamargam gogo* used during menstruation and the *yaras gogo* used in and after childbirth.[17]

According to a strict reading of biblical law, the Jewish woman is considered impure during her menstruation (that is, for seven days) and after giving birth (forty days after bearing a son and eighty after bearing a daughter). In Ethiopia, the practice was to keep the woman away from her daily routines and chores and to live in a special hut during this period. Located near but outside the village, this hut was partially surrounded by a half-circle of stones whose function was to mark the difference between the "impure" woman and the "pure" village. The woman's relatives would bring her food on special plates without ever touching her.

To Western eyes, this seems a rather gloomy predicament, but it is not at all the case from the viewpoint of the Beta Israel woman. More often than not, the woman was not alone in the hut, as it was common to several families. As a matter of fact, it was often in the "impurity hut" that the women learned from one another. For instance, one of the informants told us that it was there that she had learned to embroider her clothes.

Men too can be impure for biological reasons, for instance, if they happen to touch a corpse. However, the impurity of men occurred less often and more accidentally. Thus, it was the cyclic functioning of the woman's body which preserved the classification "pure/impure."

The Beta Israel could also be impure for social reasons. Thus, if one touched a non-Beta Israel, he would immerse in the river in order to wash away the impurity. Leslau, who was with the Beta Israel at the end of the 1940s, says that they were also called "the people who smell of water." Though this custom faded with the modernization of Ethiopia, it is still alive in the memories of the immigrants. Nevertheless, the marking of social boundaries via the purity laws has diminished, while the marking of biological boundaries—especially in the case of women—has continued.

However, by coming to Israel, the women of Beta Israel lost the space which permitted them to maintain these biological boundaries. If there is one thing from their former life in Ethiopia which the women mention spontaneously and with expressions of nostalgia, it is the "impurity hut." Indeed, the loss of this hut seems to be tantamount to a loss of touch between the woman and her body. I had the following conversation with a woman who was pregnant:

"In what month of pregnancy are you?"
"Here, I don't know. I think six or seven."
"You do not know?"
"In our country I know. When there is blood, we are outside
[in the impurity hut]."

This point struck me as very important at the time of the interview, but thus far I have not gathered additional information which permits me to expatiate about it. For the present, it is my speculation that, whereas in Ethiopia the women preserved the laws of purity (the very laws which set boundaries between the Beta Israel community and the non-Beta Israel) through their bodies and their biological functions, here in Israel they have come to produce a surrogate or vicarious object for the same purpose. With the help of their bodies—through the work of their hands—but not from within it—i.e., from the womb—they have now come to produce the artifacts which have become synonymous with their ethnicity in Israel.

Thus, the *safet* and the *injera* have become not only markers of identity, a function they certainly did not have in Ethiopia, but also spatial markers. They are the reminders of the lost "imaginary space" that Ethiopia has become.

Endnotes

1. The community calls itself Beta Israel. The name "Falasha" was given to it by the neighboring people of Amhara; it has a pejorative connotation alluding to

the immigrant and foreign status of its members. A. Z. Aescoly, *Sefer Ha-Falashim* (Jerusalem: Reuvon Mas with the Rav Kook Institute, 1943). When discovered by Western travelers, like James Bruse and later by such missionaries as J. M. Flad and H. A. Stern, the Beta Israel came to be known in the West by the name "Falasha." Bruce, *Travels to Discover the Source of the Nile in the Years 1768, 1769, 1770, 1771, 1772 and 1773*, vols. 1–5 (Edinburgh, 1790); Flad, *A Short Description of the Falasha and Kamants in Abyssinia* (Basel, 1866); Stern, *Wandering Among the Falashas in Abyssinia* (London, 1862). This name was generally used by Jewish writers as well, for instance, by the first Jewish envoys to this community, J. Halevy, "Excursion chez les Falashas ou Juifs d'Abyssinie," *Bulleting de la Societe Géographique* (1869), 5(18):270–294, and J. Faitlovitch, "The Falashas," *American Jewish Yearbook 5681*, September 13–October 2, 1921, pp. 80–99. The term "Ethiopian Jew," which is generally accepted usage in contemporary Israel, indicates that they are not different from any other Jewish group, at least from a semantic perspective.

2. I shall not discuss here other important matters that were examined, such as the new perception of marriage arrangements and the selection of husbands, the views concerning contraception, and the number of children to be desired.

3. For a general description of Absorption Centers in Israel, see R. T. Horowitz, "Immigrants in Transition: The Israeli Absorption Center," *International Migration* (1977), 15(1):288–299; for the experience of the Ethiopian immigrants, see G. J. Abbink, *The Falashas in Ethiopia and Israel: The Problem or Ethnic Assimilation*, Nijmegen Sociaal Anthropologische Cahiers (1984), vol. 15; and Tsili Doleve-Gandelman, " 'Ulpan' is not Berlitz: Adult Education and the Ethipian Jews in Israel," *Social Sciences Information* (1989), 28:121–144.

4. V. Turner, *A Forest of Symbols* (Ithaca: Cornell University Press, 1967).

5. For a general outline of the Ulpan's ideology, see Sh. Kodesh, "Ha-Ulpan be-Shmonim," *'Ed Ha-Ulpan* (1982), no. 41, pp. 20–21, and nos. 40–43, pp. 8–11; and Y. Shaked, "Shloshim shana la-Ulpan be-Israel," *'Ed Ha-Ulpan* (1980), no. 33, pp. 4–8. My own detailed examinatiom of the special case of the Ulpan for the Ethiopian Jews (" 'Ulpan' is not Berlitz") emphasizes the role of the teacher in this context.

6. It is interesting to note that some of the women in the Walkait area of Ethiopia had shifted their efforts towards "tourist art." Y. Kahana, an Israeli traveler, has described this development from the female perspective, in *Black Brothers* (Tel-Aviv: Am-Oved, 1977).

7. In the community in which our fieldwork was conducted, only one man was a regular weaver. He had begun to work in a factory, but had had to stop owing to poor health. While living on his social security pension, he built a loom and used it to produce cloth. This man had been a full-time weaver in Ethiopia and an instructor in an Ethiopian resettlement project. We also met another man who constructed a loom but rarely used it.

8. Schooling was not obligatory in prerevolutionary Ethiopia; it was the father who decided whether to send one of his children to school. As often as not, this decision depended on whether he needed his children on the farm, and the sons were needed the most.

9. At the time the Committee for Marketing Milk carried out an aggressive television campaign pointing to the supposed benefits of milk and dairy products, including this artificially prepared sweet. It is from the conversation with this

particular mother that we understood the role of television as a legitimizing source.

10. W. Leslau, *Falasha Anthology*, tr. from Ethiopian sources with an introduction by Leslau, Yale Judaica Series, Julian Oberman, ed., vol. 6 (New Haven and London: Yale University Press, 1951).

11. Doleve-Gandelman, "Comment interpreter l'intégration des Juifs d'Ethiopie en Israel," *Les Temps Modernes* (January 1986), 41:139–156.

12. Doleve-Gandelman, "La Fonction de l' 'autre' dans la production de l'identité nationale: le cas paradoxal des Juifs d'Ethiopie," *Vers des Societés Pluriculturelles: Etudes Comparatives des situations en France*, Actes du Colloque International de l'AFA (Paris: Edition de l'ORSTOM, 1987), pp. 503–508.

13. E. Goffman, *Frame Analysis* (New York: Harper & Row, 1974).

14. P. Ricoeur, *La Métaphore vive* (Paris: Editions du Seuil, 1975).

15. Ethnic food is popular in Israel, but apparently some time has to elapse between the arrival of an ethnic group and the popularization of its food. Then the food ceases to be served in its traditional context and becomes mass produced and commercially distributed. Under these conditions, the ethnic food falls into the category of "it is and it is not."

16. C. Rosen, "La Dialectique d'interaction entre les Juifs éthiopiens et israéliens," *Les Temps Moderne* (January 1986), 41:117–131.

17. A. Z. Aescoly, *Sefer Ha-Falashim*; W. Leslau, "The Black Jews of Ethiopia An Expedition to the Falashas," *Commentary* (January 1949), 7(1):216–224, and *Falasha Anthology*; and Y. Kahana, *Black Brothers*.

11
THREE WOMEN: CULTURAL RULES AND LEADERSHIP ROLES IN THE BLACK COMMUNITY
Jacquelyn Mitchell

THE SURVIVAL of organized programs in women's studies and in ethnic studies provides evidence of the tenacity of those who refuse to accept the racist and sexist forms of doublethink that have permeated this country during the first half of the twentieth century. Through the civil and women's rights movements, many unsung heroes and heroines contributed to the struggle against the inequalities and injustice of our racially, sexually, and class segregated society. While racial and sexual segregation are manifested in different ways, all of the victims—women and minorities—have been dogged by myths and images that bar full participation in this society. Thus, it is not surprising that a major concern for each movement continues to be the elimination of negative stereotypes that encourage the persistence of barriers to the complete realization of an equitable society. Chief among these are those that imply incapacity for leadership.

Once negative stereotypes are socially established, they place the victim in a double-bind. Demonstrations of ability are turned against the victims, not the stereotypes. How many of us have heard "she thinks like a man" or "he or she is not really black?" The typifications foisted on members of segregated groups not only victimize people, they make individuals participate in their own victimization. Survival often demands compliance with prescribed—and bounded—terms for economic or social mobility; compliance affirms these boundaries and confirms the stereotypes. Your *survival* becomes living proof that the system is tolerable; while your *protest* against the system is used to prove that boundaries are necessary to protect society from you. Once institutionalized, stereotypes cease to be primarily the expression of local opinions and become formalized authority shaping opinions and punishing violators.

Another unfortunate consequence of such stereotyping is that information within the society flows along the lines established by the stereotypes, ensuring that the prevailing knowledge bears some logical relationship to the stereotype. The imposition of legal barriers between groups not only reduces the interactions among them, but over time, insures that their specific collective and personal identities are linked to the stereotypical images of the prohibited other. In a sense, the overall society lacks a central core of values and is instead comprised of a multiplicity of stereotypical reflections of itself as the excluding other. Individuals' perceptions and world views are shaped from within their respective groups and incorporate their group's stereotypes of other groups. Consequently, when legal restrictions are removed, the legacy of separation persists because most of what one group knows about the other is based on stereotypes.

This is particularly true for women in America whose gender identity has been consistently subordinated to ethnic identifications. Even when racial myths of dominance proclaimed the United States "white man's country," the status of women was clearly dependent on their subservience and proximity to men. As a consequence, we frequently turn on *each other*, instead of to *each other*.

An honest valuation of what women have attained requires more than an agenda of examining the most obvious constraints; it requires an honest appraisal of historical, social, political, economic, sexual, and racial factors that impede not only the attainment of professional women in society, but the advancement of *all* women. Until we study women—whether black, white, Indian, Latina, Asian, lesbian, poor, or the aged—with special attention to their successes and failures in fashioning contexts that encourage self-esteem and survival, we cannot truly discern how women will exercise power and authority.

The question is *how* are women to exercise power in a political, economic, and social climate that is increasingly geared to professional attainment. At stake here are leadership roles that are vested with authority and power, but created primarily in our absence. The issue for women and for minorities is whether *we adapt ourselves* to the established leadership roles or whether *we adapt them to us,* infusing in them new options and greater perceptions based on our experiences in achieving professional status.

I am interested in the processes by which minorities and women develop leadership roles. That the terms "leader" and "white male" are typically synonymous indicate that the informal rules of our culture are strongly wedded to this combination, and create dissonance for those who are neither white nor male. The fact that informal cultural rules that associate leadership roles with white males operate in our society does not mean that they are any less susceptible to change than such formal rules from a century ago that prohibited women and blacks from voting. But rules that are informal are more difficult to uncover because they are a part of a cultural tradition that is difficult to articulate.[1] They are the taken for granted rules, rules with which we all abide but are unable to articulate.

In observing that our persistent association of males with leadership roles is partly a consequence of informal cultural rules, one wonders about informal rules that exist among women, rules that involve patterns of actions and behaviors comparable to those associated with public roles of authority and responsibility. If, for example, we generally agree that making rules for others to follow is an indication of authority, we might begin to ask *who* makes such rules among women, *how* are they transmitted, and *why* are they accepted? Furthermore, it seems as important to uncover these informal cultural rules that operate among women—so that they can be formalized into public roles—as it is to disclose why informal rules restrict public roles to males. A better understanding of the ways that *women* exercise authority and responsibility will enable us to prescribe patterns for de-gendering public roles, making them comfortable for members of *either sex.*

After realizing that informal cultural rules exist among women who maintain power and authority, certain patterns among some of the black women I had previously known and studied took on new meanings. Although my research has not specifically investigated female culture as such, I realized that I had accumulated an extensive array of observations, strategies, personal accounts, and values and beliefs from a cross-section of women over time: from the low-income mothers of the preschool children that I taught in a Headstart Program during the sixties, to the women I studied in a National Institute of Mental Health (NIMH) funded research project during the seventies that investigated stress among low-income black and white mothers, and the community-based teacher who is the focus of my current research.[2]

Reflecting on images of these women, I recalled their expressions, their gestures and posture, their pithy statements that at the time I dismissed though intuitively recognized as significant. Although I was unable *really* to hear their tacit messages during our interactions, their silence was far more striking than any words they might have spoken. Upon later reflection, it became clear that if taken out of the immediate context, their expressions, the gestures, those pithy statements were inexplicably puzzling.

In reconstructing intimate glimpses into the everyday lives of these women, similarities in their behaviors emerged in terms of informal rules that operate in female culture, similarities that I strongly suspect characterize many such women who hold positions of authority within their communities. Perhaps these patterns offer a special example of what anthropologist Edward Hall describes as "those implicit rules by means of which sets are arranged so that they take on meaning." Hall elaborates further that, "A given pattern is only obvious to certain categories of people. . . . In effect, groups can be defined by the relation of their members to certain patterns. The individuals of a group share patterns that enable them to *see the same thing* and this *holds them together.*"[3]

It seems logical, then, given Hall's definition, that a leadership role would entail mastering the informal rules of a culture and developing skills based upon that knowledge to hold things together and enable people to see the same thing. It also seems reasonable to assume that authority entails making rules that others accept and abide. This ability to enable others to see the same thing means giving interpretations of themselves, the historical and immediate contexts, and their relationships to the self and the situation. This mode of culture building can provide the standards of behavior and the criteria of evaluation with which established group identities resist hostile environments. Moreover, the ability to call things and people by their *true* names has, throughout human history, been recognized as a potent source of power. At the same time, standards and norms within groups provide the means to evaluate cultural knowledge and performance, and to allocate status.

For people traditionally excluded from direct participation in the dominant society—women and people of color, most especially—this function of setting the group reality offers an alternative source of self-esteem impervious to the intent of the powers that be. Members of these groups *see* their world, its realities, its patterns, and connections in a cultural way. For it is those who *see*, ones who possess this cultural knowledge, who become recognized as authorities and leaders. Our leaders, we might say, are our teachers in the sense that they invariably influence our cognitive style and development.

The basic conception that underlies the emerging perceptions of power within contexts can be illustrated by a few examples. These I believe represent the patterns that might perhaps, with more systematic study, enable us to gain broader insight and a better understanding of the ways that black women develop and maintain roles of authority. Once we establish relationships between patterns of role behavior and authority for black women, it should become possible to engage in comparative studies and examine similarities and differences among all women. Studies of this nature could collectively contribute to the development of a theory of female culture and might rectify the current asymmetry in knowledge and methods for studying women. As it stands now, we lack the knowledge that is needed to create additional options for individuals within our institutions and society. The public roles that do exist are dangerously constrained by the same static qualities that characterize the stereotypes discussed earlier. I do not mean to suggest that an examination of strategies that traditional women in black communities use to exercise authority will solve our problems. I do believe that studying ways that authority and leadership operate among different groups and at various levels might enable us to begin to comprehend some of the dynamic processes at the heart of our complex society. In this paper, I will introduce three black women who exercise power and authority and whose mastery of cultural rules has had a tremendous impact on my own personal and professional development.

The first woman I wish to discuss, at least in terms of appearance, is an unlikely person of authority and respect. Louise Johnson, the proprietor of a beauty parlor situated in a Roxbury, Massachusetts ghetto, is a heavyset, matronly, slow-moving woman who agreed to let me "hang around" her beauty parlor to investigate its social organization and cultural patterns of temporal sequencing for a fieldwork assignment (required in my graduate program at Harvard).[4] I entered the rather dilapidated shop—"the field" in academic jargon—proudly sporting my newly acquired "social scientist" hat. The hat was rather tight if one considers the multitude of attitudes, prejudices, and preconceived notions that swelled my head. But then the role was new.

As an outsider, nothing about the shop made sense. The place seemed chaotic. From my perspective, everything was disjointed, out of whack. Nonetheless, I left the shop a year later rather chastised and a great deal wiser. The experiences that I had in the shop and with Louise changed me in ways difficult to articulate. Somehow and unexpectedly during the course of events that year, Louise became my *teacher*. *I* was the "sophisticated" graduate student, so I believed. And *I* was the one who could interact comfortably among the most learned scholars in the country. Yet how did it happen that I unwittingly become Louise's pupil, the cultural dope in a setting so seemingly without organization and structure that it made no sense? A description of this women and of a few of my experiences with her will help to convey the events and processes by which this role reversal came about.

Louise Johnson was originally from the South but had been living in Boston, at the time of the study, for thirty-five years. For twenty-two of these years, she had worked as a beautician. Although Louise retained a slight trace of a southern accent, she had adopted the silent "r," common in Bostonian accents. As an expatriate New Yorker, I enjoyed hearing her ritualistic query asking when I arrived each day if I'd had trouble finding a "paking" space for my "cah." The accent seemed unfitting to ears that had only associated "paking" and "cahs" with people like the Kennedys, certainly not to black beauticians with limited education.

Louise can be described best as an outspoken women who never hesitated to say whatever she had to say, whenever she wanted to say it, and to whomever she wanted to hear it. People who were easily intimidated did not come to the shop. She once told me that she had "lost many a customer on account of [her] mouth." One of the most striking observations in my fieldnotes was the frequency and intensity with which she yelled at and denigrated the shop's patrons. But for reasons totally unknown to the researcher, the customers continued to come.

Louise's philosophy of life, "always tell the truth," was reflected on a wall poster that hung in the shop. Although I had noticed the poster my first day in the field, it had little meaning at the time and I dismissed it as unimportant. Printed beneath the idyllic scene—that familiar, Madison Avenue prototype of love, peace, and tranquility—was the following message: "The greatest kindness we can offer each other is truth." Well, people always knew where they stood with Louise. One never had to second guess her. "I don't give a damn what people think," she once said. "I always say to your face what I'll say behind your back." In realizing that talking to people in such a way was not without its risks, she once cautioned her beauticians, Marie and George, that, "You can't talk to people the way I do 'cuz they might knock you down."

George was young, naive, and gay. One day he arrived at work with a blackened eye. When I asked what had happened, he answered that he had fallen down a flight of stairs. Louise chuckled disdainfully both at his explanation and my sympathy and retorted, "You a lie. That ole man you livin' with beat you up. If you had any kinda sense you'd leave." George, with head hung low in contrition, silently acknowledged his rebuke. Louise's blunt "Yeah, you got caught with your pants down, didn't yuh, huh?", was not an attempt to make a bad gay joke funny, nor to castigate him for his sexual preference. Her indirect message entailed a common black community practice that one employs to "call somebody to task," or to "call something by its true name." Indexically, she was saying that "I'm telling it like it is, now deal with it." And though George, like all the others I met that year in the beauty parlor, took pains to avoid Louise's wrath, each evaded her close scrutiny at all costs—the researcher included, I might add.

Although everyone dreaded the humiliation of being "caught with one's pants down," the possibility of facing Louise's silence was even more threatening. On one occasion, for example, George had been absent from the shop for quite some time. When I inquired about his whereabouts he whispered a desperate plea not to refer to his absence in Louise's presence. He had vacationed in Cleveland and hadn't worked for over two weeks. Moreover, he had left town without first informing Louise of his plans. She had needed to readjust her schedule to accommodate both her customers and his, and needless to say, was in a foul mood. Occasionally she would mutter loud and distinct derogatory comments under her breath and look through George as if he wasn't there. "Ole sneaky-eyed devil," she'd mumble. "Stupid ole big-headed jerk. Never can count on a fool." George ungrudgingly welcomed Louise's upbraiding, for though she *visually denied* his physical presence, she *verbally acknowledged*, in her deprecation, the possibility of redemption and restitution. Had Louise ignored him completely, it would have indicated a withdrawal of her affection and support. The consequences of being victim to the silent treatment at the shop were foreboding and devastating, and signified a negation of one's significance and value.

At another time George wanted to invest in a shady deal and

had sought Louise's advice. She refused to offer any, citing time pressures and being behind with her appointments. After George's emotional ten minute spiel, Louise, seemingly moved by his plea, stopped washing her customer's hair—the researcher's, incidentally—and listened intently to his plan. George explained that he wanted to become a partner in a fool-proof deal that would supposedly net $60,000. Louise vehemently opposed his involvement and cautioned about a possible con. Dismissing her advice, George requested that she give him the back-pay that she had been withholding to enable him to invest in the scheme. But true to form, Louise absolutely refused. Her final words and advice admonished, "Be careful what you put your name on. Better pass that cosmetology exam and put your name on that operator's license."

Although Louise taught the beauticians the culturally appropriate rules for playing the game, she enjoyed the challenge of an occasional scrimmage. It was common knowledge that she was a firm believer in beating white folks at their own games and derived immense pleasure in her role as artful trickster. The punch lines in her "let's out-smart the whites" schemes gained admiration and respect among people in the shop and never failed to draw loud chuckles. "Never iron for white folks unless they wear the same size clothes as you do," was one such proverb. Her bitterness toward whites often surfaced whenever she talked to the women who worked in Sweet's, a pimp's, stable. All the women were white. Even to this day I'm uncertain whether her bitterness was a reflection on their race, profession, or naive dismissal of the racism that was rampant in Boston at the time. Although Sweet was in jail, the women continued to hang around the shop. "You white girls are fools," Louise chastised. "You think you can go down to the jail and see Sweet and them white folks gonna like it. White folks don't wanna see no black man with a white woman. You ain't helping Sweet at all. Why don't you keep your asses away?"

One of the women, a mother of a black baby, sought sympathy when discussing the forced family ostracism that she encountered when her child was born. Listening to her dilemma, Louise retorted angrily and unsympathetically, "White people can pet a black dog and love it to death, but they can't love an innocent black baby." The message was clear that day and everyone in the shop remained silent, both black and white.

One day, Joe, the local alcoholic who always screamed during conversations, visited the shop. Although he had ignored me in the past, he noticed for the first time, that particular day, that whenever he was in the shop, I would be constantly writing on a large legal-sized pad. My logic must have been impaired some-how because I failed to connect my professor's advice to maintain an unobtrusive participant-observer presence with my blatant but naive use of a large yellow note pad to write fieldnotes. I was jolted from my reverie into the present when Joe loudly and defiantly demanded to be told what I was writing. How does one effectively explain to a street dude that one is investigating the social organization of the beauty shop and its patterns of temporal sequencing? "You doin' what? And what temper you wanna learn about?" he screamed. My jargon-laden explanation of temporal sequencing got lost somehow between *his temper* and my sheer panic and insane but understandable desire to be far away. "I don't believe you," he yelled, even more loudly. "Lemme see what you writin' on that pad." "Aha," he shouted in triumphant after spotting his name in my notes. "When your book come out I'm gonna to sue you for one million dollars." I tried in vain to reassure him that I wasn't planning to publish when he de-manded that I delete all references about him from my pad, but my protests fell on deaf ears.

The threats escalated, especially when he failed to understand why I kept calling the beauty parlor, the local hangout, "the field." My eyes implored Louise for help as Joe's tirade got louder and more frightening, but she chose not to intervene and left me on my own to figure out how to negotiate myself out of a situation that I had created. I prayed that she would come to my defense and rescue me from Joe's verbal assault, but Louise remained calm and quiet, a rarity for a woman known for her infamous temper. I had no way of knowing that day how much she was teaching me by her silence. I can chuckle now about my dilemma, but on that day in the shop all I could think of was "hail Mary full of grace," and I'm not even Catholic.

When Joe was finally spent and left, Louise turned from her customer, looked at me and simply said, "You'll learn." Conducting research in a poor black neighborhood like Roxbury, she admonished later, entailed knowing how to handle oneself in all sorts of situations. And she was right. The experience, though frightening at the time, was a learning one. I survived and I learned. There may have been easier exercises to learn from, but I don't believe that Louise included any such lessons in her curriculum on survival.

People who visited the shop came from a potpourri of backgrounds: nurses, prostitutes, teachers, drug addicts, housewives, alcoholics, men who sold *hot* items for *bargain basement prices*, and even neophyte social scientists. Their perceptions of the social climate in the shop differed significantly from mine. And for all intents and purposes, they appeared relaxed and at home in the setting; they felt welcome. Social status, at least in this setting, was determined neither by income, education, nor profession. The visitors also came for number of reasons. The following quotes derived from fieldnotes explain why the assorted participants came to the shop and how they regarded Louise:

> Mario (a white pimp): Louise understands us. You can tell her anything.
> A Customer: Louise is more than your hairdresser. She's your friend. She'll tell you when you're wrong.
> Marie: Well, she take anybody who comes in. . . . They ain't got no place else to go.
> George: She's very outspoken. I admire her outspokenness.
> Researcher (probing further): Sometimes Louise yells at you a lot. Does this frighten you?
> George: Why you say that? I don't ever 'member Louise talkin' bad to me.

Only after having been away from the field for quite some time did I realize that like the participants I studied, I had also begun to respect Louise Johnson and wanted acceptance and inclusion in the shop. In his classic ethnography, *Tally's Corner*, Liebow describes the values and experiences of a group of black men who hung out on a Washington, D.C., street corner. In one anecdote, the men describe themselves as "dogs" and attribute their infidel-

ities and need for women other than those in their primary relationships to involuntary urges beyond their control—to their
"manly flaws." What was startling for me when I read the sce-
nario that Liebow described, was Liebow's change in role. As the
women walk past the street corner, the men—self-described
"dogs," but blameless because of "manly flaws"—comment on
and evaluate each woman's physical attributes and sexuality while
embellishing on one another's fantasies. When Liebow actively
participates in the commentary, he unconsciously but unwittingly subscribes to and validates the men's theory of manly
flaws. And as a consequence, the subjects become his cronies and
Liebow changes, at least for the moment, from an "objective"
participant-observer to a "subjective" *man*.[5]

The day my role changed from participant-observer to observ-
ing-participant in the beauty parlor is quite vivid. One morning
Louise asked me to answer the telephone in the shop and take
messages; the two beauticians had not arrived, she was busy, and
Wally, her do-everything-but-hair man was out sick. Using a sec-
retarial voice that significantly contrasted Wally's "Whaddja wont?"
when he answered the phone, I answered, "Louise's Beauty Parlor. May I help you please?" Louise seemed pleased with my
initiation and performance as a full-fledged member in the setting
and her approval pleased me. My social scientific objectivity
dissolved rapidly, and in my quest to belong I forgot momentarily, as did Liebow, that I was the *researcher*, not one of the
subjects. Louise became the *teacher* and I became the *student*.
But then again, role reversals in certain contexts make for good
ethnography.

Although no one asked specifically, customers who called were
curious and wondered who was taking messages. Later that afternoon, when Louise yelled and reproached in her odd amalga-
mated "Bostonian-Southern" accent, "You may go to Hahvad, but
you sho' is stupid," I beamed happily, realizing that having been
put to work to answer the phone, called to task and by a "true
name," and *honored* by denigration, I had survived the initiation
period and passed the final rites of passage as a member in the
shop.

Loud, rough, gruff Louise was given authority and respect from the people who frequented the shop. Her cognitive strategies for "holding things together" enabled the shop's patrons to *hear* themselves and to *see* their situations. And for me, she made visible the understanding of her role as teacher in the setting and the sense-making implicit in her interactions with the patrons. Louise offers illustrative examples of how to call things and people by their true names. The white women who frequented the shop were blind to the fact that their visits to the city jail—even in the name of love—could cause adverse reactions. The informal cultural rules of racist Boston needed exposure, not naiveté, precisely what Louise taught when she reproached the women, "You white girls are fools."

"Be careful what you put your name on. . . . Better pass that cosmetology exam and put your name on that operator's license," she had warned. George didn't protest when she called him to task for wanting to invest in a hare-brained scheme rather than passing the beautician licensing exam and investing in himself. "Never iron for white folks unless they wear the same size clothes as you do" may have caused a lot of thigh-slapping laughter in the shop, but people were also aware that cultural and shared meanings were embedded in her message. The joke held special significance for people who were poor and black.

Although Louise's reproaches may have seemed direct from an outside perspective, her instructions were in fact quite the opposite. Participants were socialized to recognize situations for what they are. Taught to *see*, rather than given answers, they had to look to themselves for solutions. I was a middle-class, book-smart doctoral candidate, but her student just the same. Louise structured the environment and provided the pedagogy that enabled me to *see* the cultural meanings and patterns that were hidden from the non-initiated. I "did learn" as she had threatened, but only retrospectively did I realize how artfully I had been trained in ethnographic research methods and how skillfully Louise had mediated my experiences to enable me to *see*.

Her crash methodology course was a lot more rigorous and effective than the ones I took in graduate school. Under her tutelage I discovered the rule-governed systems underlying the beauty parlor's social anatomy, not Harvard's. And after being assigned the gatekeeping role of answering the phone, a position of trust, when Louise decided it was time for me to get promoted—I became, in effect, a socially and culturally competent member in the setting. The shop was neither chaotic nor disorganized as I had first believed. Louise's two primary modes of instruction—criticism and encouragement—in addition to the power, authority, and knowledge that she exhibited "held things together" in the shop. While the pedagogical strategies that she employed affected the patrons' cognitive styles and development somewhat indirectly, they do illustrate how she successfully maintained an environment that required its members to develop a particular way of seeing the world.

The second black woman I want to present was a teacher in a community-based ethnographic study that I conducted in San Diego, California, to investigate the relationship between culture and cognitive development in black children. She was a true master of cultural rules, using them to create an effective learning environment. Salimu (Sä leēm' u), the adopted African name she preferred, was well-known in her southeast neighborhood. She was a powerful voice in that community and had been a long-time activist committed to educational reform and quality education for poor and minority children. Salimu was an articulate critic of educational policies and practices that affected black children, and publicly and privately confronted the principal, the teachers, and staff at the local school, as well as members of the Board of Education, on issues related to curriculum, student placement, teacher attitudes, treatment of children, cultural and ethnic matters, and on policies governing majority/minority enrollment in the magnet programs that had been launched in targeted San Diego schools.

She often proclaimed her belief that the social and academic difficulties of black children and their test performances by extension resulted more from mainstream teacher unfamiliarity with black learning styles and their unawareness of effective ways to teach the children than from the intellectual and linguistics deficiencies that are cited as the cause. Her concern over the fate of her own children in school and loss of faith in the school's ability to teach, prompted her to augment her older daughters' school instructions with activities at home. Salimu also argued that black children would experience fewer difficulties if teachers concentrated *more on teaching them how to learn* and *less on the mastery of content*. The academic activities that she arranged for her children at home were organized around this belief.

In the late 1970s, several neighbors who resided in the same apartment house as Salimu requested that she include their children in her instruction. After a relatively short time, eight children were participating in the apartment lessons. On occasion, Salimu would take them on field trips to acquire hands-on learning experiences: to the nearby canyons to collect insects, snakes, and vegetation for a science table, and on neighborhood walks to observe people at work—telephone repairmen, excavators, mail carriers, and construction workers. Salimu organized these excursions to teach the children about life in their everyday world, about things that were around and familiar. The trips to local supermarkets and shopping malls were also instructional, and the numbers, letters, and symbols on boxes and cans handy as instructional aids to develop reading and number readiness, and to teach concepts of shape, size, and color. During summers, Salimu took the youngsters on overnight and week-long camping trips. Older children accompanied them as counselors.

As more people in the community heard about the apartment lessons and the field and camping trips, and requests for inclusion increased, it became obvious that the apartment was inadequate to accommodate the growing interest in the school. Three years after Salimu initiated the out-of-school lessons, the apartment school was moved to a large house on a semi-rural dead-end street and formally named BEGIN, acronym for Basic Education Give It Now. Although BEGIN became its official name, Salimu and the children informally referred to it as "the little school."

Even at the time of this writing, I am uncertain if BEGIN was a distinct kind of organization particular to the community that I studied, or if it was a variation of a type of institution that might be quite common in other black communities. My initial and continued efforts to classify it as an established system were thwarted by a series of organizational identities that emerged during the year that I spent in the setting.

The colleague who had negotiated my entry into BEGIN shaped my initial and most persistent impression of its function and status by referring to it as a "day-care center." The confusion I experienced was compounded further when I learned, several months later, that the organization was legally licensed by the county as a particular kind of child-care arrangement called a "day-care home." Although I was able to readily accept the day-care center and home categories that outsiders attributed to BE-GIN, my bias as a former teacher caused me to unconsciously reject the "school" label that its teacher and students consistently used. I did not realize until I had left the field and was immersed in the data, that all the categories attributed to BEGIN described aspects of it to some extent, but none had been fully able to capture its purpose and complexity. BEGIN functioned as a bridge, a social, linguistic, and cognitive bridge, a bridge between home and school that was organized to ease the children's entry into school and to facilitate their future success.

Whenever Salimu discussed BEGIN during conversations with outsiders she purposefully referred it as a "preparatory school," in a conscious effort, perhaps, to qualify and legitimate its purpose and status in their thinking. Although her distinction was inappropriate from the standpoint of accreditation, her attribution deserves some consideration granted the school's educational and philosophical objectives. In this sense perhaps, BEGIN might qualify, though with a distinct specificity, considering that its teacher, a community parent, was an AFDC (welfare) recipient with neither teacher training nor a college degree, the students were all low-income and black, and the school itself was actually a large house that had been structurally renovated to function as both a home and a school. Perhaps these unique features designate BEGIN for its own idiosyncratic distinction—*home school*, a more appropriate appellation to capture the particularistic structure and function of this community institution.

In much the same way, the label "teacher" is inadequate to describe the role that Salimu assumed, the term being insufficient and far too narrow to encompass the multiplicity of functions and roles that she performed. The limits of this title become especially apparent when listening to the language that she used with the children and while observing her interactional style. Salimu's linguistic repertoire at the home school was distinctive, reflecting both the caretaker and teaching roles that she maintained, and syncretic in the sense that it embraced a unique synthesis and blend of her parent/teacher roles and socialization/pedagogical practices. As a mother who taught, her role function might be more properly redefined to that of a "mama teacher."

Salimu retires to her "office" when she arrives at the house each weekday and remains there until the official 9 a.m. opening of school. Parents en route to work or siblings walking to the local public school usually leave the morning and all-day children between 6 and 8 a.m. None of the early arrivals disturb Salimu during these hours; each prepares his or her own breakfast—usually cereal and milk—cleans the kitchen after eating, and generally amuses himself or herself with school materials such as books and games. In all cases, materials are returned to their designated places after use. Preschoolers who arrive earliest often assume teacher roles by taking out materials and organizing activities for youngsters who arrive later. If problems arise, Salimu is never approached. The children find solutions among themselves. When I asked what she would do if conflicts or problems occurred before 9 a.m., Salimu replied that "they [the children] gotta go settle it themselves."

School is officially in session from 9 until 11:30 a.m. for preschoolers and afternoon-session kindergarten children. Salimu usually conducts readiness classes around the kitchen table during these hours or works with small groups of children in the converted work/play room. When she leaves at 11:30 a.m. to take the afternoon kindergarten children to school and to pick up the morning kindergarteners, the three and four year olds are left to supervise themselves and to assume roles similar to ones they perform before the start of school. More likely than not, Salimu departs without informing the children that she is leaving for school or going on an errand. Yet there is no noticeable change in routines at the house during her absence, nor changes in the

behaviors of the children. It is unstated but clearly understood
that they will be responsible not only for themselves but for each
other. There is evidence in the collective responsibility inherent
at BEGIN that the home school is organized and operates in much
the same way as an extended family, a common arrangement and
tradition in black communities.

One day, ten of the twenty children who were present at BEGIN
stood at attention in the playroom of the house facing Salimu in
readiness to recite the home school's pledge. This was not a daily
ritual, but one more likely to occur when the public schools were
closed and older children were in attendance. After having placed
their right hands over their hearts, the children raised their left
hands as if in salute. Their outstretched arms resembled the black
felt clenched fist that was hand-sewn onto the red and green
colored banner hanging from the side wall. The fist represented
struggle. It was shackled but breaking free from its chains. Salimu
instructed the students to "make it strong." In chorus and with
fervor the children recite:

I pledge on my honor to put forth my best effort today.
I will be self-disciplined, self-demanding, and self-determined.
I will respect myself and I will respect others.
I will cooperate with my teachers and fellow students.

Later that day, the children perform elaborate ritualistic mo-
tions as they chanted in Swahili the grace that precedes their
meals:

Ja, la, tu (translation, "one, two, three")
Sisfa, otay, ena, wata, nyeusi ("all praise to black people")
Kwatu ("for us," i.e., like a toast).[6]

The pledge, the red, green, and black colored banner, and the
grace reflect the cultural nationalist ideology in which Salimu
believes and practices at the school.

After lunch, when the kitchen table was cleared and the "babies" sent to nap, Salimu selected five children to come to the
table to have a class. On this particular day she was teaching a
lesson that required the children to match the five digit number
sets that she had printed on pieces of blue oaktag with similar

number sets that she had printed on pocket-like envelopes. Earlier that day, Salimu had stapled the envelopes in symmetrical rows onto a large piece of cardboard in preparation for the lesson. The cardboard "mailbox" that she had made resembled the numbered window boxes that one sees in post offices. All of the oaktag "letters" as she called them, were prefixed with 921, the first three numbers of the San Diego zip code. Fourth place digits of zero or one were used in combination with fifth place values of one, two, three, or four. Melinda was designated the mailgirl, told to read the numbers on the oaktag letters, and hand them to the children to mail when they identified the numbers that they had been assigned. The exercise was exceptionally complex considering the variety of numerical combinations that the children needed to recognize and the fact that their ages ranged from three to five.

Like all of the lessons that are taught at the home school, this one began with the traditional type of opener that teachers in schools use to introduce a subject or topic. "One," Salimu began, "we're going to talk about numbers and their order. That means how they line up." But as the lesson progressed, it became obvious that it differed significantly from the traditional format that one expects in school. The differences were particularly apparent in the type of teacher talk that Salimu used during instruction and in her methods of social control.

The exercise was extremely difficult since the children needed to detect subtle differences between the five digit number combinations on the blue oaktag letters and five digit numbered sets printed on the envelopes. One number, for example, might be reversed with another or the numerical sequence on a card slightly altered. When the children became confused during the lesson, Salimu did not show them their errors, but offered a clue instead. "The numbers on the beginning mix me up because they be the same," she suggests. After giving this hint, she points back and forth between the two sets until the children see why they became confused and realize where the mistake was made. But Salimu pretends that she, not the children, has made the mistake and is confused. And when the children discover the origin of "Salimu's" error, she shouts excitedly, "Okay!" and sings, "I know."

When in spite of her clues three-year-old David continues to experience difficulty, Salimu alters her strategy but does not give him the answer. Instead she reminds, "Ah, check it," and encourages him to focus more: "The mailman has to have sharp eyes. These numbers are very important." It is rare for Salimu to tell a child an answer directly. When pressed for one she usually responds with such statements as, "I don't know. You're smarter. I don't go to kindergarten." Three-year-old Mimi is very capable, and because Salimu perceives her to be so, she seems even more demanding: "I can't tell you, Mimi. Everything you know is in your smart head." Elijah once asked where he should place his answer on the paper. "Wherever you think it is," he was told. "If you think that's where it belongs, put it there. Salimu's head doesn't think straight. Yours does."

In all cases, Salimu makes the child responsible for his or her own learning. Although she provided clues in the number matching exercise by pointing out that the first three numbers in the zip codes were the same, the children were responsible for finding their own mistakes. David was not only told to check his answers, but given a reason for paying close attention to detail: "The mailman has to have sharp eyes. These numbers are important."

But one of Salimu's unique pedagogical strategies was her method of providing a cognitive map for the children, a map that offered an age and culturally appropriate way of learning. In saying that "the numbers on the beginning mix me up because they be the same," for example, she provides a cognitive map that situates the point of their confusion. The map is age appropriate in the sense that she articulates children's inner speech by saying aloud what they might be thinking, "I'm confused. Okay, that's where I made the mistake."

During the lesson Earl had been growing impatient. Most of the other children's zip code numbers had been called and he had yet to receive a letter. "Ahhhh, Ahhh," he whines. "I don't got no blue things like that." "You have to be patient," Salimu responds. "Somedays we don't get any mail. Today you'll probably get a bill." Elijah was also becoming impatient and bemoaned, "I never get one." "No news is good news," Salimu sympathizes. Later when she wanted to change mail carriers and says, "I'm

going to let two people write while one person does the mailbox,"
three-year-old David cries, 'I wanna do the mailbox." Earl follows
quickly with "Yeah me. I want to do it. I wanna do it." Salimu
responds quietly and low-keyed, "Oh, I understand."[7]

Earl's behavior in the kindergarten was quite different from
what it was at the home school, especially in his interactions
with his teachers. At school he could successfully manage to turn
in incomplete sloppy work and be viewed, and even praised, for
working to the best of his ability. This was not the case at the
home school, and Salimu and Earl often engaged in verbal duels
during her efforts to make him responsible for neat, correct, and
complete work. In an ethnographic study that examined life and
language in a small Southern mill town, Shirley Brice Heath
describes episodes of playful interactions between black mothers
and their children, exchanges in which the children, from an
outside perspective, might appear somewhat defiant. Interactions
of this kind were not only encouraged in the community that
Heath studied, they were positively sanctioned. But the children,
using members' knowledge of the cultural rules embedded in
these exchanges, knew just how far they could take their sassi-
ness with adults until it was no longer considered playful and
acceptable.[8]

The following exchanges between Earl and Salimu were taken
from the transcript of a lesson that I taped in the home school. It
provides an illustrative example of Salimu and Earl interacting in
an educational situation, but one where Salimu's methods of
social control are culled from the cultural context of the black
community. In an assignment where he was supposed to have
drawn pictures and written the names of several body parts, e.g.,
neck, ears, mouth, Earl claims to have finished, but Salimu dis-
agrees:

    Salimu: Earl, Earl.
    Earl: What?
    Salimu: Don't play with me.
    Earl: What?
    Salimu: Where's your neck?
    Earl: What?
    Salimu: Where. That's what I'm asking you.

Earl: Where what?

Salimu: Where's what?

Earl: Where's what?

Salimu: What? Right here (points to place on his paper where the answer should be, but isn't). Now Earl.

Earl: What?

Salimu: Earl, Earl. You trickin' me.

Earl: What?

Salimu: Earl.

Earl: What?

Salimu: I know you don't know, huh?

Earl: No.

Salimu: Yes.

Earl: I, I, I, I, I.

Salimu: I, I, I, I, I (imitating him). Where? You're right.

Earl: I'm not finished.

Salimu: Ah, ah, ah. It's all on you Buddy.

Earl: What?

Salimu: What? I don't go to kindergarten Earl. I don't know.

Earl: I'm here.

In gaming, and by not completing his work, Earl is not honoring the goals articulated in the home-school pledge—to be "self-disciplined," "self-demanding," and "self-determined." He is aware of the cultural and indexical meanings behind Salimu's admonishment, "It's all on you, Buddy," and knows that he is being called to task, and that his performance on the assignment is being called by its true name. Earl understands the message implicit in Salimu's words:

> I ain't gonna con you, bullshit you or tell you it's for your own good or that you have to save the race. I ain't a gonna lay none of those trips on you. But I will tell you this, you want the education—go for it. I won't walk in with you, but I'll hold the door open. *It's all on you buddy*, the ultimate responsibility is yours.

Salimu believes that the intelligence of black children is a given, not displayed in ways, perhaps, that may be discernible to their teachers in school. Her instructional style and curricular content reflect this belief. Children are taught at BEGIN that the most important resource available to them in problem solving situations, either personal or academic, in school or out, is the self. They are encouraged to look to themselves for solutions to problems first, to summon up answers from their own world experiences, and to reflect on that knowledge.

It is apparent to anyone who has had occasion to visit the home school that BEGIN represents for Salimu the heart of her efforts to effect change for black people. Undoubtedly, she is an authority, a leader whose knowledge and mastery of cultural rules in the black community is having an impact. Public school teachers could learn a lot from this "mama teacher." I certainly did.

Although I met Louise and Salimu in ethnographic research projects, there is one woman whose effect preceded and shaped my awareness as a woman. The memoir presented here reflects a time in my life when I was about ten and lived with my parents and grandmother in a fairly northern urban city. This last black woman I would like to introduce to you is my maternal grandmother, Frances Cook, known to the neighbors as Miz Cook and to me as Ma.

She sat each day on the stoop like an ageless queen granting a royal audience to an endless parade of city diplomats. There were the winos, the muttering street poets, the junkie socialities, and the sanctified tambourine-playing church members on their way to daily prayer meeting. The clanging staccato rhythm made by the "doorkey" kids clinking beer cans against curbs punctuated the beat of a quartet of local street dudes harmonizing Frankie Lymon and the Teenagers' latest hit. Tired women, mothers laden with shopping bags heavy with the week's groceries, rushed to cook and clean again, having cleaned the white folks' homes all day. And gangling me with knees sidewalk-battered, face pumpkin-round, pensive, sitting silently, watching Ma's unending receiving line. Each morning around nine, her throne—a padded, yellow, vinyl and chrome chair—was positioned on the same strategic lookout stoop, and returned to the kitchen when the fireflies signaled her bedtime.

Her weathered, clay-brown face had been sculpted by labor:

sixteen babies and years of back-breaking work under a merciless Georgia sun. This face, chiseled deep with wrinkles, often brought to mind the relief map hanging on my classroom wall that portrayed the Mississippi River's tributaries meandering to their delta. Squat, toothless, with a snuff-packed lower lip, Ma nevertheless sat tall and regal in her chair, crowned with countless silver braids and dressed as always in a faded house dress and a cobbler's apron. Large floppy breasts jiggled beneath her apron bib. She never wore a bra, and would glance knowingly at me, suppressing an impish smile whenever well-meaning kin casually hinted that she'd feel much more comfortable wearing one, "it being so hot and everything."

A pair of black support shoes, which she appropriately called "my old lady comforts" complemented her queenly attire; and from them rose noticeably Caucasian-colored cotton stockings that continually defied Newton's law by obstinately remaining upright, rolled beneath her kneecaps tucked in a ball. Ma's stocking-covered legs reminded me of Park's pork sausage links— though I dared not mention this image in her presence for fear of being "smacked clean into New York City," as she often threatened. And like me, the neighbors never challenged nor questioned her matriarchal status. Ma's appearance, it seems, had little if any bearing on the position she maintained, a role I never understood completely but nevertheless accepted.

I recall the ring she wore. She had married at fourteen; the ring had been a bride's wedding gift from her late husband John. She used to say it had once been carved with forget-me-nots, but when I saw it the flowers were long since gone, worn into the thinness of a plain gold band.

The street folk paid daily homage to Miz Cook, never daring to catch her eagle-eye scan without paying due tribute. "How do you do, Miz Cook? Gittin' kinda nasty out agin, ain't it? Lawd knows we due fuh some some sunshine affa all dat rain." Many times gifts accompanied these pleasantries and Ma, reigning sage, acknowledged these befitting "gifts of state" with a slight nod. "Thank you mos' kindly fo' dat C. C. DeVore snuff yuh got me Bubba, I sho' 'nuf 'preciates it." Vanilla ice cream a frequent present, was a favorite, and though she fussed and hollered each time, I'd always get a heaping spoonful if I begged long and hard enough.

"If yuh wonts tuh know sumpn' Ax" was one of her unwritten axioms, and she always got answers. "Where was you yestiddy son? Huh? Ah didn't see yuh go by. You wuddin' tryin' tuh sneak by me now, was yuh, Boy? Huh? Hey! Dat gret big bag yuh totin' sho' looks rat heavy. Waddja hidin' in dere? Sumpn' yuh don't wonts me tuh see? Huh? Oh, Lawd ha' mussy! Ain't dat Lorritha walkin' down yonda? Ain't seen dat gal since duh night duh police took Jonnie Ruth's youngest boy 'way in duh paddy wagon fuh fightin' wid dat white man. Hey Lorritha! Yeah, you Gal! Ah's talkin' tuh you. Come over heah 'cuz Ah wonts tuh ax you sumpin'. Listen, Chile, is you in duh family way agin? Ah 'spects you is. Yuh knows you cain't fool Miz Cook, cuz Ah knows when sumpn' up duh crik ain't clean. Duh sooner yuh leave dat damn fool duh better awf you'll be. Hush now Baby. Ain't no need fuh you tuh cry. Jes' sit on down heah nexta Miz Cook an' res' uh spell. Take a load awf yo' feets. Troubles ain't near bad as they looks when yuh looks at sum'un else's. Might 'pear hard tuh yuh rat now Honey, but . . . Wait a minute, Sugah! Ain't dat Willie Sampson talkin' wid James Earl Junior fronta Abe's sto'? Wonda what lie he layin' on dis time? Dat boy wuddin' tell duh troof if it hit 'im in duh face."

After all these years I haven't discovered the magic formula of the queen who signed her pension checks with an "X." The loyal subjects paid her court, sat obediently, listened, and walked away on lighter feet. Ma died the year I left for college. She had acted high-falutin and proud that last time I saw her—the favored grandchild, all grown up, going to get a college education, going away to do the family proud. I wanted to hold on and I wanted to go, dreading the moment, yet knowing all the while that my time to leave home had come.

I returned years later to find that time again, but found instead an ordinary kitchen chair and an empty stoop enshrined in silence.

I wrote this memoir[9] well before I began thinking about the

informal rules that infuse the traditional leadership roles that a
great many women maintain in black communities. Still today I
am not quite sure how my grandmother achieved and maintained
her authority over those whose deference was implicit in the
presents they gave to her and the respect that they bestowed. But
like Louise and Salimu, she too was outspoken, quick to criticize
or comfort, and dauntless in getting to the bottom of things.

It would be easy to *dismiss* the three women that I've described
as *busy-bodies*, meddlers in the affairs of others, were it not for
the fact that people willingly subjected themselves to their inqui-
sitions. None of these women possessed the extrinsic symbols of
power associated with formal authority in our society, yet each
was vested with formal authority by those around her. Why?

Are there intrinsic attributes that these women share that explain how each came to acquire her position? And if this is the
case, do such attributes shed light on the interplay between individual and collective orientations that make leadership the personal realization of collective values and rules? At this stage in
my research I cannot provide definitive answers, nor detail precise patterns of leadership. But I do see certain shared characteristics indicative of the unifying role that Hall suggests.[10]

Each of these women is a risk-taker who insists on calling
people and events by their "true names." Both Salimu and Miz
Cook would agree with Louise that their mouths had cost them.
And both would also concur with her recognition that she could
say things to other people that would get someone else knocked
down. Thus the verbal strategies that these women use must seem
to the hearer, at the time, to go beyond the critical revelation of
the utterance.

If the direct message is critical, what is the nature of the indirect message? Recall Louise's retort when George explained how
he got his black eye, "You a lie. That ole man you livin' with beat
you up," Salimu's "You trickin' me, Earl," or Miz Cook's "Listen,
Chile, is you in duh family way agin?" This passion for the truth,
however, is not an end in itself, but a means for articulating those
inner fears that erode personal responsibility. In each case the lie
is synonymous with personal responsibility. The lies are also

synonymous with a disavowal with personal responsibility. And as attempts to deny reality, they also decrease the individual's ability to find a constructive solution to a bad situation.

Insisting that people who are poor and discriminated against take responsibility for their own lives may seem like a cruel burden to place upon them. But these women know that while we can't always control *what others* do to us, we can and must control what *we do* to ourselves. Louise's taunt "Got caught with your pant down," vividly captures George's role in sustaining an abusive relationship with his lover. After Earl finally acknowledges that he is not finished with his work, Salimu does not offer comfort with her "It's all on you, Buddy," but reaffirms his responsibility instead. Miz Cook's "Duh sooner yuh leave dat damn fool duh better awf you'll be" not only prescribes a course of action, but underscores the girl's role in staying with the man.

A third common theme among these women involves the ways in which they get people to focus on the alternative available to them. It is more than coincidental, I think, that both Louise and Miz Cook say "Leave him." Neither expect that course of action to be taken literally, but the utterances focus on possibilities. Getting adults to consider their options is perhaps more difficult than getting them to recognize their responsibility for past problems or successes. The fears that motivate people to deny what has already happened become paralytic when the issue is planning a future course of action. Miz Cook's "Ain't no need fuh you tuh cry. Jes' sit on down . . . res' uh spell. Take a load awf yo' feets," is more than just comfort and support, it is a refocusing so that the girl can see that "Troubles ain't near bad as they looks when yuh looks at sum'un else's."

Salimu does not give children answers because she is teaching them to solve problems for themselves, to think. Her graphic clues demonstrate *how* to find the solution: "The numbers at the beginning mix me up because they be the same," and *why:* "The mailman has to have sharp eyes. . . . These numbers are important." Perhaps if George had had a teacher like Salimu he would not have needed Louise's admonishment, "Be careful what you put your name on. Better pass that cosmetology exam and put your name on that operator's license."

Perhaps a succinct summary of the verbal strategies that these women use is revealed in the ways they utilize their knowledge of the people around them to get them to overcome their fears and use the knowledge in their heads to solve their own problems. Their verbal strategies interpret events that enable people to come to see the same thing. But the thing that one needs to see is *the options that are open rather than the doors that are closed.* Louise, Salimu, and Miz Cook make rules that others follow. And from their interactions we can discern that:

- They insist on calling things by their true names.
- They articulate the fears that inhibit others from acting responsibly.
- And they prescribe courses of action that focus *not* on what others have *done to them,* but on what the individual *can do.*

These women do not give up and they do not give up on those around then. It is this persistence, perhaps, that explains how they are able to "hold things together."

Only recently have black women become the subject of serious scholarship, and finally an emerging core of black women social scientists, literary critics, and historians is producing studies that analyze and describe them and document their contributions.[11] This recent scholarship, as well as future studies, offers an opportunity to question the myths surrounding black women, to reveal finally *why* they are *who* and *what* they are. But here lies the problem. Myths about black women are held by white men and women, black men, and even black women themselves. And four hundred years of misperceptions is a long time to make up.

The misconception of racial and ethnic stereotypes continue to obscure our views of each other. It is not the universality of our gender, but the particularism of the adjectives that shape our sense of self. While we are often motivated to dissolve the gender stereotypes that hinder our personal and professional growth, we continue to accept the stereotypes of race and economics. Too often we explain away the differences among us in the particularistic jargon of the social sciences without questioning its generalizability. Too often, in our haste to set things right, we *tell* rather than inquire, *conclude* rather than reflect, *bind* rather than free. We mean well but find our efforts coopted and directed in ways we didn't intend. We are making headway today as individuals achieving our goals, professional status, and sometimes power by becoming physicians, professors, attorneys, corporate executives, presidents of institutions, and members of important groups that make rules and criteria for judging people. And though we are learning that the power acquired within these settings depends on our mastery of the prevailing rules, a major challenge facing all of us today is how to exercise such power.

As we gain more political, economic, and social rights we must assume the responsibility of working for greater equality for *all* women. Once this responsibility is earnestly undertaken, the trust and respect accorded will be granted to those so deserving. Maya Angelou once said, "You have a responsibility for the time you take and the space you occupy." [12] If women take this responsibility seriously, as did Louise, Salimu, and Miz Cook, we should get that respect. Respect is a universal phenomenon that transcends the cultural and racial boundaries that often separate white women and women of color.

In the lives of black women there is much to learn and to share beyond the stereotypes. And there are many teachers out there, the Louises, Salimus, and Miz Cooks we can learn from: women who can show how one develops the respect that all of us strive for in our professional endeavors, women who can teach us how to exercise power and authority, and women who would not hesitate to tell us to call things by their true names.

It is obvious that spurting out the embarrassing truth is not always effective as a mode of leadership in bureaucratic institutions. Neither is withholding information always the most effective way to teach self-reliance. Yet my original point was that models of success must not be dawn solely from the historical precedents of a white male world; nor should the measure of achievement be tested solely against the positions, the status, and roles currently recognized in that world. Bureaucracies can evolve to accommodate more honesty, and teaching can evolve to accommodate more of the tasks of assisting transitional development and translating alternative cognitive perspectives. The full impact of women's contributions to the professions will depend less on *whether* we achieve than *what* we achieve. And the study of what some black women have been doing in maintaining roles can only help us in our quest.

Endnotes

1. S. P. Spradley, "Foundations of Cultural Knowledge," in Spradley, ed., *Culture and Cognition: Rules, Maps, and Plans* (New York: Chandler, 1972).

2. J. Mitchell, "Reflections of a Black Social Scientist: Some Struggles, Some Doubts, Some Hopes," *Harvard Educational Review* (1982), 52(1):27–44; E. Steele, J. Mitchell et al., "The Human Cost of Discrimination," in D. Bell, ed., *Lives in Stress: Women and Depression* (Beverly Hills, Calif.: Sage, 1982); and J. Mitchell, "Elijah and Earl: An Ethnography of the Social, Cultural, and Cognitive Learning Environments of Two Black Kindergarten Boys."

3. E. T. Hall, "The Organizing Pattern," in B. G. Blount, ed., *Language, Culture, and Society: A Book of Readings* (Cambridge: Winthrop, 1974), pp. 41 and 44 (my emphasis).

4. J. Mitchell, "Whaddja gettin'—press 'n curl or wet set? An Ethnography of Temporal Sequencing and Social Organization in a Black Beauty Parlor," Paper, Graduate School of Education, Harvard University, 1977.

5. E. Liebow, *Tally's Corner* (Boston: Little, Brown, 1967).

6. I cannot verify the authenticity of the Swahili nor its English translation.

7. I had also observed Earl and Elijah with their teachers in kindergarten as part of the broader study. Rather than being told that "Somedays we don't get any mail," or that "No news is good news," Earl might be told to "Shut up and wait your turn." Students are seldom if ever told that when they compete for a turn in school, compete to be first, compete for a teacher's recognition or attention, or compete to be chosen as the line leader that "Oh, I understand." It is competitive behavior, not cooperation, that is encouraged in schools; and competitive situations are seldom resolved with empathy.

8. S. B. Heath, *Ways with Words, Language, Life, and Work in Communities and Classrooms* (New York: Cambridge University Press, 1983).

9. J. Mitchell, "The Stoop Sovereign," paper, 1977.

10. E. T. Hall, "The Organizing Pattern."

11. See, for example, B. Christian, *Black Feminist Criticism: Perspectives on Black Writers* (New York: Pergamon, 1985), and *Black Women Novelists: The Development of a Tradition, 1892–1976* (Westport, Conn.: Greenwood, 1980); P. Giddings, *When and Where I Enter: The Impact of Black Women on Race and Sex in America* (New York: Morrow, 1984); B. Hooks, *Ain't I a Woman: Black Women and Feminism* (Boston: South End Press, 1981); G. T. Hull, P. B. Scott, and B. Smith, eds., *All the Women Are White, All the Blacks Are Men, But Some of Us Are Brave: Black Women's Studies* (Old Westbury, N.Y.: Feminist Press, 1982); J. Jones, *Labor of Love, Labor of Sorrow: Black Women, Work, and the Family from Slavery to the Present* (New York: Basic Books, 1985); J. Ladner, *Tomorrow's Tomorrow: The Black Woman* (New York: Doubleday, 1971); S. L. Lightfoot, *Balm in Gilead: Journey of a Healer* (Reading, Mass.: Addison-Wesley, 1988); Y. Moses,

"Black Women in Academe: Issues and Strategies," *The Project on Status of Education of Women* (Washington, D.C.: Association of American Colleges, 1989); J. Noble, *Beautiful, Also, Are the Souls of My Black Sisters: A History of the Black Woman in America* (Englewood Cliffs, N.J.: Prentice-Hall, 1978); N. Rice, "When Malindy Sings: Implications of the Formation of the National Association of Colored Women's Club for the Black Community," paper, 1980; L. Rodgers-Rose, ed., *The Black Woman* (Beverly Hills, Calif.: Sage, 1980); and B. Smith, ed., *Home Girls: A Black Feminist Anthology* (New York: Kitchen Table: Women of Color Press, 1983).

12. M. Angelou, Presentation for the "Minority Women's Lecture Series," Women's Research and Resource Center, University of California, Davis, 1982.

INDEX